Canada's Industrial
Space-Economy

General editor
PROFESSOR R. O. BUCHANAN
M.A.(N.Z.), B.Sc.(Econ.), PH.D.(London)
Professor Emeritus, University of London

A. Systematic Studies

GEOGRAPHY AND ECONOMICS
Michael Chisholm, M.A.
AGRICULTURAL GEOGRAPHY
Leslie Symons, B.Sc.(Econ.), Ph.D.
THE WORLD TRADE SYSTEM
SOME ENQUIRIES INTO ITS SPATIAL STRUCTURE
R.J.Johnston, M.A., Ph.D
LAND REFORM: A WORLD SURVEY
Russell King, B.A., M.Sc., Ph.D.

AGRICULTURE IN THE THIRD WORLD:
A SPATIAL ANALYSIS
W.B. Morgan, M.A., Ph.D.

B. Regional Studies

AN ECONOMIC GEOGRAPHY OF EAST AFRICA
A.M. O'Connor, B.A., Ph.D.
AN ECONOMIC GEOGRAPHY OF WEST AFRICA
H.P. White, M.A. & M. B. Gleave, M.A.
YUGOSLAVIA: PATTERNS OF ECONOMIC ACTIVITY
F. E. Ian Hamilton, B.Sc.(Econ.), Ph.D.
RUSSIAN AGRICULTURE: A GEOGRAPHIC SURVEY
Leslie Symons, B.Sc.(Econ.), Ph.D.
RUSSIAN TRANSPORT
(Ed.) *Leslie Symons, B.Sc.(Econ.), Ph.D. & Colin White, B.A.(Cantab.)*
AN HISTORICAL INTRODUCTION TO THE ECONOMIC
GEOGRAPHY OF GREAT BRITAIN
Wilfred Smith, M.A.
A GEOGRAPHY OF BRAZILIAN DEVELOPMENT
Janet D. Henshall, M.A., M.Sc., Ph.D. & R. P. Momsen Jr, A.B., M.A.,
Ph.D.
AN INDUSTRIAL GEOGRAPHY OF JAPAN
(Eds.) *Kiyoji Murata & Isamu Ota*

Canada's Industrial Space-Economy

DAVID F. WALKER

Associate Professor of Geography
University of Waterloo, Ontario

BELL & HYMAN

London

First published in 1980 by
BELL & HYMAN LIMITED
Denmark House
37–39 Queen Elizabeth Street
London SE1 2QB

© D. F. Walker 1980

Walker, David Frank
    Canada's industrial space–economy. –
    (Advanced economic geographies).
    1. Industries, Location of–Canada–History
    I. Title   II. Series
            338'.0971   HC120.D5

ISBN 0 7135 1210 5 (cased)
ISBN 0 7135 1258 X (paper)

Printed in Great Britain by
Biddles Ltd, Guildford, Surrey

Contents

Tables	*page*	vii
Maps and Diagrams		viii
Preface		ix
1 Manufacturing in the Canadian Economy		1
2 Regional Diversity		35
3 The Atlantic Provinces		78
4 Québec		104
5 Ontario		131
6 The Prairie Provinces		170
7 British Columbia		202
8 Municipal Industrial Development		228
9 Conclusion		243
Index		253

Tables

1.1 Gross Domestic Product at factor cost, by industry   *page* 2
1.2 Employment by industry   2
1.3 Canada's merchandise trade balance, by product group
     selected years, 1955–74   3
1.4 Gross value of production, primary, secondary and total
     manufacturing industries - selected years 1870–1957   8
1.5 Non-resident control as a percentage of selected Canadian
     industries 1926–73   9
1.6 Canada's manufacturing structure, 1975   12
1.7 Canada's major industries, 1975   13
1.8 Manufacturing value added per production worker in
     relation to the US by major industry groups - 1972   17
1.9 Output per dollar of capital stock (at replacement cost) for
     Canada and the US, by major industry groups - 1972   18
2.1 Selected statistics of manufacturing industry, by Province,
     1975   35
2.2 Canadian trade in manufactured goods 1974   37
2.3 Population by Province, selected census years   38
2.4 Components of population change, by Province   40
2.5 Personal income per person by Province   41
2.6 Gross Domestic Product *per capita*: Canadian Provinces and
     OECD countries   44
2.7 Index of labour quality in all industries, by Province, 1970 46
2.8 Multivariate analysis of the components of growth   47
2.9 Regionalism and corporate sectors for the economic
     elite, 1972   55
2.10 DREE's 1975–76 expenditures   71
2.11 Grants, contributions and subsidies to business, Canada,
     by region, 1974–75   72
3.1 Atlantic Provinces: principal statistics by industry group,
     1974   85
4.1 Québec: principal statistics by industry group, 1975   105
5.1 Ontario: principal statistics by industry group, 1975   138

(vi)

6.1 Prairie Provinces: principal statistics by industry group,
1975   176
7.1 British Columbia: principal statistics by industry group,
1975   206
7.2 Economic specializations and similarities of regions,
based on component scores (1961 data)   212
7.3 Industrial structure of B.C. census divisions, 1967   216
7.4 Classification of B.C. manufacturing industries   217

Maps and Diagrams

1.1 Manufacturing trends since 1945   *page* 11
2.1 Employment by Industry and Region, November 1975   42
2.2 Unemployment rates by Region   43
2.3 Percentage Growth of Gross Provincial Domestic Product   45
3.1 Burke and Ireland's Atlantic Core Region   87
3.2 Atlantic Provinces: Designated Special Areas   96
4.1 Montreal's Industrial Areas   119
5.1 Settlement of Southern Ontario   132
5.2 Southern Ontario: Regional Percentage of Employment
in Manufacturing   135
5.3 Ontario's Ten Economic Regions   140
5.4 Population Change By Region 1941–71   147
5.5 Urban System Concept for Ontario   165
6.1 Degraph of Rail Tonnage Flows   173
6.2 Degraph of Road Tonnage Flows   174
6.3 Winnipeg's Industrial Areas   183
6.4 Edmonton's Industrial Areas   191
7.1 Present and Potential Forest Harvest in British Columbia   207
7.2 An Economic–Geographic Map of British Columbia   214
7.3 Vancouver's Industrial Areas   220

Preface

Canada is an enormous country but its relatively small population of 22.6 million (1976) is concentrated in a narrow strip close to the United States border. It is a land of contrasts: from the harsh northern tundra to mild southwestern British Columbia; from the vast continuous forest lands of northern Ontario and Québec to the extensive Prairie wheatfields; from tiny, isolated Newfoundland outports to fast-growing metropolitan Toronto or Montréal. Its diversity results not only from the natural environment but also from its cultural heritage. In addition to the two major founding groups that have led to an official bilingualism, there is a large variety of other peoples, who frequently have retained many aspects of their culture, including language. One expects to hear conversations in Italian in Toronto, German in Kitchener, Ukrainian in Prairie towns and Chinese in most cities. There are also the native peoples, of whom the Indians are found in most parts of the country, while the Eskimos are confined to the north.

In fact it has frequently been argued that Canada is a highly artificial country, its east-west orientation being quite contrary to the more natural north-south lines of the North American continent. Regional contrasts are quite marked, are often reflected in popular attitudes and are reinforced by the federal structure, which leaves considerable power in the hands of the provinces. Yet Canada is now well past its hundredth birthday (Confederation took place in 1867) and must be considered as a single unit for many types of analysis. This is perhaps especially true in the realm of economic development because so much of what happens to the economy depends on federal policy. Thus, it is logical to begin a study such as this at the national scale, focusing on the role of manufacturing in the Canadian economy and on federal policies which influence its character and well-being.

Nevertheless, this book is about Canada's industrial space-economy and the emphasis is, therefore, squarely on the spatial pattern of manufacturing within the country.

There are three main objectives:
(1) To provide a description of the past and present pattern of industrial location in Canada;
(2) To interpret historical trends, the current situation and future prospects by drawing together the vast number of research studies that now exist on the topic;
(3) To review and evaluate planning and industrial development policies designed to use manufacturing for the benefit of Canadians.

The structure of the book, then, is to start at the national scale with a consideration of the role of manufacturing in Canada. Next comes an interpretation of the regional dimensions of the Canadian economy, which provides a framework for the later chapters that examine the regions in detail. The regional breakdown is one that is commonly employed. The four Atlantic Provinces (Newfoundland, Nova Scotia, New Brunswick and Prince Edward Island) are combined as are the three Prairie Provinces (Manitoba, Saskatchewan and Alberta). With Québec, Ontario and British Columbia that gives five regions. Admittedly the federal Department of Regional Economic Expansion links British Columbia to the Prairies in its Western Region, but here the distinctions are considered sufficient to warrant separation. In each detailed regional chapter, industry will be discussed, not only at the broader regional scale but also in terms of urban manufacturing in the larger centres. The two northern territories form another, very distinctive part of Canada but manufacturing is almost non-existent there and so the North will not be the subject of a special chapter. Following these regional chapters, each of which will include a section on provincial policy, Chapter 8 focuses on municipal industrial development as it is practised in Canada. Finally, a conclusion draws together some salient themes and speculates on the future.

Basic statistics used in this book are taken from census publications. Unless explicitly stated, population totals are for 1976. The annual Census of Manufacturers provides manufacturing data and, for national and provincial totals, 1975 is the reference year. For sub-provincial areas and cities, however, the latest figures apply to 1974. Larger cities in Canada are combined with smaller surrounding places into Census Metropolitan areas. It is to these census areas that metropolitan data will apply.

The typescript was completed in the Fall of 1978 and does not cover information and publications appearing since the end of that year.

I owe a debt to numerous academics and practitioners across the country who have helped in the preparation of this book. Many development commissioners took time to show me around their areas and Ghislain Girard, Lynn Shyluk, Ron Blake and Austin Fraser went out of their way in this regard. Criticisms of draft chapters were kindly offered by Gordon Ritchie, Mike Ray, Yves Dugal, Ron Blake, Roger Hayter, Guy Lévesque, Jack McKeown and Graham Parsons. The series editor, Professor R. O. Buchanan, also provided an ideal blend of criticism and encouragement, mainly the latter. Most of the typing was done at the University of Waterloo by Jackie Rugwell and Karen Steinfieldt and excellent editorial and research assistance was supplied by Diana Middleton. Figures were also drawn at the University under Gary Brannon's direction. Thanks to all.

David Walker

1

Manufacturing In The Canadian Economy

Although Canada is usually considered to be one of the advanced industrial nations, the share of manufacturing industry in the Gross National Product has always been relatively low compared to that of most western countries. Its rich resources have helped in the retention of an important primary sector while its large size and high degree of trade have encouraged an important element of servicing. The growth of the manufacturing sector, in fact, owed much to governmental support, especially in the form of tariff protection. Currently many industries are undergoing severe problems and Canada is still a major net importer of manufactured goods. The situation is such that some fairly radical proposals have recently been made for a restructuring of federal industrial policy.

MANUFACTURING'S ROLE IN CANADA

Table 1.1 shows the contribution of the different economic sectors to Canada's Gross Domestic Product. It can be seen that manufacturing is the largest sector but, if the commercial and service sectors are combined, their contribution is far greater and it has been growing. This reflects current trends in most developed countries, in which services have been increasing rapidly in comparison with manufacturing. Despite the fact that Canada has great natural wealth, primary production does not directly provide a large proportion of Gross Domestic Product. In employment, the picture is fairly similar, although the role of manufacturing is slightly smaller (Table 1.2). Note also the steady decline since 1951, during which time the percentage increase in the service sector has been considerable (18% to 34.3%). Currently manufacturing employs 1,302,635 males and 404,695 females in Canada.

Another picture of the role of manufacturing in the Canadian economy is obtained through an examination of the country's balance of trade. Table 1.3 shows a consistent weakness in highly manufactured products. It is clear that the country depends very

TABLE 1.1
GROSS DOMESTIC PRODUCT AT FACTOR COST, BY INDUSTRY

	1966	1971	1976
	millions of dollars		
Agriculture	2,886	2,791	5,722
Forestry	513	608	1,296
Fishing and trapping	116	135	242
Mines, quarries and oil wells	2,203	2,840	6,909
Manufacturing	14,023	19,013	36,005
Construction	3,726	5,687	12,821
Transportation	3,399	4,892	9,305
Storage	157	225	410
Communication	1,384	2,285	4,286
Electric power, gas, and water utilities	1,489	2,385	5,243
Wholesale Trade	2,746	4,195	8,703
Retail Trade	3,820	5,674	11,703
Finance, insurance, and real estate	5,917	9,666	20,646
Public administration and defence	3,671	6,152	13,456
Community, business and personal service	8,714	16,319	34,630
Total	54,764	82,867	171,377

Source: Canada, Statistics Canada, National Income and Expenditure Accounts, 1962–76. Ottawa: 1977.

TABLE 1.2
EMPLOYMENT BY INDUSTRY

	Persons employed[1]							
	1951		1961		1971		1975	
	000's	per cent	000's	per cent	000's	per cent	000's	per cent
Agriculture	939	18.4	681	11.2	510	6.3	479	5.1
Forestry	115	2.3	86	1.4	72	0.9	72	0.8
Fishing and trapping	30	0.6	18	0.3	22	0.3	23	0.2
Mining	79	1.5	80	1.3	129	1.6	132	1.4
Manufacturing	1,350	26.5	1,452	24.0	1,795	22.2	1,951	21.0
Construction	348	6.8	376	6.2	495	6.1	605	6.5
Transportation, communications and other utilities	449	8.8	563	9.3	702	8.7	806	8.7
Trade	718	14.1	1,025	16.9	1,330	16.5	1,633	17.5
Finance, insurance and real estate	154	3.0	239	3.9	385	4.8	460	4.9
Service	916	18.0	1,178	19.5	2,118	26.2	2,508	26.9
Public administration	—	—	356	5.9	520	6.4	639	6.9
Total	5,097	100.0	6,055	100.0	8,078	100.0	9,308	100.0

[1] The employment figures are annual averages
Source: Statistics Canada. Perspective Canada II. Ottawa: 1977, 116.

TABLE 1.3

CANADA'S MERCHANDISE TRADE BALANCE, BY PRODUCT GROUP, SELECTED YEARS, 1955-74[1]

	1957	1961	1965	1969	1973	1974	Three-year averages			
							1955-57	1961-63	1968-70	1971-73
Billions of dollars										
Farm, fish, and crude materials	0.6	1.1	1.7	1.8	4.2	5.1	0.6	1.1	2.2	3.4
Partly manufactured	0.9	1.4	1.7	2.3	4.1	4.3	1.0	1.5	2.6	3.3
Highly manufactured	-2.1	-2.4	-3.3	-3.3	-6.4	-8.9	-2.1	-2.4	-3.1	-4.9
Total trade balance	-0.6	0.1	0.1	0.8	1.9	0.5	-0.5	0.2	1.7	1.8
Balances as a percentage of GNP										
Farm, fish and crude materials	1.81	2.73	3.10	2.27	3.55	3.63	1.76	2.67	2.76	3.20
Partly manufactured	2.73	3.54	3.02	2.93	3.41	3.12	3.22	3.45	3.31	3.14
Highly manufactured	-6.32	-5.95	-5.88	-4.19	-5.35	-6.38	-6.65	-5.63	-3.96	-4.64
Total trade balance	-1.77	0.32	0.24	1.00	1.60	0.38	-1.67	0.50	2.10	1.69

[1] Exports in each group and the total include re-exports. Balances are derived from Trade of Canada figures, since product group breakdowns are not available in the balance-of-payments accounts. A negative sign represents a deficit (imports greater than exports).

Source: Economic Council of Canada (1975), 22.

heavily on primary and semi-finished goods in order to pay its way. Forest products are the largest earner, followed by metals and agricultural exports, with energy also important. Many of these items are slightly processed (e.g. pulp, refined metals and foods) but nevertheless manufactured goods form the major net import group. The poor showing of recent years is particularly worrying because trade in manufactured goods was stimulated in 1965, when the automobile pact was signed with the United States. This enables 'North American automobile companies to ship vehicles and parts across the border without paying tariffs' (Powrie and Wilkinson, 1974, 60) and had an appreciable effect in increasing Canada's share of production in the industry for a number of years. Yet in the mid-1970s, Canada's trade in highly manufactured products is worse than in the early 1960s. In general, Canada has not demonstrated a comparative advantage in many manufacturing industries.

HISTORICAL EVOLUTION

At the time of Confederation in 1867, when several countries had already experienced several decades of the 'Industrial Revolution', Canada had a population of only 3,690,000 (Easterbrook and Aitken, 1956,384). Settlement was confined almost entirely to the more accessible areas of the eastern provinces (Newfoundland, Nova Scotia, New Brunswick, Prince Edward Island, Québec, Ontario) with a scattering over the rest of the country. It was a rural economy, with some 80 per cent of the people engaged in agriculture and the extractive industries (Harris and Warkentin, 1974, 322–3). Manufacturing, such as it was, took the form largely of small, craft operations. Economically, the country depended on its export staples, just as it had done since white settlement began.

Export staples are the subject of the basic theme of economic development in Canada until at least 1900 and have also become the subject of a theory of economic growth for pioneer countries (North, 1955; Watkins, 1963). A staple is a natural or very slightly processed item, which is exported and provides a major source of income. Good examples would be furs, wheat or refined metals. The staple theory of economic growth holds that development occurs as a result of foreign demand for staples, this being the generator of income in the country. In a highly specialized system of trade, the new country provides foodstuffs and raw materials, which enable it to pay for its other requirements, especially manufactured products from already industrialized countries. The characteristics of development under such a system depend greatly on the nature of the staple (Watkins, 1963). Furs, for example, demand that trappers are frequently on the move, and permanent settlement is not required except at one or two export centres. In contrast, wheat requires a permanent settlement of farmers, who with their families generate demands for goods and services, thus providing the basis for potential growth through multiplier effects. Caves (1971, 433–7) has listed the linkages which appear to be important in affecting growth rates.

This staple theory has been largely worked out and developed by Canadian economic historians, who have visualized Canada's growth as being very closely related to a series of staples (Easterbrook and Watkins, 1967, 1–98). The earliest white settlement was on the east coast and based on dried fish, an item in great demand in the Roman Catholic countries of Europe. The Banks off the coast provided a superb fishing area and attracted the fleets of several European countries by the early sixteenth century. At first, the English established semi-permanent bases in Newfoundland and they had a 'permanent foothold' there by the end of the century (Easterbrook and Aitken, 1956, 27). Nevertheless, fish did not require many settlers nor did it encourage the opening up of the interior. In the latter process, furs played an important role in the second half of the sixteenth century and during the seventeenth and eighteenth centuries. Because furs were soon exhausted in any one area, the trapping of fur-bearing animals attracted men to all parts of the country. In addition, it encouraged large transcontinental commercial operations such as the Hudson's Bay Company, which not only encouraged some settlement but also improved lines of communication in the interior. On the other hand, the companies were the enemies of large-scale settlement, because permanent agriculture destroyed the sources of furs.

The dominant role of furs in the Canadian economy was eventually replaced by timber. In the eighteenth century, Britain was highly dependent on external supplies of timber, especially for shipbuilding, which was so essential both to her trade and to her martial prowess. Supplies, however, were not difficult to obtain from New England nor from the Baltic until they were jeopardized respectively by the American Revolution and the Napoleonic Wars. At that point Britain began to foster timber production in Canada

(Lower, 1967, 30). Eastern Canada, of course, had vast areas of forest which were fully capable of supplying large amounts of ships' timber, including pine masts. Thus from around 1784 and especially in the early nineteenth century, the timber trade grew, aided by high preferences for colonial timber in Britain. During this period the timber trade spread from the eastern provinces and became extremely important in the St Lawrence and Ottawa Valleys. In the St Lawrence valley, there was a close relationship between lumbering and agriculture: farmers usually cleared the land and sold lumber to the timber firms. Along the Ottawa Valley, however, the timber firms had to clear the less attractive land themselves and farmers followed. Gradually, agricultural products came to occupy an increasingly important place in Canada's exports. Their heyday as a vital staple, however, came only in the early twentieth century, when wheat played an essential role in the economy. This was largely associated with the opening up of the Prairie Provinces and its effect has been discussed by Caves (1971, 405-19).

Timber and wheat both made demands that were far in excess of those of earlier staples. In particular, they were bulky, relatively low-value products which required new transport forms. They helped to stimulate the extensive development of canals and railways in the country. In addition, because the number of workers required to produce them was far higher than for fish or furs, the boost to settlement was greater. They encouraged an increasing density of population in all the more hospitable parts of the country, playing a major role in the gradual westerly spread of people and communications.

Canada's economic development, however, is not just a history of staples: one of the strongest criticisms of the staples approach is that it has encouraged a relative neglect of other aspects of the economy. As the country has grown, the economy has inevitably become more complicated and the home market has assumed a greater role. This is reflected also in the gradual strengthening of the manufacturing sector. In a country whose expansion has been governed so much by primary products and commerce, manufacturing has been assigned a secondary role. It was, in fact, still of minor importance and mainly of a craft type as late as the 1871 census. In the last quarter of the nineteenth century and the early part of the twentieth, however, it expanded, diversified and modernized (Bertram, 1967, 81). Bertram's work indicates annual growth rates of the gross value of manufacturing output of 4.4 for the decade 1870–80, 2.4 for the 1880s, 4.8 for the 1890s and 6.0 for 1900–10. Actual figures can be seen in Table 1.4. Some of this manufacturing is initial processing of primary products (primary manufacturing) but secondary manufacturing was growing faster in this period. Concentration of Canadian industry in Ontario, especially iron and steel, also became more pronounced (p.97). By 1920, Canada was a modern industrial nation despite its dependence on staple exports.

During the twentieth century the manufacturing sector has become increasingly complex but Canada's dependence on manufactured imports has nevertheless continued. Staples have remained the major exports with an increasing volume of metals, pulp and paper added to wheat. More recently, energy exports have also grown but, owing to declining reserves, this phenomenon will not last. While the country's openness has remained, there has been a significant switch in the orientation of its trading patterns to an increasing dominance by the United States. Moreover, the country has continued to have a persistent balance of payments deficit that is only counteracted by large capital imports. Thus, foreign indebtedness has been increasing and is particularly noticeable in manufacturing and the newer staples. Further, much of the twentieth century investment has been in a direct form as opposed to nineteenth century British portfolio investment (Levitt, 1970, 58–70). Table 1.5 illustrates the trend since 1926. The situation has become especially significant since 1945, with very heavy American involvement. In 1975 Americans provided 81 per cent of long-term foreign investment in the country (Canada, Statistics Canada, 1978, 1).

Although Canada is often identified with the spirit of individualism and private enterprise of the United States capitalist system (or former system), the country's economic development has in fact been associated with a very high degree of state action. Aitken argues that 'the creation of a national economy in Canada and, even more clearly, a transcontinental economy was as much a political as an economic achievement' (Aitken, 1967, 184). Nationhood involved a good deal of economic action on the part of the federal government. In transport, there was the Confederation promise of a rail link to the Maritimes, which was finally completed with the Intercolonial from Rivière du Loup to Truro in 1876. In 1871, a similar agreement was made with British Columbia, when it joined the Dominion of Canada. Although the government did not even-

TABLE 1.4

GROSS VALUE OF PRODUCTION, PRIMARY, SECONDARY AND TOTAL MANUFACTURING INDUSTRIES STANDARD INDUSTRIAL CLASSIFICATION OF 1948

Selected years 1870–1957[1] – (in 1000's of dollars)

	Primary		Secondary		Total		Index[2] 1935–39 =100
	Current	Constant	Current	Constant	Current	Constant	Constant
1870 Includes estimate for P.E. Island	81,691	102,370	137,534	172,348	219,225	274,718	79.8
1880	102,993	143,444	200,497	279,244	303,490	422,688	71.8
1890	156,529	233,277	296,054	441,213	452,583	674,490	67.1
1900 All Firms Adjusted plus correction factor	199,300	319,380	335,300	537,320	534,600	856,700	62.4
1910 All Firms Adjusted plus correction factor	429,170	546,700	769,630	980,400	1,198,800	1,527,100	78.5
1915 Firms of over $2500 plus correction factor	494,000	538,130	851,700	927,770	1,345,700	1,465,900	91.8
1919[3]	879,195	503,260	2,283,376	1,307,027	3,162,571	1,810,287	174.7
1926[4]	1,070,680	821,704	2,038,036	1,564,111	3,108,716	2,385,815	130.3
1929	1,202,276	964,909	2,676,589	2,148,145	3,878,864	3,113,054	124.6
1933	627,638	718,121	1,325,266	1,516,322	1,952,904	2,234,443	87.4
1939	1,192,048	1,201,661	2,280,780	2,299,173	3,472,828	3,500,834	99.2
1946	2,773,121	1,996,487	5,259,977	3,785,880	8,033,099	5,783,367	138.9
1957[5] Excludes Newfoundland	6,572,205	2,890,152	15,397,048	6,770,909	21,969,253	9,661,061	227.4

[1] Years 1870–1915 computed for this study. For methods of computation see G. W. Bertram, 'Historical Statistics on Growth and Structure of Manufacturing in Canada, 1870–1957,' Canadian Political Science Association, Conference on Statistics, 1962, Table I.

[2] Dominion Bureau of Statistics, *Prices and Price Indexes*, 1949–52 and 1958. Wholesale price index.

[3] Special study of Dominion Bureau of Statistics, preliminary, 1960. Data arranged according to Standard Industrial Classification of 1948. Division between primary and secondary industries estimated on basis of 1915 proportions.

[4] Data for years 1926–46 from worksheets of the staff of the Royal Commission in Canada's Economic Prospects, supplied by the D.B.S. Value added is net of cost of fuel and electricity.

[5] Data refer to selling value of factory shipments. Computed from D.B.S., *The Manufacturing Industries of Canada, Summary for Canada, 1957*.

Source: Bertram (1967), 81.

TABLE 1.5
NON-RESIDENT CONTROL AS A PERCENTAGE OF SELECTED
CANADIAN INDUSTRIES 1926–1973

Percentage of total controlled by all US residents	1926	1939	1948	1963	1973
Manufacturing	35	38	43	60	59
Petroleum and natural gas	—	—	—	74	76
Mining and smelting	38	42	40	59	56
Railways	3	3	3	2	2
Other Utilities	20	26	24	4	7
Total of above and merchandising	17	21	25	34	35
Percentage of total controlled by US residents					
Manufacturing	30	32	39	46	44
Petroleum and natural gas	—	—	—	62	59
Mining and smelting	32	38	37	52	45
Railways	3	3	3	2	2
Other utilities	20	26	24	4	4
Total of above and merchandising	15	19	22	27	26

Source: Levitt (1970), 61 and Statistics Canada (1978), Canada's International Investment Position, 1974. Ottawa.

tually build such a link itself, its land grants of 25 million acres in the West plus a direct subsidy of $25 million were very influential in persuading the Canadian Pacific Railway to do so (Easterbrook and Aitken, 1956, 425-30). The CPR was completed in 1885, a mammoth engineering task which was the culmination of years of argument, government defeats and scandal. Rail policy after Confederation does not stand as an isolated example of federal initiative in the transport field. Canadian governments have been prominent in the St Lawrence canal system from the 1821 Lachine Canal (Montréal) to the 1959 Seaway. In the early twentieth century, the federal government consolidated a number of rail lines to become owner of the Canadian National, while it also dominates the air with Air Canada.

Another vital element of policy worked out in the post-confederation years has been of fundamental importance to the position of manufacturing in Canada. This was the new tariff policy, often referred to as the 'National Policy', which was designed to reduce Canada's dependence on export staples and build up indigenous manufacturing. It took the difficult years of the 1870s depression and the failure to obtain Reciprocity with the United States to convince the government, but high tariffs were eventually introduced in 1879. Under the new arrangements, Canada's integration would be strengthened by development of wheat in the West, manufacturing in central Canada and new rail links across the country (Aitken, 1967, 208-9). 'Duties on semi-finished goods and industrial materials ranged from 10 to 20 per cent, those on fully manufactured industrial equipment and machinery were in the neighbourhood of 25 per cent and on finished consumer goods in common use up to 30 per cent' (Easterbrook and Aitken, 1956, 393-4). The system remained much the same until 1930 and tariffs on most manufactured goods are still high.

An important complement to tariff policy was that on patents. Before the 1872 Patent Act, many new ideas were brought into Canada by immigrant Americans or even by copying processes operating south of the border. Naturally, the United States was not happy about either arrangement. The new act therefore protected their patents but only on condition that the process was carried out in Canada. As a result many United States firms worked out licensing arrangements in Canada. The arrangement brought new processes quickly into the country but it also increased the attitude of dependence and reduced the number of patents granted to Canadians (Naylor, 1975, vol. 2, 38–64). In the 1890s, the combination of tariff and patent policy encouraged large-scale direct investment by the American multidivisional firms which had resulted from a wave of mergers in the United States (Naylor, 1975, vol. 2, 70–7). Thus Canadian manufacturing has been greatly supported by commercial policy leading not only to considerable growth but also, in the view of many economists, to substantial inefficiency (Economic Council of Canada, 1975, 25–37). The latter has come about especially through the relatively small scale of operation and the fact that many industries have no real comparative advantage.

The Current Situation

The most recent (1975) figures indicating the scale of Canadian manufacturing showed that 30,100 establishments in the country produced a value of shipments worth over 88,000 million dollars. Employment of production workers totalled 1,272,051 and the value added in manufacturing was nearly 39,000 million dollars. Figure

1.1 illustrates the main trends in these data since World War II. Unfortunately, a change of procedure in 1960 reduces to some extent the comparability of the data before and after that date as illustrated by the listing of 1959 according to both new and old procedures. Value added in manufacturing was rising fairly steadily during this period, while the number of plants declined after 1955, and employment figures fluctuated.

Amongst the major industrial groups, the largest in terms of value added in manufacturing are food and beverages, transport equipment, paper and allied industries, primary metal, metal fabricating, electrical products and chemical industries. These can be seen in Table 1.6, which also shows that the picture is somewhat different when based on employment figures. The clothing group, for example, is a major employer, while the chemical group is stronger measured by output than by employment.

The major industrial groups are, of course, composites of industries. Canada's top ten specific industries, ranked by value added in production, can be seen in Table 1.7. If this list were ranked according to employment, it would include both men's and women's clothing.

These facts about Canada's industrial structure emphasize once

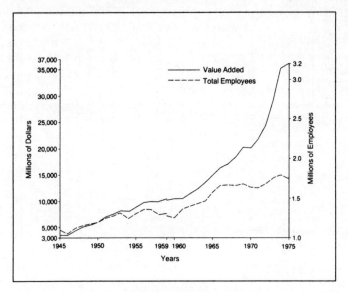

Figure 1.1   Manufacturing trends since 1945.

TABLE 1.6
CANADA'S MANUFACTURING STRUCTURE, 1975

	No. of Establishments	Total Employees No.	%	Value Added in Manufacturing $'000	%
1. Food and beverage industries	4,740	220,415	12.66	5,375,417	13.88
2. Tobacco products industries	27	9,686	0.56	366,845	0.95
3. Rubber and plastics products industries	771	52,963	3.04	1,030,971	2.66
4. Leather industries	415	26,834	1.54	316,474	0.82
5. Textile industries	923	71,050	4.08	1,099,789	2.84
6. Knitting mills	306	24,682	1.42	294,497	0.76
7. Clothing industries	2,094	100,528	5.77	1,143,188	2.95
8. Wood industries	2,920	97,717	5.61	1,689,596	4.36
9. Furniture and fixture industries	1,959	49,688	2.85	724,645	1.87
10. Paper and allied industries	665	127,342	7.31	3,469,803	8.96
11. Printing, publishing and allied industries	3,618	92,912	5.34	1,899,375	4.91
12. Primary metal industry	380	120,335	6.91	2,948,174	7.61
13. Metal fabricating industries	3,882	150,899	8.65	3,278,286	8.47
14. Machinery industries	1,098	92,290	5.30	2,046,762	5.29
15. Transportation equipment industries	991	159,642	9.17	4,208,537	10.87
16. Electrical products industries	805	125,868	7.23	2,631,778	6.80
17. Non-metallic mineral products industries	1,199	55,932	3.21	1,502,408	3.88
18. Petroleum and coal products industries	101	17,264	0.99	865,952	2.24
19. Chemical and chemical products industries	1,046	80,251	4.61	2,663,040	6.88
20. Miscellaneous manufacturing industries	2,160	65,247	3.75	1,160,062	3.00
All industries – Total	30,100	1,741,545	100.00	38,715,600	100.00

Source: Canada, Statistics Canada *Manufacturing Industries of Canada: National and Provincial Areas,* 1975. Ottawa, 1977; 4–13.

TABLE 1.7
CANADA'S MAJOR INDUSTRIES, 1975

Value Added in Manufacturing $000	Rank	Industry	S.I.C. Code	Employment	Rank
2,569,050	1	Pulp and Paper Mills	271	64,329	1
1,348,021	2	Iron and Steel Mills	291	42,169	3
1,227,889	3	Miscellaneous Machinery and Equipment Mfts.	315	43,573	2
1,171,006	4	Motor Vehicle Mfts.	323	31,694	8
1,008,394	5	Motor Vehicle Parts & Accessories	325	34,907	5
849,323	6	Sawmills and Planing Mills	2513	40,788	4
844,537	7	Smelting and Refining	295	22,932	13
843,736	8	Communications Equipment Mfts.	335	26,328	10
789,783	9	Petroleum Refining	3651	6,806	33
783,782	10	Commercial Printing	286	32,955	6

Source: Same as Table 1.6.

again the country's continuing dependence on primary products. Many of her major manufacturing industries involve early-stage processing of the products of mine, farm and forest. On the other hand, many types of secondary manufacturing remain relatively weak, although there is also growing strength in some areas (motor vehicles, metals and machinery, electrical products and chemicals, for example). Since 1961, the major groups which have increased most in value added in manufacturing include rubber (almost five times the 1961 figure in 1973), metal fabricating, machinery and transport equipment (all over three times as large), as well as the traditional wood products and furniture groups.

The Resource Base

Canada's historic and current reliance on primary activities and primary manufacturing reflects her rich base of natural resources. From this point of view Canada is certainly one of the more fortunate countries of the world. While these resources are not limitless and more careful conservation measures are needed than were practised in the past, the country can look ahead with reasonable assurance of good supplies.

Only a small proportion of Canada's land is suitable for farming but the total number of hectares is still large. Nearly 31 million hectares are considered as arable land (Classes 1 to 4). Unfortunately, only about 4.5 million of these are of Class 1 quality and half are in Ontario, where competition from urban development is greatest (Canadian Imperial Bank of Commerce, 1977; Geno and Geno, 1976, 16). Climatic limitations restrict the range of farm products so that exports are mainly of wheat, barley, other grains, live animals and animal products. As far as farm produce for processing is concerned, the country also supplies a variety of vegetables and fruits, as well as tobacco. Although British Columbia and Newfoundland are short of arable land, other regions have a fair share.

Vast areas of the country are forested, including over two-thirds of the land south of the 60th parallel. Thus it is not surprising that lumber, pulp and paper are so important to the Canadian economy. The resource is primarily in the form of softwoods. In 1975, for example, production of softwoods was 26,315,000 cubic metres compared to only 993,000 of hardwoods (Canada, Statistics Canada, 1977, 26). This production is well below the output potential.

A third major renewable resource, the fishery, has been suffering from overuse but the Government's imposition of a 200 mile limit on 1 January, 1977 is expected to help stocks to rise again. The 1970s showed a steady decrease in the tonnage of fish caught, down to 981,000 tonnes by 1975 (United Nations, Food and Agriculture Organization, 1976), which represents 1.4 per cent of the world catch as compared to 2.34 per cent in 1968. The greatest decline has been in the east coast fishery, where competition from non-Canadian vessels is very severe, but the west coast and inland fisheries exhibit the same tendencies. Currently, over four-fifths of the landings are on the east coast while the west coast is roughly three times as important as the inland fishery.

Canada's other major renewable resource is hydro-electricity, which plays a major role in supplying about one quarter of the country's total energy requirements. Once current projects such as James Bay are completed, however, there will be few good remaining sites for development. Thus by the end of the century, it is expected that both thermal and nuclear power stations will become more important for electricity generation (Canada, Department of Energy, Mines and Resources, 1976, 68). The country's main supplies of energy come from oil and gas (about two-thirds). Canada on balance has been exporting substantial amounts of both natural gas and petroleum. In the light of reductions in estimates of Canada's reserves, however, exports have declined since 1973. In fact, it is now calculated that Canadian supplies of crude oil will be insufficient to meet domestic demand as early as 1982 (National Energy Board, 1976, 15). The situation for natural gas is consider-ably better. Estimates, of course, vary greatly from year to year as exploration, mainly in Alberta and the North but also off the east coast, continues. In any case, Canada can also fall back on the enormous, though expensive to recover, Athabaska tar sands as well as very large coal reserves (mainly in Saskatchewan, Alberta and British Columbia with smaller amounts on Cape Breton Island). It is fortunate that total energy supplies are great because Canada is a heavy user as a result of the long, cold winter and the vast distances which necessitate high energy use for transport.

Finally, and of considerable importance to manufacturing indus-try, Canada possesses rich and varied mineral resources. Production (excluding fuels) was worth $6,693 million in 1975 (Canada, Statistics Canada, 1976). By value, the most important items were iron ore, nickel, copper and zinc. It is amazing that in 1974 Canada was the largest world producer of asbestos, nickel, silver, zinc and potash, was second for gold and molybdenum and third for gypsum, platinum, copper, lead and iron ore (Canada, Department of Energy, Mines and Resources, 1974). Most of the metal ores are found in the Canadian Shield although the Western Cordillera are also important. Potash is concentrated in Saskatchewan, asbestos in Québec, while other minerals tend to be somewhat more wide-spread. Supplies are plentiful and shortages are not expected in this century.

Scale, Ownership and Efficiency in Canadian Manufacturing

Canadian manufacturing has frequently been criticized for its inefficiency, usually in comparison with its counterpart in the United States. The Royal Commission on Canada's Economic Prospects, published in 1957, indicated that net output per man-hour in Canadian manufacturing was 35–40 per cent below that in the United States (Fullerton and Hampson, 1957, 154). A more recent Economic Council of Canada study suggested that this differential had continued until the late 1960s (Daly, et al. 1968,9), noting at the same time that manufacturing costs were also higher in Canada (p.12). Calculations indicated that between the countries a volume difference per employed person in manufacturing amounted

16   CANADA'S INDUSTRIAL SPACE-ECONOMY

to some 30 to 36 per cent (p.13). The Economic Council study further pointed out that the differential for manufacturing was greater than for the economy as a whole (p.14).

It was an appreciation of this general situation that led the Economic Council into a study of 'Scale and Specialization in Canadian Manufacturing' (Daly, *et al.* 1968). Economists in Canada have usually seen a close link between scale and productivity in the country's manufacturing sector but the Council's study examined the concept of scale in more detail, considering four possible meanings: size of market, size of firm, size of plant, size of production run and capacity of equipment (p.17).

Size of market varies by product and is influenced by a large number of factors (e.g. transport costs, tariff and trade barriers, marketing practices). The Canadian market is relatively small but the national market as such is not very relevant to most firms, who either supply to regional or local markets, or export as well as shipping to Canadian buyers. In a majority of industries, manufacturing is more concentrated in Canada than in the United States, reflecting a large number of small firms in the latter country (p.18) and this despite the fact that the USA has some giant operations. A similar pattern is found in plant size (p.20). The Economic Council felt that the key difference between the two countries was related to the length of production run. Canadian plants usually produce a much greater range of product and must frequently halt machinery for change-over or adjustment (pp.20–3). The viewpoint of Daly and his colleagues was substantiated by means of interviews, which indicated that *'the limited extent of specialization* has turned out to be not only an important, but also a pervasive factor adversely affecting costs and productivity in manufacturing in Canada'. Interviews by the Council revealed that many manufacturers were well aware of this fact and of the gains to be made by greater specialization (p.44). They seem to have been inhibited from acting on their knowledge by the facts that (1) so many of their materials were expensive and their high prices reduced potential gains in productivity, and that (2) some firms did not feel that reduced costs would benefit their profit levels because of relatively inelastic demand for their products (pp.45–6).

That the productivity problem is severe is shown by a study of the Department of Industry, Trade and Commerce (1976) which covers both returns to labour (labour productivity) and capital (capital productivity). In comparison with the United States, labour productivity improved during the 1960s and early 1970s but remained about 20 per cent behind in 1975 (p.9). Moreover, many other countries did very much better during the same period, thus increasing competition in labour intensive industries. Matthews (1977) has documented the character of the challenge from developing countries in this area. Despite tariff protection, imports have been increasing in five broad areas: leather goods, textiles, hosiery and knitted goods, clothing, and electrical and electronic products. Although wage rates in these industries are relatively low compared with the Canadian average, they are still generally unable to compete against countries with even lower wages.

These labour-intensive industries are not the ones for which the United States provides strong competition. Nevertheless, Table 1.8 shows that United States labour productivity was better than Canada's for those and almost all other industry groups. The problem is equally severe for capital productivity as shown by Table 1.9. Thus the return to capital and labour combined in Canadian manufacturing was 37.7 per cent below that in the United States (Canada, Department of Industry, Trade and Commerce, 1976, 22).

The Economic Council takes the view that a major cause for the

TABLE 1.8
MANUFACTURING VALUE ADDED PER PRODUCTION WORKER
IN RELATION TO THE US BY MAJOR INDUSTRY GROUPS – 1972

Canadian Industries where level of VA/PW Productivity was above that of the US		*Canadian Industries where VA/PW was Less than 10% below that of US*	
	%		%
Petroleum and Coal Products	15.24	Textile Industries	4.99
Non-Metallic Mineral Products	1.43	Wood Industries	6.97
		Primary Metals	9.32
Canadian Industries where VA/PW was between 10% and 20% below that of the US		*Canadian Industries where VA/PW was 20% or more below that of the US*	
Rubber and Plastics	11.29	Leather Industries	21.34
Transportation Equipment	16.15	Food and Beverages	22.00
Furniture and Fixtures	17.12	Machinery Industries	22.02
Clothing	17.80	Knitting Mills	23.72
Paper and Allied Products Ind.	18.21	Chemical and Chem. Products	27.91
Metal Fabricating	18.74	Miscellaneous Manufacturing	30.10
Tobacco Products	19.15		
Printing, Publishing and Allied	18.69		
Electrical Products	11.74		

Source: Canada, Department of Industry, Trade and Commerce, (1976), 20.

TABLE 1.9
OUTPUT PER DOLLAR OF CAPITAL STOCK
(AT REPLACEMENT COST) FOR CANADA AND THE US,
BY MAJOR INDUSTRY GROUPS – 1972

	Canada Value Added/Gross Capital Stock	Rank	United States Value Added/Gross Capital Stock	Rank	Percentage Difference Canada/US
Food and Beverages	0.592	14	1.155	10	-47.9
Tobacco Products	0.973	5	0.619	19	77.2
Rubber Products	1.037	4	1.374	3	-24.5
Leather Products	1.162	3	1.293	7	-10.1
Textile Products	0.420	15	1.234	9	-66.0
Knitting Mills	0.904	8	1.106	11	-19.3
Clothing	2.903	1	1.346	5	115.9
Wood Products	0.684	13	0.782	16	-12.5
Furniture and Fixtures	1.568	2	1.847	1	-15.2
Paper and Allied	0.227	19	0.923	13	-76.4
Printing, Publishing and Allied	0.875	10	1.520	2	-43.4
Primary Metal	0.267	18	0.717	18	-63.8
Metal Fabricating	0.856	11	1.357	4	-37.0
Machinery	1.027	9	0.909	15	12.9
Transportation Equipment	0.859	12	0.756	17	13.6
Electrical Products	1.062	7	0.912	14	16.4
Non-Metallic Minerals	0.411	16	1.257	8	-67.3
Petroleum and Coal	0.144	20	0.276	20	-47.8
Chemical and Chemical Products	0.352	17	0.990	12	-65.5
Miscellaneous Manufacturing	1.053	6	1.332	6	-21.0
Total	0.521		0.969		-46.3

Source: Canada, Department of Industry, Trade and Commerce (1976) based on Statistics Canada, Cat. No. 31–203 (1976); 1972 Census of Manufactures, US Department of Commerce.

current situation is the Canadian tariff. Thus a reduction in tariff levels would reduce the cost of manufactured products and lead to the dropping of some less productive lines. In order to be profitable, firms would then be forced to improve productivity, whereas 'the past level of high effective tariff rates has made it both possible and profitable to produce items using much more labour and capital than were being used by comparable US plants' (p.46). This view is widespread amongst Canadian economists. Powrie and Wilkinson (1974) argue that the tariff policy has worked quite well in fostering manufacturing in the country but that Canada has one of the highest tariff structures in the world and that 'the hope that Canadian manufacturing would outgrow the need for protection continues to be disappointed' (pp.62–3).

On the other hand, Canadian manufacturers do face some high factor costs. Average wage rates are now amongst the highest in the world, having risen rapidly in the last decade to a mid-1970s level above that of the United States *(Financial Times of Canada,* 1977b). Costs of capital are also higher in Canada and the gap with the United States has widened in the mid-1970s. Further, costs of plant and equipment are high for reasons of climate, inefficiencies in construction, expensive transport and tariff protection for the machinery industry (Canada, Dept. of Industry, Trade and Commerce, 1976, 12). Thus high factor costs more than offset some of the savings which result from Canada's resource, especially energy, endowment.

Tariff policy is also blamed by many analysts for being at least partially the cause of another feature of Canada's industrial situation; the high proportion of foreign ownership. The National policy in the 1870s was certainly designed to encourage foreign manufacturers to locate in Canada, and high tariffs have continued to have this effect to the present day. One result has been the tendency for many major United States firms in a given industry to develop a branch in Canada and more or less to replicate their US product range despite the much smaller size of the Canadian market (Safarian, 1969, 3). In consequence, the degree of specialization is greatly reduced, and another reason for low productivity can be identified.

The ownership characteristics have been a great cause for concern in Canada, especially in the last decade. On the economic side, many criticisms have been made of foreign-owned subsidiaries.

Safarian (1969, 3) lists the main ones at the beginning of a study, which attempted to compare the performance of these foreign-owned firms with Canadian ones. They are that such firms:

(a) limit the opportunities for Canadians to serve in senior management ranks and on the boards of their Canadian subsidiaries;

(b) limit severely the decision-making permitted to the Canadian subsidiaries;

(c) prevent the subsidiary from being export-oriented, to avoid its competing with the parent and perhaps other affiliates abroad;

(d) require the subsidiary to buy from its parent or other foreign affiliates, or from such affiliates' foreign suppliers, to the detriment of Canadian production of these items;

(e) centralize their research and development facilities in the parent company, thus inhibiting research spending, along with the employment of scientific personnel in Canada;

(f) adopt financial policies that give precedence to the needs of the parent, thus involving the subsidiary in heavy payments abroad as well as in the pricing of exports and imports contrary to Canadian interests;

(g) are not as efficient as they might be and consequently supply products and services in Canada at higher costs than necessary.

In seeking to explore such complaints, Safarian was frequently limited by somewhat inadequate data. While recognizing great differences from firm to firm, however, he did not find that the performance of comparable Canadian and foreign owned operations were substantially different. In many cases, his evidence suggested that the advantage lay with the foreign-owned firm. Thus, for example, these firms tended to export more than comparable Canadian ones (p.35), to pay less in dividends and plough more money back into the operation (pp.72–4), and to have a higher value added in manufacturing per employee and per establishment (p.81). Safarian also found a substantial number of Canadians in important executive positions in the subsidiaries (half the Presidents and two-thirds of the next three senior officers, although few Chairmen, (p.8)), a high degree of decentralization in both operations and policies (p.17) and a research effort at least as good as Canadian counterparts (p.53). In conclusion, Safarian argued that:

While Canadians have worried too much about the efforts of private decision-making within international firms, they have not

given sufficient thought to the serious questions raised by the
extraterritorial extension of US laws and government regulations
to Canada through the medium of subsidiary firms (p.6).

Other writers have been equally concerned about the fact that
plants operating in Canada are subject to the laws and regulations of
a government other than Canada. The so-called Watkins Report, for
example, argued that:

> The most serious cost to Canada of foreign ownership and control
> results from the tendencies of the United States government to
> regard American-owned subsidiaries as subject to American law
> and policy with respect to American laws on freedom to export,
> United States anti-trust law and policy, and United States
> balance of payment policy (Canada Privy Council Office, 1968,
> 360).

The difficulty as seen by the authors of the report is that the
so-called multinationals are mainly American rather than really
multinational. Levitt (1970, 117) raises the same issue, noting that
American subsidiaries were not allowed to trade with Communist
China, North Korea and North Vietnam even though Canada was
trying to develop such trade.

Technology and Entrepreneurship

One can argue that Safarian's analysis of the performance of
foreign owned subsidiaries in Canada presents too sanguine a
picture. It is all very well to compare these plants with equivalent
Canadian ones, but perhaps their presence in such large numbers in
Canada has-had a bad effect on the whole manufacturing structure.
Levitt (1970,118) argues, 'Direct American investment has
not . . . secured the basis of continued growth'. She claims that
Canada has fallen back in comparison with other industrial countries. The weakness of Canada's position can best be seen in the
areas of skills, technology and entrepreneurship.

It is a well-established fact that the educational level of the
Canadian workforce, including that of the managerial levels, is
below that of the United States. It has been calculated that the
higher educational attainment of the United States workforce was
responsible for well over one third of the productivity difference
between the two countries, and Lithwick (1967, 2) suggested that
Canada was about 30 years behind in extending education to most

of its young people. The situation seems to be especially bad with respect to management education. In comparison with the United States, 'the average differences between the two countries in this regard appear to be wider than in almost all other major categories of the labour force' (Economic Council of Canada, 1965, 62). By the beginning of the 1970s, however, things were looking much more promising and Canada was said to be:

> rapidly moving out of an extended period of persistent shortages for many types of higher-level manpower into an extended period of relatively ample supplies of such manpower – although there will be, at least for a time, a concentration of such manpower among the younger age groups in which there will have been little opportunity yet for experience (Keys *et al.*, 1971,11).

The gap in educational levels is closing and there is no reason why it should not disappear. It certainly cannot be blamed on foreign ownership of Canadian manufacturing. In fact, it can be argued that American companies have been important in bringing up-to-date ideas to Canadian management practice (Safarian, 1969, 13). Nevertheless, a real problem can be discerned in the fact that so many of these companies allow only a restricted level of decision-making to their management or directorships and that the way to the top flight is to leave for their head offices elsewhere. Thus the scope for the exercise of the highest levels of management and entrepreneurship within Canada is limited and this is bound to have a somewhat stultifying effect. Levitt (1970, 73) argues that the operation of the multinationals leads to 'increasing dependence on entrepreneurial initiatives originating in the metropoles'. Some of the left-wing analysts refer to Canadians in executive positions with multinationals in Canada as the 'comprador' elite, an implied comparison with nationals in China and elsewhere who aided the colonialists in the nineteenth century (Clement, 1975, 119). Studies of the Canadian corporate élite have been extremely interesting in their revelation of the fact that the core of this élite has its economic base in finance and commerce and has essentially ignored the manufacturing sector, at least in taking an entrepreneurial role (Porter, 1965; Clement, 1975). This, of course, reflects Canada's economic history as a trading nation but it has led to a situation in which financial institutions, especially, are very powerful while manufacturing and resource development have been left open for the outsider. Canada's financial institutions have a reputation for being cautious, and prefer to invest in well-established multinationals rather than to provide venture capital or take a risk with new Canadian initiatives (Science Council of Canada, 1971a, 30). Small Canadian companies must frequently go to the United States for capital to develop these new ideas, and this is one reason for frequent takeovers (Perry, 1971, 72–81).

The subject of innovation in Canadian manufacturing has received a good deal of attention from the Science Council of Canada, whose concern initially was with a faltering employment of scientists and technologists beginning about 1968. Manufacturing growth during the early 1960s had been closely associated with those industries dependent on science and technology (Science Council of Canada, 1971a, 17). The Council also pointed out that 'Industrial R/D activity in Canada is still far below that of most other industrial countries' and that it appeared that companies were turning away from research and development as a means of attaining technological proficiency (p.19). While it is clear that Canada will always need to import technology from other countries, the Council argued that 'Acceptance of this fact does not detract from the importance of innovation generated internally, particularly in the small specialized company taking advantage of opportunities peculiar to Canada' (p.25). Canada should seek to build on its two fundamental strengths, 'our increasingly skilled population and our wealth of resources' (p.25).

Innovations in Canada seem to have been hindered by a number of related factors. Secondary industry in Canada has developed historically by means of direct investment and technology transfer from the United States, without the establishment of a strong technological base in Canada itself. Moreover, the protection of Canadian industry by means of tariff and other barriers has encouraged inefficiency and limited the incentive to innovate. While a large market is needed to encourage expansion and innovation, it is in fact fragmented by having too many firms in many industries and reduced by allowing high imports of many products, while other countries, especially the United States, restrict access to Canadian manufactured items. Moreover the conservatism of Canadians in their investment practices makes financing for innovation difficult to obtain and government policy has not greatly improved the situation. It is likely that the relatively low level of managerial skills also impedes innovation (Science Council of Canada, 1971a, 28–31).

The role of the multinationals in this situation has received special attention through an investigation of their actual research operations (Science Council of Canada, 1971b). It is possible to distinguish two types of laboratory, the international interdependent type and the support laboratory. In the first, the laboratory is involved in a full-scale research effort, being part of the firm's international research and development operation. It may have little to do with the firm's manufacturing plants in Canada, and the products it develops will probably not be manufactured in the country but transmitted 'to the parent company for worldwide exploitation' (p.44). Thus research success in Canada will provide little more than jobs for science graduates. In fact the country:

> may actually sustain a net loss if these graduates' services could have been better used on other problems of higher priority in the country (p.44).

The second and much more common type of laboratory in Canada is the support laboratory which essentially brings in new technology from the parent and adapts products to the Canadian market. Most of the firms in the Science Council's study derived '60–80 per cent of product and production technology from the parent operation' (p.47). Generally, it was concluded that the transfer of technology through such support laboratories does not bring much benefit to Canada (p.48). Moreover, evidence is quoted to suggest that the research effort of multinationals is likely to be centralized, so that they probably will never carry out much basic research outside their home country (p.49).

Canada's weak record in innovation and research cannot, however, be blamed entirely on foreign ownership. In fact, the record of Canadian companies is generally worse than the subsidiary. Moreover, government support for industrial research and development has been falling as a percentage of federal expenditure (Science Council of Canada, 1977, 15). The problem seems to be pervasive. This could be a very dangerous situation and is probably behind Canada's weak long-term growth in the whole area of finished manufactured products as opposed to raw or semi-finished ones. In exports of such products, 'by comparison with virtually all the West European countries and a number of non-European countries Canada fell behind and industrialized at an abnormally slow rate' in the 1960s and early 1970s (Science Council of Canada, 1977, 19). On the other hand, Daly (1977, 23–5) argues that it is not so much the initial research that matters as the fast adoption of new technology. He recommends 'giving a higher priority to earlier adoption of new technology than to basic research and development' (p.25).

TOWARDS AN INDUSTRIAL STRATEGY

In the late 1960s and the 1970s, calls for an industrial strategy for Canada have become frequent. The proposals made by various interests and individuals reflect a growing dissatisfaction with the current status of manufacturing industry in the country, and with federal government policy or lack of policy on diverse matters relating to manufacturing. In reading some proposals, one has the impression that Canada has no policy in this area but in fact there exist already several relevant policies. Problems seem to involve their modification to suit present conditions, and their co-ordination to provide an integrated strategy. These tasks are still underway and contributions come forth with some regularity (Breton, 1974; Gordon, 1975).

The conventional view of economists has been to focus on some of the weaknesses of Canada's industrial structure, especially lack of specialization and the problems of small scale production. They have pointed to low productivity in comparison with the United States. Their solution is to reduce the high tariff levels, which protect Canadian manufacturing and which have been the main reason for its inefficiency. The key objective is to 'improve the performance of manufacturing firms in Canada, *irrespective of where ownership* is located' (Daly, 1972, 9). A reduction in the tariff would lead to the dropping of high-cost, low productivity items plus a specialization in products which would be able to compete in world markets. Another area of concern is the quality of Canadian management, which should receive attention in any industrial strategy (Daly, 1972, 17). Canada, according to Daly, has a comparative disadvantage in its management and scientists and technologists, a fact reflected in weak research and development and lack of competitiveness on a world scale (pp.24–5).

Most other proponents of industrial policies find the conventional approach of economists too narrow. The Science Council (1971a, 38) has argued that Canada must endeavour to build on its advantages, 'its growing population of skilled people, and its store of

natural resources'. The Council suggests an industrial strategy that
stresses medium and high-technology manufacturing in fields related to production of resources. This naturally reflects the Science
Council's interest in jobs for scientists and technologists. On the
other hand, they argue that such industries will create a good
multiplier effect and help to expand other types of employment over
a five-to-ten year period. They suggest that the various levels of
government should place more stress on innovation and co-ordinate
their policies, seek to negotiate trade pacts which would allow
Canadian high-technology industries access to wider markets, try to
encourage these industries through their purchasing powers and
give special help to certain promising programmes (pp.39–40). The
Council recognizes that industry's attitudes are hampered by its
ownership pattern and that it 'must work to overcome its subsidiary
mentality, the main characteristic of which is an extremely short
time horizon'(p.41). All in all, this approach can be considered as an
attempt to develop real comparative advantage in a number of
growing industries, fully recognizing that comparative advantage is
not a static but a dynamic concept. This would lead to a reduction of
many labour intensive industries, in which Canada finds it difficult
to compete with developing countries. According to Williams (1977,
18–19), Canada's comparative advantage is in items processed from
iron and metal ores and forest resources.

Most other suggestions for a new industrial policy focus directly
on the question of foreign ownership, taking the view that it has
harmful effects from both an economic and a political point of view.
Studnicki-Gizbert (1972), for example, argues that Canada already
makes use of numerous policy instruments, covering improvement
to infrastructure, incentives, control over some industries, long-term
capital to industry through the Canadian Development Corporation
and aid for exports, but 'what we do not have is an instrument to
deal with qualitative control over foreign investment and the
operation of foreign-owned firms' (p.61). Since he wrote, however, a
policy has been implemented in the Foreign Investment Review Act
(FIRA). The act was passed at the end of 1973. At first it applied to
takeovers by foreign companies, who were expected to demonstrate
that takeovers would be of significant benefit to Canada. Ten
criteria have been used to assess the benefits including compatibility
with existing policies, improved productivity, increased employment, new investment, new products and innovation, Canadian

participation, increased resource processing or use of Canadian parts and services, enhanced technological development, improvement in competition and increased exports (*Financial Times of Canada*, 1975). In 1975, part two of the Act was applied to expansions by foreign-owned companies into new product lines.

This agency does not satisfy most critics because it deals only with takeovers and expansions and does nothing to help Canadians to regain control of firms which already belong to foreigners. In a recent book, Walter Gordon (1975), a former Minister of Finance, makes specific proposals to deal with this situation. He notes that 'about eighty per cent of the increase in foreign control each year is represented by the expansion of existing foreign-controlled companies in Canada' (p.97). Mr. Gordon proposes that the House of Commons pass a resolution, which would cause the largest foreign subsidiaries to sell out to Canadians. He suggested that those with assets of over $250 million should qualify, noting that only 32 (not all in manufacturing) would be involved as of the end of 1973 (p.106). Control would be transferred gradually in five stages. The first three stages would involve the largest resource companies (forestry, oil and mining) and be completed within five years. Most of the manufacturing operations would be taken over in the following two years. Apart from the automobile companies and Canadian General Electric, these are mainly concerned with early stage processing of resources (p.108). The way in which control changed hands would be up to the owners but no more than 25 per cent of shares should ultimately remain in foreign hands, and not more than 12 per cent under a single person or group. Although Mr Gordon envisages the possibility that the Canadian Development Corporation (a publicly-owned corporation) could take over some companies, he does not expect a large degree of nationalization would be established. He feels that, in the proposed time span, this programme is feasible by using Canadian funds and converting foreign equity capital into other forms such as long-term government bonds. He argues:

> It would be difficult to claim that the cost of regaining effective control of the Canadian economy is beyond our financial capacity (p.111).

Socialists, who generally agree with Gordon's assessment of the effects of foreign ownership, consider that the essential requirement in Canada is for a greater degree of public ownership. The replacement of foreign capitalists by Canadian ones does not fully satisfy them because, they argue, capitalists do not serve the Canadian people at large. The socialist analysis stresses the fact that Canadian independence and nationalism are threatened by North American capitalism (Watkins, 1973, 267) and that Canadian corporations, if they become large and multinational, will tend to move their managerial function out of Canada into the larger market areas (p.258). Thus, capitalism itself is a major problem.

Not only have specific policies been proposed, but there are now suggestions as to how these might be combined into an overall integrated strategy. Thus, it would seem that much of the ground-work has been laid, even if opinions as to many details differ. One of the areas in which differences are considerable and must be resolved is the very basic one of goals to be pursued and the relative importance of such objectives as high economic growth and the maintenance of Canadian independence. No individual strategist can resolve this issue, which must somehow be dealt with at a political level. Nevertheless, its resolution is basic. Mintzberg (1972) suggests that once goals are set, a strategy would involve some evaluation of Canada's strengths and weaknesses, and of world trends which can be expected to affect the country. The next step would be to define major problems and opportunities suggested by this evaluation. The research is essentially complete on both of these steps. Mintzberg outlines the necessary components of a strategy to include:

(a) Primary-Industry Strategy relating to Canada's resources, their development and export.

(b) Secondary-Industry Strategy, which would encourage rationalization within some industries.

(c) Sector Strategy designed to aid specialization in sectors that merit particular attention. Tariff changes and support pro-grammes would encourage only certain industries which have inherent strength.

(d) Trading Strategy. Some effort is required to avoid the possibility that Canada becomes isolated as a result of the development of trading blocks such as the European Common Market.

(e) Financial Strategy designed to improve the financial situation for Canadian entrepreneurs and to reduce foreign direct invest-ment.

(f) Manpower Strategy, including the special area of improving managerial and entrepreneurial talent.

In 1975 the Economic Council of Canada, representative of the main-line economists, came forward with a strong statement in favour of free trade but with explicit recognition of some of the limitations of the approach and the necessary adjustments that it would entail. The most beneficial situation for Canada is one of multilateral free trade, that is the removal of all trade barriers (Economic Council of Canada, 1975, 81–3). This would have the effect of moving productivity in Canadian manufacturing up to United States levels through larger scale economies and greater specialization. It would open up new opportunities for innovation in specialized activities which would have a very large market. Thus high-technology industries and those requiring special skills would be encouraged. In short:

> Multilateral free trade would provide the most remarkable improvement in the economic well-being of Canadians that could result from a single step by a government today – or at any time since the Great Depression (p.82).

The Council also reviewed various free trade options that appear to be practical at the present time, including combinations involving the United States, the European Economic Community and Japan. They concluded that, because of the close trading relationship with the USA, any step would have to include that country (p.99).

Any major step towards free trade would necessitate some major adjustments and the Economic Council recommends a ten year period within which these could be worked out (p.101). Some manufacturing industries would have severe problems because of low-cost competition – for example, textiles, clothing and footwear. It would, however, be possible even within these industries for certain specialized high quality lines to be competitive (pp.77–8). Nevertheless, areas concentrating on such industries can be expected to have major adjustment problems. In general, the reorganization would bear most severely on the heavily industrialized provinces, Ontario and Québec. A lower tariff would bring cheaper products to the western and eastern provinces and lead to 'substantial gains with relatively little adjustment and reorganization' (p.79). On the other hand, after the period of reorganization, the two central provinces would benefit most because of the efficient, modernized manufacturing sector. The Council argues that the first few years of the new policy could be very difficult but that policies similar to existing ones can be used to overcome the temporary problems (pp.166–86).

To those who are concerned about foreign investment, the Economic Council answers that its suggested policies would probably 'reduce the relative importance of foreign investment in Canada' (p.184) because higher incomes would provide more finance, and indigenous enterprise would be encouraged. It feels the need for the continuation of some kind of review policy over foreign enterprise and recommends international initiatives to work out a code of behaviour for multinationals.

Not surprisingly the Science Council has failed to be convinced by the free traders and has countered with the view that Canadian manufacturing is too truncated to benefit from a freer market. A long history of weak innovation and poor research and development means that there is too restricted a base in high technology industry to compete effectively. The call then is for technological sovereignty with support for Canadian-owned companies and a regulation of the import of technology (Britton and Gilmour, 1978).

While these discussions on broad industrial strategy continue, day-to-day policy goes on, mainly under the direction of the Department of Industry, Trade and Commerce. This department has always been concerned with servicing the manufacturing sector as a whole and has administered numerous policies to this end. Recently, however, some noticeable shifts of emphasis have taken place and they are primarily in the direction of improving service to small and medium-sized business. In view of some of the studies complaining about the small scale of Canadian manufacturing, this new approach may seem strange. Many of the studies quoted above, however, showed that it was lack of specialization rather than scale of operation which is the major problem in Canada. Smaller plants can in fact be very efficient. Moreover, it has been shown that differences in productivity between small plants in the United States and Canada are considerable (Canada, Department of Industry, Trade and Commerce, 1976, 25–6). Further, if plants in some industries were to be increased in size to their most efficient level, it would be incompatible with a reasonable degree of competition (Gorecki, no date, 47–8). In addition, a strong lobby in favour of small business has grown up under the leadership of the Canadian Federation of Independent Business, while studies have argued that the small business sector can be extremely useful to the country (Peterson, 1977).

The government has established a Minister of State for Small Business and reorganized its complex system of aid into one Enterprise Development Program (EDP). The EDP is designed 'to enhance the growth in the manufacturing and processing sectors of the Canadian economy by providing assistance to selected firms to make them more viable and internationally competitive' (Canada, Department of Industry, Trade and Commerce, no date, 1). The idea is to help promising small and medium-sized firms through a whole product life cycle; – concept, development, pre-production, production and marketing. Forms of assistance include:

(1) Grants to develop proposals for projects eligible for assistance.
(2) Grants to study market feasibility.
(3) Grants to study productivity improvement projects.
(4) Grants for industrial design.
(5) Grants for innovation projects.
(6) Loans or loan insurance for adjustment projects.
(7) Special purpose forms of assistance.

A special effort has been made to publicize the programme to the small businessman. In addition, regional boards, including private sector representatives, will consider applications. As of May 1978, further policies to aid smaller businesses are being proposed, including help in taxation and venture capital areas.

Another element in small business support is the work of the Federal Business Development Bank. Formerly the Industrial Development Bank, this is a lender of last resort. The main effect of the reorganization, apart from expansion, is to increase the bank's role as an advisor to small business (*Financial Times of Canada*, 1977a).

CONCLUSIONS

It is clear that Canadian manufacturing in 1978 is in a relatively weak position. From many quarters proposals for change are being made and a recent work expresses the situation clearly:

La politique canadienne est parvenue a la croisée des chemins. Le choix de nouvelles voies est urgent, car tout retard risque d'entrainer la politique commerciale et l'économie dans son ensemble dans un cul-de-sac.(Fréchette *et al.*, 1975, 432).

The decisions to be made in the next few years will be of

fundamental importance to the location of industry in Canada. Tighter controls on foreign investment could make it almost impossible for the peripheral areas to obtain new manufacturing industry, could lead to a very slow growth of the sector everywhere and to the closure of many branch plants. A switch to freer trade would involve major readjustments everywhere but especially in Ontario and Québec, while some towns specializing in non-competitive industries such as textiles could lose their economic base. Whatever policies are pursued, however, the next decade seems likely to be one that will involve some major adjustments in the country's manufacturing sector.

REFERENCES

Aitken, H.G.J. (1967), 'Defensive expansion: the State and economic growth in Canada', in W.T. Easterbrook and M.H. Watkins (eds), *Approaches to Canadian Economic History*, (Toronto: McClelland and Stewart), 183–221.

Bertram, G.W. (1967), 'Economic growth in Canadian industry, 1870–1915', in W.T. Easterbrook and M.H. Watkins (eds.) *Approaches to Canadian Economic History*,(Toronto: McClelland and Stewart), 74–98.

Breton, Albert (1974), *A Conceptual Basis for an Industrial Strategy*. Ottawa: Economic Council of Canada.

Britton, J.N.H. and Gilmour, J.M. (1978), *The Weakest Link*. Ottawa: Science Council of Canada.

Canada, Department of Energy, Mines and Resources (1974), *Towards a Mineral Strategy for Canada*. Ottawa.

Canada, Department of Energy, Mines and Resources (1976), *An Energy Strategy for Canada: Policies for Self Reliance*. Ottawa: Energy Policy Sector.

Canada, Department of Industry, Trade and Commerce (1976), 'Productivity and competitiveness in the Canadian economy', mimeo. Ottawa: Office of Policy Analysis, 28 October.

Canada, Department of Industry, Trade and Commerce (no date), *The Enterprise Development Program (EDP)*. Ottawa.

Canada, Privy Council Office (1968), *Foreign Ownership and the Structure of Canadian Industry*, Report of the Task Force on the Structure of Canadian Industry (The Watkins Report). Ottawa: Privy Council.

Canada, Statistics Canada (1976), *Canada's Mineral Production 1976*. Ottawa.

Canada, Statistics Canada (1977), *Canadian Forestry Statistics, 1975*. Ottawa.

Canada, Statistics Canada (1978), *Informat*. Ottawa, 20 January.

Canadian Imperial Bank of Commerce (1977), 'Canada's Food Land Resource', *Commercial Letter*, No. 3.

Caves, R.E. (1971) 'Export-led growth and the new economic history', in J.N. Bhagwati *et al.* (eds.), *Trade, Balance of Payments and Growth*, (Amsterdam: North Holland), 403–42.

Clement, Wallace (1975), *The Canadian Corporate Elite*, Toronto: McClelland and Stewart.

Daly, D.J. (1972), 'Vulnerability and efficiency', in A. Rotstein (ed.), *An Industrial Strategy for Canada*, (Toronto: New Press).

Daly, D.J. (1977), 'Adaptation in Canadian Manufacturing', mimeo prepared for the Conference on Industrial Adaptation, Montreal. Ottawa: Economic Council of Canada, June.

Daly, D.J. *et al.* (1968), *Scale and Specialization in Canadian Manufacturing*. Ottawa: Economic Council of Canada.

Easterbrook, W.T. and Aitken, H.G.J. (1956), *Canadian Economic History*. Toronto: Macmillan of Canada.

Easterbrook, W.T. and Watkins, M.H. (1967), *Approaches to Canadian Economic History*. Toronto: McClelland and Stewart.

Economic Council of Canada (1965), *Second Annual Review: Towards Sustained and Balanced Economic Growth*. Ottawa: Queen's Printer.

Economic Council of Canada (1975), *Looking Outward: A New Trade Strategy for Canada*, Ottawa: Economic Council of Canada.

Financial Times of Canada (1975), 'Gillespie raises FIRA's veil', 10 March, 23.

Financial Times of Canada (1977a), 'FBDB: Making the loans no one else will take on', 22 August, 3.

Financial Times of Canada (1977b), 'Productivity rising faster in Canada than U.S.', 28 November–4 December, 21.

Fréchette, P. *et al.* (1975), *L'économie du Québec*. Montréal: Les éditions HRW.

Fullerton, D.H. and Hampson, H.A. (1957), *Canadian Secondary Manufacturing Industry*. Ottawa: Queen's Printer.

Geno, B.J. and Geno, L.M. (1976), *Food Production in the Canadian Environment*. Ottawa: Science Council of Canada.

Gordon, W.L. (1975), *Storm Signals: New Economic Policies for Canada*. Toronto: McClelland and Stewart.

Gorecki, Paul K. (no date), *Economics of Scale and Efficient Plant Size in Canadian Manufacturing Industries*. Ottawa: Dept. of Consumer and Corporate Affairs, Bureau of Competition Policy, Research Branch.

Harris, R.C. and Warkentin J. (1974), *Canada Before Confederation*. New York: Oxford University Press.

Keys B.A. *et al.* (1971). *Meeting Managerial Manpower Needs*. Ottawa: Economic Council of Canada.

Levitt, K. (1970), *Silent Surrender*. Toronto: Macmillan of Canada.

Lithwick, N.H. (1967), *Economic Growth in Canada: A Quantitative Analysis*. Toronto: University of Toronto Press.

Lower, A.R.M. (1967), 'The trade in square timber', in W.T. Easterbrook and M.H. Watkins (eds.), *Approaches to Canadian Economic History*, (Toronto: McClelland and Stewart), 28–48.

Matthews, Roy A. (1977), 'Canadian Industry and the developing countries', mimeo prepared for the Conference on Industrial Adaptation, Montreal. Ottawa: Economic Council of Canada, June.

Mintzberg, H. (1972), 'A framework for strategic planning', in A. Rotstein (ed.), *An Industrial Strategy for Canada*, (Toronto: New Press), 63–74.

National Energy Board (1976), *Annual Report 1975.* Ottawa: Information Canada.

Naylor, R.T. (1975), *The History of Canadian Business 1867–1914.* 2 vols. Toronto: James Lorimer and Co.

North, D.C. (1955), 'Location theory and regional economic growth', *Journal of Political Economy,* 63, (June), 243–58.

Perry, R.L. (1971), *Galt, U.S.A.* Toronto: Maclean-Hunter.

Peterson, Rein (1977), *Small Business: Building A Balanced Economy.* Erin, Ontario: Press Porcepic.

Porter, John (1965), *The Vertical Mosaic,* Toronto: University of Toronto Press.

Powrie, T.L. and Wilkinson, B.W. (1974), 'Canadian trade patterns and commercial policy', in L.H. Officer and L.R. Smith (eds.), *Issues in Canadian Economics,* (Toronto: McGraw-Hill Ryerson), 56–68.

Safarian, A.E. (1969), *The Performance of Foreign-Owned Firms in Canada.* Montreal: Canadian-American Committee.

Science Council of Canada (1971a), *Innovation in a Cold Climate.* Ottawa: Information Canada.

Science Council of Canada (1971b), *The Multinational Firm, Foreign Direct Investment, and Canadian Science Policy.* Ottawa: Information Canada.

Science Council of Canada (1977), *Uncertain Prospects: Canadian Manufacturing Industry, 1971–1977.* Ottawa: Science Council Committee on Industrial Policies.

Studnicki-Gizbert, K.W. (1972), 'Policy instruments', in A. Rotstein (ed.), *An Industrial Strategy for Canada,* (Toronto: New Press), 54–74.

United Nations, Food and Agriculture Organization (1976), *Yearbook of Fishing Statistics, Volume 41.*

Watkins, M. (1963), 'A staple theory of economic growth', *The Canadian Journal of Economics and Political Science,* 29, (May), 141–58.

Watkins, M., (1973), 'Contradictions and alternatives in Canada's future', in R.M. Laxer (ed.), *Canada Ltd.,* (Toronto: McClelland and Stewart), 250–69.

Williams, J.R. (1977), 'Canada's comparative advantage', mimeo prepared for the Conferences on Industrial Adaptation, Montreal. Ottawa: Economic Council of Canada, June.

2

Regional Diversity

The preface to this book drew attention to the tremendous regional variety within Canada. After considering the economy as a single unit, it is now necessary to return to that theme. This is essential not only because of large differences in the resource and locational endowment of the separate parts of the country but also because of significant variations in historical development. Above all, it must always be remembered that Canada is a federal country and that, within limits, each province is free to follow an independent line. In the realm of industrial policy this is highly pertinent: a successful strategy depends on the co-operation of federal and provincial governments and the co-ordination of their policies, something which is easier said than achieved.

The contemporary situation with respect to the position of manufacturing at a provincial level is well illustrated by Table 2.1. The dominance of Ontario and Québec is immediately apparent, especially in the value added in manufacturing. Ontario has almost half of Canadian manufacturing employees and about 52 per cent of value added. Québec, with 31 per cent and 27 per cent for the same

TABLE 2.1
SELECTED STATISTICS OF MANUFACTURING INDUSTRY,
BY PROVINCE, 1975

	No. of Establishments	No. of Employees	Employees %	Value Added $000	%
Newfoundland	270	13,000	0.75	224,139	0.58
Prince Edward Island	117	2,353	0.14	36,741	0.09
Nova Scotia	689	37,365	2.15	700,019	1.81
New Brunswick	559	29,300	1.68	610,085	1.58
Québec	9,375	532,932	30.60	10,458,512	27.01
Ontario	12,245	850,291	48.82	20,122,934	51.97
Manitoba	1,215	55,010	3.16	1,080,398	2.79
Saskatchewan	653	19,213	1.10	455,185	1.18
Alberta	1,821	64,678	3.71	1,638,347	4.23
British Columbia	3,131	137,138	7.87	3,383,285	8.74
Yukon and Northwest Territories	25	265	0.02	5,956	0.02
Canada	30,100	1,741,545	100.00	38,715,600	100.00

Source: Statistics Canada, *Manufacturing Industries of Canada, 1975.* (Ottawa: 1977).

items is also strongly represented. Only about 20 per cent of manufacturing activity is left to the other provinces combined. The Atlantic Region produces about 4 per cent of value added, the Prairies a little over 8 per cent, and British Columbia nearly 9 per cent. The share of the two northern territories is negligible.

These differences partly reflect size of population but also diffe-rent economic structures. In Ontario, manufacturing produces just under 70 per cent of the value added by goods-producing industries, and in Québec the figure is only slightly less at 65 per cent (Canada Year Book, 1975, 833). Elsewhere, this figure is much lower. In the east, where construction and primary activities are still very impor-tant, it varies from 21 per cent in Prince Edward Island to 44 per cent in New Brunswick and Nova Scotia. In the Prairies also, agriculture, mining and construction play a major role so that manufacturing's share of value added by goods-producing industries varies from only 12 per cent in Saskatchewan to 36 in Manitoba. In British Columbia, the figure stands at 45 per cent. In that province, forestry is particularly important amongst the primary activities.

In terms of trading patterns, the provinces are less well integrated than might be expected. In 1974, most provinces shipped more manufactured goods to other countries than to any one other province (Table 2.2). Not surprisingly, the provinces at the two extremes of the country were most oriented to foreign trade but substantial proportions of exports also characterized New Bruns-wick, Nova Scotia and Ontario. The highest degree of provincial integration, in terms of manufactured goods, was found between Ontario and Québec, with Québec especially forming an important market for Ontario's products. An earlier survey, in 1967, showed substantially similar patterns, although both the Prairies and Atlan-tic Provinces produced a higher proportion of their requirement of manufactured goods in 1974 than seven years earlier (Canada, Statistics Canada, 1971).

SOME FEATURES OF THE REGIONAL ECONOMIES

Provincial population statistics tell an important story in them-selves. The figures in Table 2.3 illustrate immediately the dominant position of the two central provinces, Ontario and Québec, which together are the home of over 60 per cent of Canadians. These two provinces, however, are no longer the fastest growing: Québec,

TABLE 2.2
CANADIAN TRADE IN MANUFACTURED GOODS 1974 (%)

From: \ To:	Nfld.	P.E.I.	N.S.	N.B.	Que.	Ont.	Man.	Sask.	Alta.	B.C.	Y./NWT	Abroad	Total[1] ($ bill.)
Nfld.	22.1	—	1.0	1.5	9.8	0.9	X	X	X	X	—	64.6	0.712
P.E.I.	8.1	37.0	19.7	10.4	6.8	8.0	X	X	X	X	X	9.7	0.094
N.S.	4.8	3.1	38.1	5.3	9.8	9.1	0.7	0.2	0.4	0.8	—	27.6	1.696
N.B.	2.7	1.8	7.5	31.8	9.8	9.9	0.3	0.2	0.4	0.4	—	35.1	1.586
Que.	0.9	0.4	1.4	1.5	53.3	20.8	1.5	1.0	2.0	2.4	0.1	14.7	22.397
Ont.	0.7	0.2	1.2	1.0	12.0	53.7	2.1	1.3	2.9	3.2	0.1	21.7	41.404
Man.	0.2	0.1	1.1	0.8	5.9	12.9	52.2	6.1	6.7	3.6	0.3	10.2	2.280
Sask.	0.2	0.1	1.7	0.8	4.6	6.5	7.6	53.7	8.7	4.5	0.2	11.6	1.045
Alta.	0.1	—	0.1	0.1	7.4	3.3	2.7	6.2	58.4	13.1	1.0	7.7	3.821
B.C.	0.1	—	0.3	0.3	1.8	3.6	1.4	1.3	6.0	43.5	0.4	41.3	7.411
Y & NWT.	—	—	—	—	—	—	—	—	—	—	—	—	0.009
All Provs.	1.0	0.3	2.0	1.7	21.7	34.0	3.2	2.2	5.6	6.9	0.1	21.2	
Total ($ bill.)	0.743	0.267	1.559	1.321	16.669	26.175	2.493	1.671	4.301	5.274	0.114	16.287	82.455

Note: Percentage figures exclude custom and repair work and shipments so far unallocated.
X – Confidential.
— Less than 0.05%.
[1] Includes custom and repair work and shipments so far unallocated.
Source: Financial Times of Canada. May 2, 1977, based on material later published in Statistics Canada (1978): Destination of Shipments of Manufacturers, 1974. Ottawa.

TABLE 2.3
POPULATION BY PROVINCE, SELECTED CENSUS YEARS

	1951		1961		1971		1976	
	No.	%	No.	%	No.	%	No.	%
Newfoundland	361,416	2.58	457,853	2.51	522,104	2.42	557,725	2.43
P.E.I.	98,429	0.70	104,629	0.57	111,641	0.52	118,230	0.51
Nova Scotia	642,584	4.59	737,007	4.04	788,960	3.66	828,570	3.60
New Brunswick	515,697	3.68	597,936	3.28	634,557	2.94	677,250	2.95
Québec	4,055,681	28.95	5,259,211	28.85	6,027,764	27.94	6,234,445	27.12
Ontario	4,597,542	32.82	6,236,092	34.19	7,703,106	35.72	8,264,465	35.96
Manitoba	776,541	5.54	921,686	5.05	988,247	4.58	1,021,505	4.44
Saskatchewan	831,728	5.94	925,181	5.07	926,242	4.29	921,320	4.01
Alberta	939,501	6.71	1,331,944	7.30	1,627,874	7.55	1,838,040	7.99
B.C.	1,165,210	8.32	1,629,082	8.93	2,184,621	10.13	2,466,610	10.73
Yukon	9,096	0.06	14,628	0.08	18,388	0.09	21,835	0.09
N.W.T.	16,004	0.11	22,998	0.13	34,807	0.16	42,610	0.19
Canada	14,009,429	100.00	18,238,247	100.00	21,568,311	100.00	22,992,600	100.00

especially, has slipped back in this respect. Its annual rate of growth between 1966 and 1971 was well below the national average, and its proportion of the Canadian population declined from about 29 per cent in 1951 to roughly 27 per cent in 1976. At the same time, Ontario increased its percentage share from a little under 33 to nearly 36. Fast growth has occurred recently in Alberta, British Columbia and the North, although the absolute figures for the territories are small. In contrast, the populations of the Atlantic Provinces and Manitoba have been growing very slowly while Saskatchewan has the dubious distinction of being Canada's only province to register an absolute population decline in the inter-censal periods from 1966 to 1971 and 1971 to 1976.

Those provinces with a slow population growth tend to have been losing many of their native-born through out-migration. In fact, as Table 2.4 shows, only Ontario and British Columbia had a positive net migration in all three 5-year periods from 1961 to 1976. Québec's attraction seems to have declined since the mid-1960s, while that of Alberta and the North increased. These basic statistics indicate a lack of regional equilibrium in the country, posing some major problems for provinces that are failing to hold their own. The tendency for out-migrants to be from the younger and better-educated groups aggravates the difficulties of maintaining adequate governmental services in the face of higher costs and a slow growth of population.

The best indicator of the welfare of the population is probably income per person, that is the total income of all types divided by its population. This figure is also a good reflection of economic strength despite the distortion that may be brought about through transfer payments from the federal government. In comparison with the population trends, the personal income figures (Table 2.5) indicate many similarities. One feature is noticeable though; Eastern Canada is worse off than expected while the West appears more favourably. Saskatchewan, for example, which was losing population in the late 1960s and early 1970s has a better income situation than Nova Scotia, the richest Atlantic province. Its problem is extreme fluctuations related to dependence on farming. Slow-growth Manitoba has personal income levels only slightly below the national average. In contrast, the poorer eastern provinces, Prince Edward Island and Newfoundland, have risen from around half to just over two-thirds the national average. The rather weak position of Québec is also evident.

TABLE 2.4
COMPONENTS OF POPULATION CHANGE, BY PROVINCE

	Total Population Change			Natural Increase			Net Migration		
	1961–66	1966–71	1971–76	1961–66	1966–71	1971–76	1961–66	1966–71	1971–76
Newfoundland	35,543	28,708	35,600	59,577	49,096	44,600	−24,034	−20,388	−9,000
P.E.I.	3,906	3,106	6,600	8,506	5,207	4,500	−4,600	−2,101	2,100
Nova Scotia	19,032	32,921	39,600	59,526	37,418	32,300	−40,494	−4,497	7,300
New Brunswick	18,852	17,769	42,700	53,229	35,233	33,200	−34,377	−17,464	9,500
Québec	521,634	246,919	206,700	457,717	288,727	222,900	63,917	−41,808	−16,200
Ontario	724,778	742,236	561,400	487,852	373,072	327,900	236,926	369,164	233,500
Manitoba	41,380	25,181	33,300	70,340	49,260	45,200	−28,960	−24,079	−11,900
Saskatchewan	30,163	−29,102	−4,900	75,691	50,867	38,100	−45,528	−79,969	−43,000
Alberta	131,259	164,671	210,100	134,607	105,293	95,700	−3,348	59,378	114,400
British Columbia	244,592	310,947	282,000	104,103	88,494	82,800	140,489	222,453	199,200
Yukon and N.W.T.	5,494	10,075	11,200	6,745	6,720	6,400	−1,251	3,355	4,800
Canada	1,766,633	1,553,431	1,429,200	1,517,893	1,089,387	933,600	258,740	464,044	495,600

Sources: Statistics Canada, *Canada Year Book 1973* (Ottawa: 1973), 209 and personal communication with Statistics Canada.

TABLE 2.5
PERSONAL INCOME PER PERSON BY PROVINCE

	1951		1961		1971		1976	
	$	%	$	%	$	%	$	%
Newfoundland	579	48.3	961	58.2	2190	63.8	4603	68.3
P.E.I.	653	54.5	971	58.8	2170	63.2	4650	69.0
Nova Scotia	829	69.1	1284	77.8	2662	77.5	5313	78.8
New Brunswick	804	67.1	1122	68.0	2482	72.3	5064	75.1
Québec	1007	84.0	1488	90.1	3047	88.7	6253	92.8
Ontario	1418	118.3	1954	118.4	4020	117.0	7367	109.3
Manitoba	1209	100.8	1557	94.3	3231	94.1	6357	94.3
Saskatchewan	1285	107.2	1172	71.0	2759	80.3	6709	99.5
Alberta	1331	111.0	1651	100.0	3399	99.0	6999	103.8
British Columbia	1429	119.2	1897	114.9	3745	109.0	7318	108.6
Territories	1040	86.7	1595	96.6	2981	86.8	6780	100.6
Canada	1199	100.0	1651	100.0	3435	100.0	6741	100.0

Source: Statistics Canada. *National Income and Expenditure Accounts*. Catalogue: 13–201.

Since 1951, these personal income figures have been levelling up across the country. On average the poor are less poor and the rich less rich than they were. Despite this, studies on low-income families indicate that their percentage for the country as a whole (15.9) is exceeded in every province except Ontario and British Columbia. The worst situation is in Newfoundland and Prince Edward Island, where in 1971, approximately 34 per cent of all families fell into the low-income category. Saskatchewan followed at about 28 per cent, while New Brunswick, Nova Scotia and Manitoba were fairly comparable at 24.1, 23.0 and 19.4 per cent respectively. Finally Québec and Alberta were very similar with a little under 18 per cent.

Closely related to this pattern of personal incomes across the country is the state of employment. Figure 2.1 provides an interesting picture of the percentage breakdown by employment type on a regional basis. The goods-producing sectors, including construction, employ the highest percentage of the labour force in Ontario, closely followed by Québec. Manufacturing, on the other hand, is weakest in the Prairies and the Atlantic Provinces, which are both relatively highly dependent on primary activities. This is much as expected. Unemployment figures, however, are somewhat surprising. The lowest level of unemployment during the last 20 years has been consistently in the Prairies, not in the two richest provinces, Ontario and British Columbia (see fig. 2.2). Moreover, in this respect British

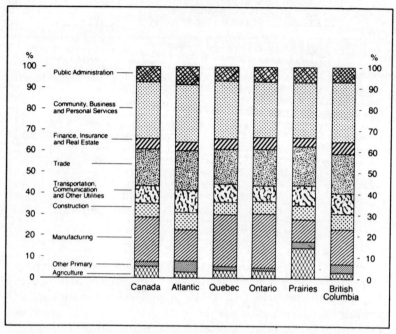

Figure 2.1   Employment by Industry and Region, 1975.
Source: *Perspective Canada*, Ottawa, (May, 1977)

Columbia has a record almost as bad as Québec's. At the bottom of the table again is the Atlantic Region, where unemployment is consistently high.

A shift-share analysis of the 1961–70 period has highlighted the recent regional trends (Martin, 1976). Using an 82-category employment breakdown, Martin showed that the major determinant of regional performance was the tertiary sector. The initial 1961 employment structure had a large bearing on Ontario and the Prairies but regional conditions were more important in the Atlantic region, where their effect was negative, and British Columbia, where it was positive. The largest relative changes in the 1960s were in the periphery (B.C., Prairies, Atlantic). The poorest employment performances were in the Atlantic region, as a result of poor regional performance, and the Prairies, which had a bad industrial structure (i.e. one with a high proportion of low-growth industries).

There are quite considerable differences of output per capita across the country as well. Table 2.6 is particularly interesting

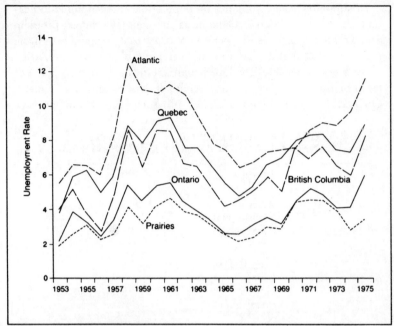

Figure 2.2   Unemployment Rates by Region.
Source: *Perspective Canada*, Ottawa, (May, 1977)

because it lists Canadian provinces along with the OECD countries, Alberta and British Columbia are in a very strong position ahead of any OECD country while Ontario is not far behind. The underlying strength of Saskatchewan and Manitoba, despite moderate income levels, is also brought out while Québec is further behind and the Atlantic Provinces, as in the case of other economic indicators, bring up the rear. The Economic Council argues that such variations in productivity are largely due not to differences in industrial structure but rather to differential output by workers in the same industry, or labour quality (Economic Council of Canada, 1977, 70–81). Developing an index based on age, sex and education, the council calculated provincial measures of labour quality as shown in Table 2.7. The index does in fact conform closely to output performance. The council's calculations of labour quality for manufacturing alone show a weaker situation in the Atlantic Region, Saskatchewan and Manitoba than portrayed in Table 2.7. In the growth of provincial output since 1961 as well, the western provinces come out strongly (figure 2.3).

In summary, these statistics on population and economic indicators all point to Atlantic Canada as the country's major problem area and to Ontario as the location of consistent economic strength. On the other hand, the Prairie region with a slow population growth and a weakly developed manufacturing structure, has not fared badly in terms of incomes, economic growth and employment. Québec, a strong manufacturing province, has below average

TABLE 2.6
GROSS DOMESTIC PRODUCT PER CAPITA:
CANADIAN PROVINCES AND OECD COUNTRIES

Provinces OECD Countries	GDP/ capita
Alberta	**$8,871**
British Columbia	**7,053**
Switzerland	6,970
Ontario	**6,912**
Sweden	6,880
United States	6,600
Canada	6,460
Saskatchewan	**6,448**
Iceland	6,280
West Germany	6,200
Manitoba	**6,066**
Denmark	6,030
Luxembourg	5,950
Australia	5,880
Norway	5,850
Belgium	5,470
Québec	**5,466**
Netherlands	5,110
France	5,060
Finland	4,710
Nova Scotia	**4,708**
New Brunswick	**4,475**
New Zealand	4,440
Austria	4,370
Japan	4,130
Newfoundland	**3,895**
P.E.I.	**3,541**
Britain	3,370
Italy	2,710
Ireland	2,180
Greece	2,150
Spain	2,100
Portugal	1,300
Turkey	750

Source: Financial Times of Canada, 23 August, 1976, 6 based on statistics from OECD and the Conference Board in Canada.

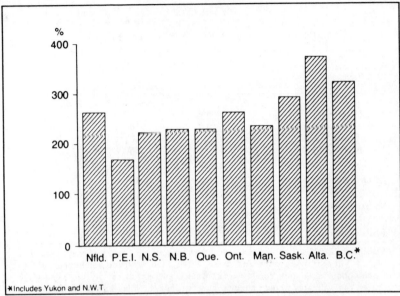

%

*Includes Yukon and N.W.T.

Figure 2.3   Percentage Growth of Gross Provincial Domestic Product, 1961–1974.
Sources: *Financial Times of Canada*, (June, 1977), and Statistics Canada, *Provincial Economic Accounts 1961–1974*, Ottawa, (1977)

income levels and is beginning to find it difficult to hold its population. In the West, fast growing and rich British Columbia is generally strong, despite a high level of unemployment, while growth in the North has not been matched by high average personal incomes.

DIMENSIONS OF CANADIAN REGIONALISM

Studies by Ray and his colleagues have done much to clarify the dimensions of regional patterns in Canada and to identify some of the causes of regional differentiation in the country. In his initial research, Ray examined eighty-five variables for cities and seventy-six for counties using the results from the 1961 census (Ray, 1971, 2). The variables – mostly economic, demographic and cultural – were then subjected to factor analysis. The analysis for the county data, which were most comprehensive because they included both urban and rural areas, yielded the major components listed in Table 2.8. Also shown in the table are the variables which load highly on these components. In a later study of population growth, Ray and

TABLE 2.7
INDEX OF LABOUR QUALITY
IN ALL INDUSTRIES, BY PROVINCE, 1970

	Men	Women	Average
		(Canada = 100)	
Newfoundland	93	94	95
Prince Edward Island	97	102	97
Nova Scotia	98	102	100
New Brunswick	96	100	97
Québec	97	96	97
Ontario	102	101	101
Manitoba	100	99	99
Saskatchewan	100	103	100
Alberta	103	105	103
British Columbia	103	105	105

Labour quality index[1]

[1] Estimates are based on national wage rates paid to full-time employees, male and female, in five age groups and at six levels of educational attainment. If, by assumption, male and female workers had been paid at exactly the same wage rates, the estimates would change somewhat, but the relationships would remain essentially the same.

An ideal measure of labour quality should include other factors such as degree of motivation, work effort, aptitudes, and attitudes, which may or may not have some bearing on provincial variations in labour quality. To some extent, however, these factors may be reflected in levels of education and labour for participation rates.

Source: Economic Council of Canada (1977), 72

Villeneuve (1975, 105) examined the relationship of the six components to the relative growth[1] of population in the counties from 1911 to 1971. Relative growth, as the independent variable, was explained by the six components in a multiple regression analysis. In Table 2.8, the 'leverage' column shows the regression coefficients for each component and provides an indication of their contribution to relative growth in the 60 year period.

Ray and Villeneuve's interpretation of these results draws heavily on the 'core-periphery' concept operating at different scales. At the international scale, east–west trends reflect Canada's early development as a periphery to the European heartland, which demanded its staples. The gradual spread of settlement westwards is now reflected in increasing ethnic heterogeneity as one moves westwards across the country, with East European immigrants and their descendents becoming more and more numerous. Nationally there is a strong

[1] Relative growth is growth of the county compared to the nation so that, if both grow at the same rate, relative growth equals 1.0. See Ray (1975, 96) for more detail.

TABLE 2.8
MULTIVARIATE ANALYSIS OF THE COMPONENTS OF GROWTH

Components	Associated Characteristics (high loadings in factor analysis)	Leverage (regression coefficient)	Statistical Confidence (t test)
Centre-Periphery Gradients			
rural-urban	higher incomes, house values, education levels and more post World War II immigration in urban areas	0.400	16.81
metropolitan	financial and manufacturing activity, Jewish and Italian ethnicity	0.072	3.04
heartland-hinterland	unemployment, income disparity, logging, fishing, and other primary activities in hinterland	0.206	8.74
east-west	ethnic heterogeneity, with substantial East European representation established by pre-1931 immigration and farming tending to increase east to west	−0.050	−2.12
Non-Gradient Components			
English-French	contrasts in age-structure and family size, immigration rates and education and occupation structure	−0.186	−7.83
U.S. control of manufacturing	mainly secondary manufacturing activity	0.180	7.62

Note: The leverages exerted by each component are determined by multiple regression analysis in which the dependent variable is the relative growth rate for each of the 229 census counties.

The independent variables are the components which are measured using standardized factor scores. The components are described in detail elsewhere (by D. M. Ray, *Dimensions of Canadian Regionalism*. Information Canada, Ottawa, 1971). The multiple correlation coefficient for the six components is 0.83 and with an F ratio of 80.27. The overall model and individual regression coefficients are all statistically significant at the 0.01 level. The regression intercept is the unweighted mean of the relative growth rates: 0.655.

Source: Ray and Villeneuve (1975), 105.

tendency for increasing primary activities, unemployment and income disparity away from the Québec City to Windsor corridor. Finally at the local scale, rural-urban contrasts and the metropolitan component reflect the increasing attraction of urban areas and their importance for secondary and tertiary activities. The authors also identify two components which do not operate as part of such a scheme: the strong cultural contrasts which separate French from English Canadians, and the effects of United States control on manufacturing activity.

THEORY OF POLARIZATION AND ITS APPLICATION TO CANADIAN DEVELOPMENT

The factors identified in the discussion of Canadian growth by Ray and Villeneuve relate closely to the theory of polarized development which has been elaborated by John Friedmann over the last few years. Friedmann(1966) first outlined the core-periphery concept in the first part of his book on Venezuela, but it has since been expressed more formally (1972).

Friedmann first notes the crucial role of innovation in the development process. Innovation may be technical or institutional. While growth essentially consists of more of the same, innovation leads to a transformation of some aspect of society. Innovations are not necessarily the result of inventive activity within the society, for they may be borrowed or imitated from elsewhere. Thus the early technical inventions of the 'Industrial Revolution' took place in England but were accepted by an ever-increasing number of countries as innovations, eventually leading to major transformations of their industrial structure. The same can be said of American management practices in the twentieth century. A complete process is characterized by Friedmann (1972, 87) in the following way:

> The cumulative effect of successive innovations is to transform the established structure of society by attracting creative or innovative personalities into the enclaves of accelerated change by encouraging the formation of new values, attitudes and behavior traits consistent with the innovation: by fomenting a social environment favorable to innovative activity; and by bringing into existence yet further innovations.

Six conditions that govern the likelihood of acceptance of innovation are outlined:

(1) The degree of success achieved by traditional means in solving problems. If this is low, innovation is more likely.

(2) The extent to which different mental frames of reference clash, leading to the interaction of opposing ideas and viewpoints.

(3) The character of the social system in relation to the acceptance of

change. Friedmann argues that centrally-controlled hierarchical societies are particularly resistant to innovation.

(4) The frequency of innovative personality traits in societies.

(5) The ability to carry the innovation right through society.

(6) The character of social rewards for innovative activity. If rewards are high, such activity will be encouraged.

Historically, there has been a close connection between large urban centres and innovation, although the two are not perfectly correlated.

A successful innovator obtains a real advantage over his competitors and with it the possibilities for control and power. If the innovation is socially compatible, the innovator is usually rewarded but there are other cases in which innovators may be in conflict with the existing authority group (élite). Such conflicts may lead to the suppression of the innovators (counter-élites), to the latter's success in overthrowing the existing group, or to some intermediate solution. If the innovators gain control, there will be a considerable change in the social situation as authority-dependency relationships are transformed.

All of this, of course, takes place in a spatial framework. Innovations tend to take place in a small number of centres, designated as 'core' regions by Friedmann. Corresponding to the authority-dependency relations amongst people are those between core regions and their dependent 'peripheries'. While there may well be conflicts as a result of peripheral challenges to established authority, the core's position tends to be strong and self-reinforcing for the following reasons:

(1) Dominance effects – resources, people and capital are continually drawn to the core.

(2) Information effects – a high degree of interaction within the core encourages further innovation there.

(3) Psychological effects – conditions favourable to innovation are present in the core.

(4) Modernization effects – 'social values, behavior, and institutions' are transformed in the core (1972, 95).

(5) Linkage effects – innovations tend to breed further innovation by creating new markets and new demands for services.

(6) Production effects – increasing returns and reduced costs in the core.

The final element in this scheme of polarization outlined by

Friedmann is the geographical scale factor. Core-periphery relationships are evident at several scales in 'a nested hierarchy of spatial
systems' (1972, 96). Thus a core can be observed at a world scale
but also in the form of a metropolis with its surrounding region.

Polarization in Canada

The outline of Canada's economic development in Chapter 1
showed how the main thrusts of early expansion were related to the
exploitation of staples designed for the European market. In the
international economy, Canada was a periphery initially under the
colonial powers of France and Britain, later just of Britain. Traders
and settlers came to find a succession of products – fish, furs, lumber
wheat, etc. – which were sent back to furnish the expanding
motherland with essential raw materials and foodstuffs. The whole
economy of the Canadian colonies was tied to that of the homeland
cores and, even when centres such as Montréal increased in size,
they were highly limited in their range of power. Given the origin of
capital and population, it is not surprising that this pre-
Confederation expansion took place with a strong east-to-west
component, eastern areas being exploited first and settled population tending to spread gradually westward.

Power relationships were greatly modified at Confederation in
1867, when Canada became independent. Not only was the authority of Canada as a national power established *vis-à-vis* the outside
world but the formerly independent provinces were combined into a
federal state. Sufficient internal relationships were formed to provide
the framework within which a national core-periphery would develop and this was encouraged by commitments to build a railroad
to the east coast and later to the west. The interesting questions in
1867 were, who would gain power in Canada and where would it
reside?

From today's perspective the answers to these questions seem
self-evident. In 1867, things were far from clear. The 1871 Census
showed a population of 1,620,951 for Ontario, 1,191,516 for Québec
and 767,415 for the three Maritime Provinces. The Maritime
Provinces were enjoying a high degree of prosperity based on
exports of timber, lumber products, fish and ships, and had the
wealth to develop into the new manufactured products. In fact, the
Maritime business community looked forward to prosperous times

under the new arrangements and those established by the National Policy of 1879 (Acheson, 1972, 3–4).

The fact that Canada's core eventually developed in Southern Ontario and Québec reflects several important features of the country, as well as the manoeuvres of the business community. Firstly, it must be recognized that in this central Canadian region, settlers found extensive areas of good productive land which, in combination with the climate, provided the base for prosperous farming. The relatively dense farm settlement encouraged the expansion of services, trade and consumer industries such as clothing, food and beverages. Gilmour (1971) has shown how this process led gradually into a more diversified industrial structure in Ontario. These happy circumstances form a sharp contrast to most parts of the Maritimes, where soils are poor and the climate harsher (Black and Maxwell, 1972).

In the period of growing industrialization after Confederation, the expanding population of central Canada was a great boost to manufacturers in the region because it provided a ready market and a large and varied workforce. In materials for the manufacturers as well, there were advantages: the farm products, the enormous forest reserves at first in the south and later further north on the Shield, numerous and varied metal ores that were gradually discovered mainly on the Shield, abundant water resources which were ideal for water power and, after 1900, cheap hydro-electricity. Whatever was not locally available, notably coal, was readily obtainable from nearby sources (Walker, 1971). While the Maritimes also had many of these materials, it was in almost every case in smaller amounts or lower quality.

Perhaps the major disadvantage for the east coast locations, however, was simply their relative location in a country which could only expand away from them. Central Canada was better placed to obtain maximum benefit from the opening up of the North and West. Meanwhile, the Maritime Provinces were cut off by tariff barriers from their nearest markets in New England and hampered by a stagnation of their own population which has lasted until today.

Another element of relative location that has gradually increased in importance over the years has been the spread of United States' influence into the Canadian economic scene. Canada, once a European periphery with strong ties to the east, is now in many ways part of the United States' periphery. This can be seen in the strong north-south trading patterns involving Canadian exports of essentially staple products in return for mainly manufactured goods. Even more, however, it is clear in the high degree of ownership of Canadian resources and, especially, manufacturing industries. American capital replaced that of Britain as Canada's main foreign supply as early as World War 1 (Ray, 1967, 69).

The area within Canada to gain most from United States capital has been the Québec City-Windsor axis, a fact reflecting its location near to the American manufacturing belt. In manufacturing, the National Policy and the continuation of high tariffs encouraged American capital to move over the border to capture the Canadian market. But a strong tendency to remain close to the border has benefited the area between Toronto and the border cities of Windsor and Niagara Falls. Ray (1965) examined the locational pattern of American subsidiaries and developed the concept of economic shadow, which was designed to help explain why some areas had a concentration of subsidiaries and others did not. Three elements of the shadow concept were outlined:

(1) Interactance decay – 'the number of subsidiaries established within a region by all parent companies in a city located beyond that region is directly proportional to the total number of firms in that city, and inversely proportional to its distance from the region' (p 27). This is essentially a form of gravity model.

(2) Sectoral Affinity – 'these subsidiaries tend to be located in the sector of the region lying between the parent company and the primary market centre within the region' (pp. 27–8). This element particularly benefits South West Ontario which lies between Toronto and most of the United States' manufacturing belt.

(3) Sectoral penetration–'hypothesizes that there is a direct relationship between the distances of the subsidiary and the parent company from the international boundary' (p. 105). A parent which is close to the Canadian border will tend to keep its branches very close as well (e.g. Detroit parent, Windsor branch) but more distant parent companies will tend to locate in Toronto.

Ray tested his ideas with a series of mathematical models and established the validity of the concept in Ontario, showing how eastern Ontario was in the shadow, while the south-west received considerable capital investment from the United States. The strong spatial element in the economic shadow concept tends to reinforce the view that a low degree of shadow is essentially a measure of high integration into the United States core region. Table 2.8 shows that United States manufacturing investment has been an important element in twentieth century growth rates. Its spatial influence, however, has been very restricted to the Canadian core region.

With all of these resource and locational advantages, it is not at all surprising that Southern Ontario and Southern Québec have established themselves firmly as the Canadian core region during the last century. The process was not automatic, however, and power was not easily or willingly given up by the Maritimes. In the 1880s and 1890s, as local groups established manufacturing companies, there was a flurry of activity in many Maritime cities. These entrepreneurs possessed 'the enterprise and the capital resources necessary to initiate new industries' (Acheson, 1972, 4) and were involved in a variety of manufacturing, with special emphasis on textiles and iron and steel. Most of the new manufacturers had been successful in traditional staple and trading activities of the area and were willing to import technical and management skills to help them in their new ventures (p. 11).

A major problem, however, proved to be a lack of strong financial institutions to provide the essential back-up for the entrepreneurs (Acheson, 1972, 7). In the depression period of the mid-1880s, this hit many manufacturers hard. The British lumber market deteriorated and cut off a traditional source of Maritime income. In the meantime, the new pattern of internal trading within Canada began to hurt the area. Central Canada was buying Maritime primary products but was also shipping its manufactured goods eastwards. In fact, the National Policy had led to over-production of some manufactured goods by 1886 and Maritime producers blamed high rail costs for their inability to sell their products in central Canada (pp. 13–14). The solution to the problem was not beneficial to the Maritimes. Montréal interests gradually took over many of the manufacturing companies there with the objective of restricting output and limiting expansion (p. 17). In other words, the new core area in Canada asserted its financial strength by systematically removing the competition, especially in cotton and sugar refining. Acheson lays partial blame on the lack of enterprise in the larger metropolises of the area, which had taken a very passive role during the 1880s and 1890s. Some lessons were learned by the Halifax business community, which set up a consortium in 1894 to provide capital for industry and took an active role in financing the growing

Nova Scotia steel industry (p. 25). Nevertheless, competition from Montréal remained strong and, by 1920, had combined with Halifax and London interests to finance the new giant British Empire Steel Corporation, a consolidation of two Nova Scotia companies. 'The event,' writes Acheson, 'marked both the final nationalization of the region's major industrial potential and the failure of its entrepreneurs to maintain control of any significant element in the industrial section of the regional economy' (p. 27).

Meanwhile, Canada was expanding westwards and there, despite occasional Indian problems and threats from the south, the central Canadian business interests had things much their own way. The building of the transcontinental railroads and the settlement of the Prairies brought a large market for manufactured products from Ontario and Québec, especially for rails and farm machinery. The tariff wall kept out foreign competition and a pattern of westward flowing manufactured products and eastward movement of grain and other foodstuffs was set up that has remained characteristic. As the population of the West grew, so local production of consumer items expanded, but the manufacturing base is still very narrow and many of the plants are owned by Ontario and Québec interests.

Since the Second World War the western provinces have become increasingly in a position to assert themselves. The discovery of oil in Alberta in 1947 and the subsequent exploitation of oil and natural gas reserves plus its coal deposits have greatly increased the province's wealth. Currently, in fact, with the energy crisis, Alberta is in a very strong position. British Columbia also has rich and varied resources. The four western provinces are beginning to co-operate in attempting to remedy what they see as some of the injustices of the present situation, including rail freight rates (Canada, Grain Handling and Transportation Commission, 1977, 273 –311), and the weak base of manufacturing in the West. It seems to be a classic case of one of Friedmann's challenges by a sub-core. The West has been making gains, especially through oil revenues[1], but it remains to be seen how things will go in the future. Already, though, Alberta and British Columbia are among the rich provinces, while Québec has joined the poor.

As a summary of the current situation with respect to economic

[1] In 1976–7 the Alberta Heritage Savings Trust Fund, administering profits from non-renewable resource sales, invested nearly $700 million in capital projects and had current assets of over $1,400 million.

TABLE 2.9
REGIONALISM AND CORPORATE SECTORS
FOR THE ECONOMIC ÉLITE, 1972

| | Birth Place | | | | |
Sector	West	Centre	East	Total	(Number of Positions[1])
Finance	21.4%	70%	8.6%	100%	454
Utilities	34.3	56.5	9.3	100	108
Trade	23.1	74.7	2.2	100	91
Manufacturing	17.9	74.4	7.7	100	117
Resources	31.8	59.7	8.4	100	154
Total Élite	23.4	67.8	8.8	100	924
Population (1921)	28	60	12	100	
	(158)	(456)	(59)	(673)	

[1] Number of positions does not total to 673 because one person may hold a position simultaneously in more than one sector.
Source: Clement (1975), 228.

power in Canada, a recent study of the corporate élite is instructive. Clement (1975) examined the élite in 1972 based upon directorships in what he termed 'dominant' corporations, essentially those with assets over $250 million and income of over $50 million (p. 128)[1]. He showed a considerable interlocking of directorships, with the Canadian banks particularly linked to all other sectors of the economy. In fact, the Canadian control of finance, utilities and trade is dominated by a group of families which has been in a similar position for a long time (p. 150). In the manufacturing and resource sectors, however, Canadian control is weak, reflecting the takeover by American companies and Canada's peripheral position in the international scale of things (p. 152). Clement's second book (1977) analyzes these international links, showing how the Canadian élite has mainly kept to its narrow range of financial, commercial and transport interests and chosen to invest in United States' resource and manufacturing companies, which exhibited technological, management and marketing expertise. Meanwhile the pattern of direct investment by these U.S. firms in Canada severely restricts the influence of Canadians on manufacturing in Canada.

Within Canada also, Clement's (1975) study illustrates the continued economic power of Ontario and Québec. Table 2.9 shows that central Canada has more directorships in dominant companies

[1] For a detailed list see Clement, pages 400–28. There were 113 dominant corporations.

than its population warrants, although its strength in utilities and resources is lower. While Atlantic Canada plays little role in the country's major boardrooms, it can be seen from the table that the West is in a position to challenge. Directorships for westerners, however, are disproportionately high in the foreign-controlled subsidiaries, which implies less real power than the table suggests (p. 229). In the core area, despite some contemporary complementarities (Kerr, 1968), there is also a long-standing struggle between Toronto and Montréal. Since the Second World War, Toronto has been forging ahead. Montréal still has some major corporate head offices, especially those of Canadian commercial companies (e.g. Canadian National, Canadian Pacific, Royal Bank of Canada) but it has not attracted as many foreign-owned subsidiaries as Toronto. Moreover, the current situation in Québec, with a separatist government, is causing great uncertainty. A number of firms have moved out parts of their head office operation and one major insurance company (Sun Life of Canada) caused a furore in late 1977 by announcing its intention to move to Toronto.

Urban Polarization

Friedmann's theory stipulates the operation of polarization at several scales. The discussion so far has focused on the international and national levels, but the same kind of factors also operate within the Canadian regions. Table 2.8 showed that a rural-urban dimension was the major component in the growth trends of the 1911–71 period. Urban areas are associated with higher incomes, house values, education levels and post-World War II immigration. During this period also, Canada became far more urban, so that the rural population declined from 58.2 per cent to 23.9 (Canada, 1974, 9). Recently the largest metropolitan areas have been increasingly dominating the population scene and now have over 55 per cent of Canada's population (Canada, 1974, 10).

In Ray and Villeneuve's study, metropolitan location was associated with financial and manufacturing activity (Table 2.8). The rapid expansion of modern office blocks in the centre of Canada's largest cities dramatically attests their importance in commercial and financial activities. Their strength in manufacturing is perhaps less obvious because it is mainly evident in the suburbs. The pull of the largest centres for manufacturing activity, however, is great. It was already evident in the late nineteenth century, when Gilmour examined trends in manufacturing in Southern Ontario. He showed that between 1851 and 1891, the so-called 'Manufacturing Belt' (York, Peel, Halton, Wentworth, Lincoln, Brant and Waterloo Counties) increased its share of the manufacture of Southern Ontario consumer goods from 33.1 to 47.1 per cent. This was achieved with a declining share of population (24 per cent in 1891 as opposed to 26 per cent in 1851) (Gilmour, 1972, 143).

Many of the reasons causing such a concentration of manufacturing at that time still apply today. Gilmour reasoned that arguments based on the theories of industrial location and regional development would lead one to expect spatial concentration (p. 119). Growth would concentrate in the first settled areas, which would benefit from the process of cumulative mechanisms that encouraged population growth, higher incomes, technological improvements and reduced transport costs. Such growth tendencies influence industrial location by;

(1) Encouraging existing industries to concentrate in growth centres through the closing of some of the earlier sites. This was often encouraged by mergers and/or technological change (Walker, 1974, 58–61).

(2) Providing favoured sites for new industries as they develop. Such industries tend to establish in the most industrialized areas.

A recent outline by Norcliffe (1975) sets such tendencies within a wider theory of manufacturing places based on current tendencies in industrial location. He argues that traditionally important factors such as transport and labour are now less influential and that three others, which can be considered as characteristics of places, are increasingly evident. The three are:

(1) Infrastructure availability – provision of essential services at a site e.g. water, sewage, electricity.

(2) Internal and external economies of scale – essentially those features identified as agglomeration economies in the literature. Norcliffe adds centralization economies, which operate at regional scale in a similar way that urbanization economies work for the urban one.

(3) Linkage and contact patterns – face-to-face contact is becoming more important at the upper levels of administration, encouraging administrative units to locate close to each other.

Norcliffe argues that these trends all encourage a tendency for manufacturing to shift to larger urban centres. A gradual increase in plant size makes it more difficult for smaller places to afford the infrastructure for the larger plants, agglomeration economies continue to encourage the growth of large centres, and contact patterns also operate best in the metropolis. Combining these trends with the core-periphery concept operating at the national level, permits one to outline an expected distribution of manufacturing activity. First, however, four categories of manufacturing should be distinguished:

(1) Processing – using raw materials as the major inputs;

(2) Fabricating – major inputs have already been processed but are modified further;

(3) Integrative – assembly industries, combining items which are already mainly finished;

(4) Administrative – no physical inputs, except perhaps for research and development.

Processing activities occur everywhere but can be expected to be pushed more and more into the periphery as urban development spreads outwards from the core. In contrast the other activities, as a result of factors already mentioned, will largely concentrate in the core, the only exceptions being peripheral cities which have high amenity value and are attractive as places to live. Within the core area, Norcliffe argues that current trends will all encourage manufacturing to develop in urban areas. Moreover, the larger the plant, the more likely it will be to operate in a large centre. The plant's function will also be important. Administrative operations are tending to concentrate in metropolitan areas to obtain face-to-face contacts, but the increasing rents and congestion in these same areas encourage some decentralization of fabricating activities into medium- and small-sized towns in the core. Norcliffe's outline has not yet been carefully tested but it is intuitively reasonable and seems to fit much of the evidence in Canada.

In its effect on income, Ray and Villeneuve (1975, 111) argue that city size is a crucial factor and outweighs the national core-periphery differences. For any particular size class of cities, for example 1–24,999 or 100,000–199,999, the spread of average income is not more than 20 percentage points from region to region and Atlantic Canada is usually not below 90 per cent of the Canadian average. The problem is that the area lacks any city in the largest, richest category of over 1 million population and has few even above 100,000. Thus the degree of urbanization suggests a focus for policy responses. On the other hand, it is also important to ask why such a situation has arisen and whether there are fundamental reasons for it, such as the coastal orientation, lack of good sites or political fragmentation.

A detailed discussion of urban polarization for particular areas will follow in the relevant regional chapters. It has been sufficient here to stress its importance as a Canada-wide phenomenon and, therefore, one that must be considered in federal regional policy.

MANUFACTURING INDUSTRY AND FEDERAL REGIONAL POLICY

While various regional programmes operated earlier, regional policy did not really get off the ground in Canada until the 1960s. A new mood, which involved the resolve to deal with the needs of areas that faced economic problems, especially high unemployment and low income levels, seemed to sweep the country at that time. As a result, several important policies were introduced by the federal government. In response to rural problems, the Agricultural Rehabilitation Development Programme (ARDA) was established in 1961, supplemented in 1966 by a programme for comprehensive rural development (FRED). Slow growth areas were aided by the Area Development Agency (ADA), which attempted to encourage manufacturing to locate there. The Atlantic Region received additional support through the Atlantic Development Board (ADB), which concentrated mainly on the improvement of infrastructure such as roads and power plants. A review of all of these programmes is out of place here, but they have been examined by Brewis (1969). It is relevant, however, to discuss the role of manufacturing and the success of the Area Development Programme.

The Area Development Agency

The Area Development Agency (ADA) was established under the Department of Industry in 1963 and represented the first Canada-wide attempt to influence the location of industry. The programme was designed to help areas with severe economic problems. 'On the basis of high levels of unemployment over a number of years and slow rate of economic growth', thirty-five areas in Canada were 'designated' (Canada, Department of Industry, 1964, 26–7). Designation allowed financial aid for manufacturing and processing industry in the form of capital cost allowances on new machinery, equipment and buildings. In addition, a three-year Federal tax exemption was allowed for new plants.

After a relatively short time, the Area Development programme was considerably expanded in August, 1965, following a new act in June. The new programme provided for a much greater emphasis on financial grants rather than tax allowances, and the designated area was enlarged. Three main benefits were available to manufacturers: (1) A Development Grant in the form of cash or an equivalent tax credit of up to one-third of the capital cost of new machinery and equipment and new buildings. The Development Grant was exempt from federal income tax and did not reduce the amount of capital costs which would be used for tax purposes.

(2) Accelerated Capital Cost Allowances of up to 50 per cent per annum on new production machinery and equipment.

(3) Accelerated Capital Cost Allowances of up to 20 per cent per annum on new buildings and significant extensions to existing buildings (Canada, Department of Industry, Area Development Agency, 1967, 5).

These incentives were applicable only if the new plant or facility would increase employment. The firms were required to notify the local employment agency of job vacancies. While manufacturing and processing activities were eligible for support, energy production and publishing not related to printing were specifically excluded.

Areas were designated on the basis of criteria related to income and employment. The areal unit was the area of the employment service, responsible for helping people to find jobs, but such units could be combined. In order to qualify for inclusion, an area had to satisfy at least one of three conditions:

(1) (For areas with an average family income below the national average.) During the previous five years there had been
    a) an unemployment rate of 200 per cent of the national average or greater,
or b) an unemployment rate of 150 per cent of the national average and a rate of employment growth less than half of it.

(2) In the previous five years, employment declined at an annual rate of more than 10 per cent.

(3) a) Average family income was below $4,250 p.a. (The national average was $5,449 at the time)

b) 40 per cent or more of families had an average annual income below $3,000 (Canada, Department of Industry, 1965).

A Critique of the ADA Programme

The federal government commissioned a number of studies to provide a detailed evaluation of the results of the Area Development policy. Those on Nova Scotia (Comeau, 1969), New Brunswick (Larsen, 1969) and the Georgian Bay area of Ontario (Yeates and Lloyd, 1969) were all released and provide a wealth of information on the subject although they were completed before the full impact of the programme could be seen. In addition many other evaluations have been completed by independent researchers and commentators.

While the ADA programme provided many jobs directly in manufacturing and some indirectly in other sectors, it was the object of a great deal of criticism. Perhaps the most basic problem was its orientation as a welfare operation, designed to increase employment in areas with very high unemployment. Politically such a goal is important but it is likely to lead to short-term answers to what in most cases are problems of long-range economic planning. In the long run, solutions to local and regional unemployment problems are likely to be solved only after a careful matching of the attributes of the areas with the requirements of various economic activities. Brewis (1969, 109) has argued that the need is not for 'a blanket form of assistance to all areas suffering from chronically high unemployment . . . but rather a programme of assistance based on the specific needs and potentialities of individual areas'. Some problem areas lack scope for most types of manufacturing activity, others have tremendous potentialities but require capital to begin the process of growth, while a third group may be undergoing adjustment as a result of the decline of formerly-important industries (Smith, 1971, 443–5). In addition, certain forms of manufacturing activity are more appropriate to some areas than others, so that incentives should not necessarily be the same for different industries in the same area.

Under the ADA programme, no consideration was given to the planning of either the structural or the spatial effects of the incentives provided for manufacturing. In the Atlantic Provinces, existing types of industry tended to receive the bulk of the support, as noted by both Comeau (1969, 32) and Larsen (1969, v–17). It has been argued that modifications to the Atlantic Region's industrial structure are essential, particularly to increase the proportion of industries which are growing and which themselves encourage further growth (Brewis, 1969, 169–172; Larsen, 1969, vii–1, vii–3). It would also be helpful if the manufacturing expansions provided higher wages than existing industries but the opposite has been the case. Partly because of an increase in female labour, many new jobs have been paid poorly (Comeau, 1969, 116). On the other hand, the Georgian Bay experience was much better. Much of the investment was in new, growth industry (motor vehicle and electronic components), and job opportunities and wage levels rose (Yeates and Lloyd, 1969, 64).

Spatially, the ADA programme tended to encourage decentralization of manufacturing investment (Cannon, 1970, 178–9). This was partly because the unit area for designation was so small. (These areas were those used in connection with unemployment services – National Employment Service areas – later called Manpower areas). In the Atlantic Provinces a scattering of plants was encouraged by the fact that the only areas not designated were those around the largest urban centres – Halifax-Dartmouth, Saint John and Fredericton. Such a situation was criticized severely within the region (Atlantic Provinces Economic Council, 1968, 12–13). Industrial location theory indicates the importance of agglomeration economies to manufacturing (Isard, 1956, 172–88; Hoover, 1971, 75–88) while empirical studies have shown the continued attraction of larger urban areas (Alonso, 1970). Thus from a development point of view one might have expected an emphasis on, rather than a neglect of, the larger centres. Other spatial strategies are possible: the real problem with the ADA programme was the lack of any such strategy.

Another difficulty during most of the 1960s was the existence of such a multiplicity of programmes each with some bearing on economic development. Each province had its own programmes, while the several federal programmes operated independently. There are too many such bodies to consider here, but Richards (1965) has reviewed some of the complexities and Whalen (1965) provides a picture of the numerous agencies in the Atlantic region. The essential point is that most agencies reported to different controlling bodies and that co-operation was therefore difficult to achieve even it it was actively sought.

The Department of Regional Economic Expansion

In 1968, Canada elected a majority Liberal government under Pierre Trudeau, who had only recently taken over the leadership of his party. A number of major policy changes followed this election, one of the first being the announcement, in July 1968, of a new Department of Regional Economic Expansion (DREE), which was designed 'to encourage economic expansion in regions of Canada where the growth of employment and income has been lagging' (Canada, Department of Regional Economic Expansion, undated a). The overall policy of this department represents a significant response to many of the criticisms levelled at earlier programmes.

DREE is designed to co-ordinate all regional work, and all of the existing separate programmes such as ARDA and ADA were placed within its wing, frequently being modified considerably in the process. A determined effort was therefore made to develop a united approach to regional problems and to remove former conflicts between the separate federal programmes. Officers were appointed within the department who were responsible for specific regions.

Within this broad framework of a department concerned with all aspects of regional development, a new incentive scheme for manufacturers was soon announced. In July 1969, it was put into legislation as the Regional Development Incentives Act (RDIA). A feature of the statement of purpose is that the programme is to help areas both with economic expansion and with social adjustment, thus widening the scope from a narrowly economic framework. A system of regions designated as being eligible for support was again used but their minimum size was larger than under the Area Development Agency (5000 square miles). The criteria for designation are less tightly defined than under the ADA scheme so that greater discretion is possible. They are:

(1) Exceptionally inadequate opportunities for productive employment;

(2) That new or expanded facilities will significantly help economic development or social adjustment (Canada, 1969, 1242–3).

The second criterion makes this programme more than a welfare one. It indicates that designated areas should have potential for development or improvement. Also because the whole Atlantic region except Labrador was (and is) designated, a regional approach to the location of manufacturing can be followed in that area.

One of the more interesting changes was implemented in March 1970 with the arrangements for Special Areas. These respond to arguments for growth centres which were so frequently made in criticism of the ADA scheme. Special Areas were designed 'to promote economic expansion in selected areas by enhancing their attractiveness as locations for new job-creating activities' (Canada Department of Regional Economic Expansion, 1972, 16). Relatively small-sized areas (usually urban ones) were provided with finances to improve their infrastructure – for example water supply, transport, sewage treatment facilities, industrial parks, schools or assembly of residential land. The places were chosen on the basis of some existing attractiveness for growth and potential for development. The intent of the special area approach was to make them even more attractive by concentrating available funds into them.

Some special arrangements were also made which tended to strengthen the encouragement of growth centres. The first of these was New Brunswick Multiplex Corporation Ltd., a federal-provincial crown corporation set up in February 1971. This corporation has been concerned with the planning and development of an integrated industrial complex of metalworking industries in Saint John (Luttrell, 1972). Unfortunately, Multiplex did not succeed in attracting the desired manufacturers and was absorbed in a new New Brunswick department in 1976. Another federal-provincial corporation was established for Halifax-Dartmouth in September, 1972. This was MAGI (Metropolitan Area Growth Investment Ltd.), which invested in and promoted business ventures in the Halifax area. It was hoped that MAGI would stimulate entrepreneurial talent and lead to job creation in the area. In 1977, however, its name was changed to Mainland Investments Ltd. and its activities became available to all of mainland Nova Scotia. Both of these corporations were financed jointly by a province and the federal government. It is clear now that such direct support of specific areas is not to be pursued.

The actual incentives available under the Regional Development Incentive Act (RDIA) are subject to certain maxima but until 1974 could not easily be worked out by an applicant according to a definite formula. Maximum grants vary according to region, with the highest available in the Atlantic provinces. The Ministry considered specific details concerning the plant and its location, trying to allow for costs that the new plant would impose on the local authority, potential pollution, etc. Thus, there was considerable discretion involved in computing the inventive offer, which is open to the firm for 90 days. There are a few conditions placed on the incentives, the most important being:

(a) Approved capital costs (which do not include land costs) must be at least $30,000 for an expansion and $60,000 for a new plant.

(b) The firm must have at least 20 per cent of approved capital costs in equity capital for a new plant and, for expansions, 20 per cent of the value of the existing facility plus approved capital costs.

(c) Firms must co-operate with Canada Manpower centres for recruitment of the labour force. As far as possible also, local labour must be employed.

(d) Satisfactory control of pollution is required.

(e) Canadian manufacturers must be given an opportunity to supply machinery and equipment.

These incentive criteria reflect a continued interest in job creation and a recognition that the local impact of new plants is likely to be greatest if the payroll is high. This should be interpreted not only as a welfare consideration (to take up unemployment slack) but also as recognition that wages paid will be reflected in local spending and will boost other sectors of the economy. It should be noted too, that stipulations regarding the purchase of equipment and machinery are designed to keep as much of the grant money within Canada as possible. On the other hand, within Canada, many of the regions eligible for support will need to import this equipment, mainly from Ontario or Québec. Thus the Atlantic and western provinces will lose some of the indirect benefits of the grants. It is almost impossible, however, to avoid this problem.

An Evaluation of the DREE's Early Years

The DREE Programme was welcomed by most observers as a significant improvement over earlier policies. It reflected acceptance of most of the major criticisms levelled at the ADA scheme. Regional policy was co-ordinated in one department, the whole Atlantic Region was designated, and growth centre approaches were encouraged. In the Atlantic Region there were some nagging doubts that perhaps too much of Canada was designated and that the region would have difficulty in competing with designated areas closer to the economic centre of the country (APEC *Newsletter*, 1969, 1). Nevertheless, on the whole, there was an enthusiastic reaction.

Criticisms soon began to surface in the Atlantic Region particularly within the Atlantic Provinces Economic Council (APEC), an independent organization with a long history of interest in the region's economic development. They reflected some dissatisfaction with the results of the DREE programme in the region and can be categorized into two groups. In the first place, the feeling seemed to be growing that DREE was too centralized. It was argued in APEC's (1971) Fifth Annual Review that, for true regional planning to take place, more important DREE officers should be based in the regions. Only in such circumstances could regional needs be adequately appreciated and good co-operation be built up with provincial officials. APEC recommended that 'all DREE planning, implementation, industrial intelligence and promotion for the Atlantic Provinces be transferred to a regional office headed by an assistant deputy minister' (p. 100). The specific administration of RDIA incentives, however, should remain in Ottawa. Criticism of DREE's organization was picked up in other areas of the country and became an issue in the 1972 federal election, which was won by the Liberal party with only a very narrow majority over the Conservatives and which left the new government in a minority position in the House. After the election, changes were promised and the DREE programme underwent a major reorganization during fiscal year 1973–4.

The second type of criticism of the DREE programme has resulted from an examination of the way in which the grants have actually been used. A summary of offers made under the RDIA across Canada by 1972 showed that Canada's major problem region, the Atlantic Provinces, received 18.0 per cent of accepted offers, 17.6 per cent of expected costs, 17.1 per cent of employment and 25 per cent of incentive grant money. These totals were high relative to the area's manufacturing and population size. More important, however, is the character of recipients of the grants. If the Atlantic Region is to advance, it is generally considered that some changes in industrial structure are needed. The ADA scheme had been criticized for failing to encourage many such changes, but it appears that the RDIA programme was operating in the same way (APEC *Newsletter*, 1973, 3–4). The same criticism was also levelled in Québec (Fréchette, *et al.*, 1975, 377–8.)

The reason for these results may be that the incentive grants rarely influence the decision-making of manufacturers. In a study involving a small sample of thirty-one firms which had received grants, Springate (1973) found little evidence that the location of the plants was influenced significantly. Larger companies usually decided on a region for their location before contacting DREE and within a region the grants do not vary much. Smaller firms generally considered expansion on existing sites first, and if they were not suitable, moved as short a distance as possible. Thus the scope for influencing the small firms is not very great.

The discretionary nature of RDIA incentives before 1974 could have been disadvantageous because it precluded calculation of the financial advantages of location at specific places. The desired effects would be more likely to be attained if firms knew exactly the benefits available for making a particular choice. In addition, however, many of the businessmen interviewed by Springate took the view that their decisions should not be influenced by the existence of grants.

Spatially, the larger urban centres in Atlantic Canada were still not generally receiving as many supported manufacturing plants as might be expected, despite the infrastructure support designed to encourage their attractiveness and the special bodies responsible for Saint John and Halifax-Dartmouth. Up to December 1972, 10.9 per cent of the region's RDIA induced jobs went to Halifax-Dartmouth (11.3% population), 8.5 per cent jobs to Saint John (5.4% population), 4.5 per cent to Moncton (3.6% population) and 4.4 per cent to St. John's (6.7% population) (APEC *Newsletter*, 1973). Under the operation of a real growth centre strategy these figures should be increased. Moreover, as noted above, Ray and Villeneuve have suggested that the regional problem in Canada may be more a problem of differential urban development than anything else. In other words, the cities of the Atlantic Provinces have income levels that are often reasonably similar to other Canadian cities of comparable size, but there is a shortage of large, high-income metropolitan areas. Thus a strong growth-centre strategy based only on the largest centres may be warranted.

DREE's New Look

The criticisms based upon the first few years of operation by the Department of Regional Economic Expansion led to a major reorganization during 1973–4. Two principal elements were involved in the changes: firstly, a greater degree of decentralization and secondly, a move towards overall regional economic planning.

In response to charges that Ottawa-based officials are too far removed from regional situations to be able to respond to their real needs, the department committed itself to a policy of basing about 70 per cent of its staff outside of the capital. Four regions were set up, each under an Assistant Deputy Minister, with regional headquarters at Moncton (Atlantic), Montréal (Québec), Toronto (Ontario) and Saskatoon (Western). The regional offices have considerable power and can authorize incentive grants for projects with capital costs between $500,000 and $1.5 million and up to 100 jobs. At the same time, provincial offices were also enlarged and can deal with smaller grants. By 1975, over 60 per cent of DREE personnel were located outside Ottawa and the proportion of senior executives was over 70 per cent (Canada, Dept. of Regional Economic Expansion, 1975, 2–3).

In April 1974, also, some modifications were made to the Regional Development Incentives programme (Canada, DREE, 1974). The changes allowed smaller projects (capital costs of only $25,000 or five new jobs) to become eligible for support as well as allowing greater flexibility for large developments. The other major change was the standardization of most incentives so that a company can work out its grant from a formula.

Decentralization was closely linked with an increase of co-operation between the federal government and the provinces. Before 1974 federal regional policy tended to be imposed upon the country, but the new system involves consultation leading to the signing of Ten-Year General Development Agreements between Ottawa and each province. These agreements map out the main elements of a socio-economic strategy, which Ottawa will support within the province. By 1975 an agreement had been signed with every province except Prince Edward Island, for which a comprehensive plan already existed. More detailed subsidiary agreements are regularly signed, covering specific sectors or areas.

This thrust towards overall regional economic development follows a series of working papers produced by DREE during the reorganization and published in 1973 under the title 'Economic Circumstances and Opportunities'. A separate report on each province and region evaluated past performance and suggested future policies. Another series in 1976 was entitled 'Climate for

Development'. The whole approach, described in Canada, Dept. of Regional Economic Expansion (1976) has moved to one of regional economic planning, with defined regional objectives and a conscious effort to work to the policy objectives. The success of this approach will not be clear for some years but at least it is conceptually sound. Closer interrelationship with the provinces is also welcome because each province has its own policies and, in the past, these have not always been in harmony with the federal approach.

As an example of the new agreements, we can take Saskatchewan. The General Development Agreement was signed in February 1974, with the following objectives:

(a) to increase the aggregate economic growth of the provincial economy in order to increase employment opportunities, encourage balanced growth between rural and urban centres and help ensure a continuing, vibrant, dynamic society.

(b) to preserve and enhance the value of the province's natural resources and optimize the value added from processing and manufacturing of these resources.

(c) to diversify the province's economic base to reduce its dependency on primary production and thereby help stabilize the provincial economy.

(d) to increase the number, range and type of employment opportunities within the province in order to utilize more effectively the human resources of Saskatchewan.

(e) to increase the opportunity for people in northern Saskatchewan to participate more fully in the social, cultural and economic life of the province. (Canada, Dept. of Regional Economic Expansion, 1977, 171–2).

Following this agreement, subsidiary agreements were later established and now include:
– Mineral Exploration and Development in Northern Saskatchewan
– Iron, Steel and Other Related Metal Industries
– Interim Northlands
– Planning
– Qu'Appelle Valley
– Agribition

It will be seen that such subsidiary agreements can cover areas or sectors. The agribition one is even designed to support an agricultural exhibition so their scope is very wide, allowing maximum flexibility for individual provincial variety. The importance of these

agreements in DREE's budget is well-illustrated by the department's 1975–6 expenditures (Table 2.10). In comparison, the
incentive programme now plays a minor role.

Regional Development Incentives

Even though it accounts for under 20 per cent of spending by the
Department of Regional Economic Expansion, the incentive programme (RDIA) has always received a good deal of publicity and
criticism. In business circles such 'hand-outs' are not popular while
other forms of grant or subsidy designed to improve efficiency are
considered to be legitimate. Some spectacular failures of supported
companies have reinforced this belief (Mathias, 1971; *Financial Post*,
1976). On the other extreme, left-wingers are unhappy about public
money being given directly to private companies. As noted above in
criticisms of the ADA and DREE programmes, the actual operation
of the inventive schemes has done little to improve either the
industrial structure or the spatial pattern of manufacturing.

Woodward (1974) argues that these schemes contradict regional
policy by encouraging capital-intensive rather than labour-intensive
projects. The grants lower the cost of machinery more than the cost
of labour and thus do not maximize job creation. In 1975, Woodward examined the new arrangements begun in April 1974 and
showed that capital bias remained (pp. 225–7). His findings,
however, are not universally accepted. Ratcliffe (1974), by analysing
specific cases, shows that the opposite effect may well be created.
What is clear from Ratcliffe's examples is that the effect of grants
depends heavily on the character and scale of corporate taxation.
This is because grants are not tax-deductible and therefore reduce
the size of investment upon which depreciation is allowed. Another
relevant figure in the calculations is the interest rate on loans; the
lower it is, the less beneficial the grant. Ratcliffe's conclusion with
respect to a labour bias in the incentives arises because the grants
favour investment in buildings rather than machinery (p. 9). His
major criticism of the incentive programme is that grants have less
influence on profitable companies than unprofitable ones because, in
the former case, they are smaller relative to the value of the
company (p. 11). The kind of companies which could really help
peripheral regions, however, are go-ahead profitable ones. The key
question for incentive schemes therefore, should be how to attract
such companies.

TABLE 2.10
DREE'S 1975–6 EXPENDITURES ($000s)

Province	Planning and Administration	Subsidiary Agreements	Industrial Incentives	Other Programs Budgetary	Other Programs Non-Budgetary	Total
Ottawa Head Office	18,181					18,181
Newfoundland	1,101	46,332	3,167	7,332	8,260	66,192
Prince Edward Island	435		829	32,869		34,133
Nova Scotia	1,123	18,423	9,624	7,629	5,753	42,552
New Brunswick	1,096	33,460	9,618	13,505	3,281	60,960
Atlantic Regional Office	2,904			3,948		6,852
Atlantic Development Council	284			445		729
Québec	3,972	38,060	33,122	26,257	12,550	113,961
Ontario	1,866	15,148	13,606	7,765		38,385
Manitoba	1,107	12,116	5,269	11,449	1,237	31,178
Saskatchewan	1,134	9,584	4,702	22,474	2,134	40,028
Alberta	677	4,701	5,721	5,399	1,249	17,747
British Columbia	777	2,779	879	4,953		9,388
Western Regional Office	3,195					3,195
Total	37,852	180,603	86,537	144,025	34,464	483,481

Source: Canada, DREE, (1977), 57.

TABLE 2.11
GRANTS, CONTRIBUTIONS, AND SUBSIDIES TO BUSINESS, CANADA,
BY REGION, 1974–75

	Atlantic region	Québec	Ontario	Prairie region	British Columbia	Canada	Total assistance
			(Dollars per capita)				($ Million)
IT & C industrial assistance programs	8	6	9	1	11	7	158.7
DREE	8	6	1	3	—	3	69.7
Agriculture	3	19	12	35	3	16	357.1
M & I industry training program	3	2	1	1	2	2	36.9
Total	23	33	23	40	17	28	622.4

Source: Economic Council of Canada (1977), 1970.

Regional Implications of Other Federal Policies

It is often forgotten that enormous sums of money are spent across the country by the federal government in programmes with no specific regional intent. These can, and often do, counterbalance the regional programme of the Department of Regional Economic Expansion, even though the latter is designed to co-ordinate region-al policy and does consult with other departments. Table 2.11, for example, shows *per capita* aid, including DREE grants, to businesses of various kinds. Support from Industry, Trade and Commerce is higher in Ontario and British Columbia than in Atlantic Canada and Québec, reflecting its existing industrial strength. The Atlantic Provinces particularly lose out because high *per capita* agricultural support programmes do not help them much. If these *per capita* figures are translated into dollar terms, it can easily be seen how large are federal supports to the richer parts of the country.

On the other hand, much larger amounts are transferred to people and provinces as part of the overall social welfare programme. These sums do benefit the poorer areas most. Transfers to people under pensions, children's allowances, unemployment insurance and job-creation programmes amounted to $537 *per capita* for the Atlantic Region in 1974–5 compared to $384 for Ontario (Economic Council of Canada, 1977, 186). Moreover, transfers to provinces are de-signed to promote equality of service for taxes paid anywhere in the country (Graham, 1964) and this leads to large equalization pay-ments to the poorer provinces (e.g. nearly $400 *per capita* in Prince Edward Island and Newfoundland as compared to only $30 *per capita* in Ontario). These payments are unconditional, that is the province can use them as it wishes. Other federal payments for health, education and welfare also favour poorer provinces (Econo-mic Council of Canada, 1977, 241).

Finally, there is a number of federal economic policies, which clearly have regional effects but ones that are hard to estimate. Chief among these are tariff and transport policies. As indicated in Chapter 1, tariff policy in Canada has been protective. Manufactur-ing has grown up mainly in Québec and Ontario so that tariff protection benefits the two central provinces but often prevents the peripheral areas from obtaining products cheaper at nearby United States locations or from offshore. Thus the cost of living is increased and manufacturers needing semi-finished products or machinery must cope with higher costs. Transport policy is more controversial in its effects. Rail policy, for example, opened up the West while port expenditures clearly benefit coastal areas. On the other hand, easterners claim the St Lawrence Seaway benefits central Canada at their expense while westerners complain about unfair rail freight rates, which encourage shipment of raw materials eastward for manufacturing (see Chapter 6). All in all, it would seem that both of these policies reinforce core-periphery relationships within Canada.

SUMMARY

Like most countries, Canada exhibits regional disparities in a number of key indicators related to economic health and personal welfare. The country's major regional problem has for decades concerned the Atlantic Provinces but difficulties have also been pointed out in Québec, Manitoba and Saskatchewan. Moreover, the rural-urban contrast is found everywhere. It has been shown that the theory of polarization seems to apply well to the Canadian case and that manufacturing activity has been important both in establishing and in confirming the country's core area and in bringing the country strongly under the influence of the United States. In the light of the national situation, federal regional policy seemed at first to be 'ad hoc' and relatively ineffective. Regular policy changes in the last 15 years, however, have established an approach which appears to be more able to cope with Canada's economic realities. Each province can not only receive attention to its overall situation vis-à-vis the national scene but also deal with internal polarization or other problems, such as the decline of mining areas.

So far the degree of success in changing the regional pattern of economic indicators in Canada has been small. This is perhaps particularly true for the spatial pattern of manufacturing activity which has changed little in the last two decades. Given the control of this sector from Ontario and the United States, it will probably require much stronger policies than are currently acceptable in Canada before results congenial to the peripheral regions are obtained. The country's federal structure, however, will encourage challenges on the political front, and sustained pressure by the relatively strong but in some ways disadvantaged provinces (e.g. Québec, Alberta) could bring some changes. Moreover, lacking success within the current framework, the provinces may press for more power in a reorganised federation. They may then break the strength of the current élites by means of nationalization and the encouragement of indigenous enterprise. Indeed, moves in these directions have already been taken. Only time will tell how seriously such approaches will be pursued.

REFERENCES

Acheson, T. W. (1972), 'The National Policy and the industrialization of the Maritimes, 1880–1910', *Acadiensis*, (Spring), 3–28

Alonso, W. (1970), 'The economics of urban size', *Papers, Regional Science Association*, 26, 67–83.

APEC Newsletter (1969), 13, 6, (September).

APEC Newsletter (1973), 17, 5, (May).

Atlantic Provinces Economic Council (1968), *Second Annual Review. The Atlantic Economy. Summary*. Halifax, N.S.: APEC.

Atlantic Provinces Economic Council (1971), *Fifth Annual Review. The Atlantic Economy*. Halifax, N.S.: APEC.

Black, W. A. and Maxwell, J. W. (1972), 'Resource utilization: change and adaptation', in A.C. Macpherson (ed.), *Studies in Canadian Geography: The Atlantic Provinces*, (Toronto: University of Toronto), 73–136.

Brewis, T. N. (1969), *Regional Economic Policies in Canada*. Toronto: Macmillan Company of Canada.

Canada (1969), *Acts of the Parliament of Canada. 17–18 Elizabeth II*. Ottawa: Queen's Printer, 1241–52.

Canada (1974), *Perspective Canada*. Ottawa: Information Canada.

Canada, Department of Industry (1964), *Annual Report 1964*. Ottawa: Queen's Printer.

Canada, Department of Industry (1965) *News Release: Area Development Program Announcement*. Ottawa, 5 August.

Canada, Department of Industry, Area Development Agency (1967), *Canada – Incentives for Industrial Location*. Ottawa: Queen's Printer.

Canada, DREE (Department of Regional Economic Expansion) (1972), *Annual Report 70–71*. Ottawa: Information Canada.

Canada, DREE (1974), *Regional Development Incentives, 1974 – Questions and Answers*. Ottawa.

Canada, DREE (1975), *Annual Report 1974–75*. Ottawa: Information Canada.

Canada, DREE (1976), *The New Approach*. Ottawa.

Canada, DREE (1977), *Summaries of Federal-Provincial General Development Agreements and Currently-Active Subsidiary Agreements*. Ottawa.

Canada, DREE (undated) a), *Regional Economic Circumstances and Opportunities in Canada*. Ottawa.

Canada, Grain Handling and Transportation Commission (1977), *Report: Grain and Rail in Western Canada, Vol. 1*. Ottawa: Queen's Printer.

Canada, Statistics Canada (1971), *Destination of Shipments of Manufacturers, 1967*. Ottawa: Information Canada.

Canada, Statistics Canada (1975), *Canada Year Book 1975*. Ottawa.

Cannon, J. B. (1970), 'An analysis of manufacturing as an instrument of public policy in regional economic development; Canadian Area Development Agency Program 1963–1968', Unpublished Ph.D. Dissertation, University of Washington.

Clement, Wallace (1975), *The Canadian Corporate Elite*. Toronto: McClelland and Stewart.

Clement, Wallace (1977), *Continental Corporate Power: Economic Linkages between Canada and the United States*. Toronto: McClelland and Stewart.

Comeau, R. L. (1969), *A Study of the Impact of the Area Development Program in Nova Scotia*. A Report submitted to the Area Development Agency. Halifax, N.S.: Department of Economics, Dalhousie University.

Economic Council of Canada (1977), *Living Together: A Study of Regional Disparities*. Ottawa.

Financial Post (1976), 21 February, 1, 3–4.

Fréchette, P. *et al.* (1975), *L'économie du Québec*. Montréal: Les éditions HRW.

Friedmann, John R. P. (1966), *Regional Development Policy: A Case Study of Venezuela*. Cambridge, Mass.: M.I.T. Press.

Friedmann, John R. P. (1972), 'A general theory of polarized development', in N. M. Hansen (ed.), *Growth Poles in Regional Economic Development*, (New York: Free Press), 82–107.

Gilmour, James M. (1972), *Spatial Evolution of Manufacturing: Southern Ontario 1851–1891*. Toronto: University of Toronto, Department of Geography.

Graham, John F. (1964), *Fiscal Adjustment in a Federal Country*. Toronto: Canadian Tax Foundation.

Hoover, E. M. (1971), *An Introduction to Regional Economics*. New York: Alfred A. Knopf.

Isard, W. (1956), *Location and Space-Economy*. Cambridge, Mass.: M.I.T. Press.

Kerr, D. P. (1968), 'Metropolitan dominance in Canada', in J. Warkentin (ed.), *Canada: A Geographical Interpretation*, (Toronto: Methuen), 531–55.

Larsen, H. K. (1969), *A Study of the Economic Impact Generated by ADA – Assisted Manufacturing Plants Located in the Province of New Brunswick*. Report submitted to the Area Development Agency. Fredericton, N.B.: Department of Economics, University of New Brunswick.

Luttrell, W. F. (1972), 'Industrial complexes and regional economic development in Canada', in A. Kuklinski (ed.), *Growth Poles and Growth Centres in Regional Planning*, (Paris: Mouton), 243–62.

Martin, Fernand (1976), *Regional Aspects of the Evolution of Canadian Employment*. Ottawa: Economic Council of Canada.

Mathias, P. (1971), *Forced Growth*. Toronto: James Lewis and Samuel.

Norcliffe, Glen B. (1975), 'A theory of manufacturing places', in L. Collins and D. F. Walker (eds.), *Locational Dynamics of Manufacturing Activity*, (London: John Wiley), 19–58.

Ratcliffe, A. T. (1974), 'Incentives and disincentives', paper presented at the Department of Economics, University of New Brunswick, 28 Feb. Fredericton: New Brunswick Development Corporation.

Ray, D. M. (1965), *Market Potential and Economic Shadow*. Chicago; University of Chicago, Department of Geography.

Ray, D. M. (1967), 'The location of United States subsidiaries in Southern Ontario', in R. L. Gentilcore (ed.), *Canada's Changing Geography*, (Scarborough, Ontario: Prentice-Hall of Canada), 149–62.

Ray, D. M. (1971), *Dimensions of Canadian Regionalism. Geographical Paper No. 49*. Ottawa: Department of Energy, Mines and Resources, Policy Research and Coordination Branch.

Ray, D. M. and Villeneuve, Paul Y. (1975), 'Population growth and distribution in Canada: problems, process and policies', in A. R. Kuklinski (ed.), *Regional Development and Planning*, (Leyden: Sijthoff-Leyden), 91–120.

Richards, J. Howard (1965), 'Provincialism, regionalism and federalism as seen in joint resource development programmes', *Canadian Geographer*, 9, (Winter), 205–25.

Smith, D. M. (1971), *Industrial Location: An Economic Geographical Analysis*. New York: Wiley.

Springate, D. (1973), *Regional Incentives and Private Investment*. Montreal: C. D. Howe Research Institute.

Walker, David F. (1971), 'The transportation of coal into Southern Ontario, 1871–1921,' *Ontario History*, 63, 15–30.

Walker, David F. (1974), 'Energy and industrial location in Southern Ontario, 1871–1921,' in D. F. Walker and J. H. Bater (eds.), *Industrial Development in Southern Ontario*, (Waterloo, Ontario: University of Waterloo, Department of Geography), 41–68.

Whalen, H. (1965), 'Public policy and regional development: The experience of the Atlantic Provinces', in A. Rotstein (ed.), *The Prospect of Change; Proposals for Canada's Future*, (Toronto: McGraw-Hill), 102–47.

Woodward, R. S. (1974), 'The capital bias of DREE incentives', *Canadian Journal of Economics*, 7, (May), 161–73.

Woodward, R. S. (1975), 'The effectiveness of DREE's new location subsidies', *Canadian Public Policy*, 1, (Spring), 217–30.

Yeates, M. H. and Lloyd, P. E. (1969), *Impact of Industrial Incentives: Southern Georgian Bay Region, Ontario*. Ottawa: Department of Energy, Mines and Resources, Policy and Planning Branch.

3

The Atlantic Provinces

The Atlantic Provinces are generally considered to form the country's problem area. There incomes are low and large numbers are out of a job; it is a kind of economic backwater that didn't quite make it to the mid-twentieth century. The country's regional policy has been greatly influenced by conditions on the east coast, an expression perhaps of guilt feeling for what Confederation and economic growth in Central Canada have done to the poor Maritimers. The visitor, however, might be forgiven if he is struck not by seediness but by beauty and a happy independent people. Some of the problems seem to be mainly in the minds of outsiders! Maritimers and Newfoundlanders are not all convinced of the advantages of modern ways but see the positive features of independence (in fishing, farming, wood operations, small businesses), life in small settlements rather than the large city, clean air and a beautiful environment. Perhaps this has been forced on them, perhaps these vestiges of an earlier lifestyle cannot last, but certainly Atlantic Canada's problems seem greater in the Toronto newspapers than they do in Kentville or Shediac.

THE EVER-PRESENT PAST

Just as the Northern Irish constantly refer back to the events of the seventeenth century and Québecois to the Conquest, so Maritime commentators reminisce about Confederation and its role in the region's relative decline. Of course, the Newfoundlander has a different perspective as a result of joining Canada only in 1949. People on the island have not yet fully assessed the pros and cons of the move but many do still regard the mainlanders as foreign. Throughout the Atlantic Region there is a feeling that Confederation has benefited Central (Upper) Canada, and a resentment of economic dependence on Québec and especially Ontario.

Confederation coincided with a peak in the prosperity of the Maritime Provinces. In the early nineteenth century the economy was based on two staples, fish (especially in Nova Scotia) and forest products (especially in New Brunswick). The area depended on trade and shipped its products mainly to Britain, from which most manufactured goods were obtained. Shipbuilding, which developed as a major industry to service trade and fishing, was also competitive enough to provide exports itself. By the 1860s, this economy, though unrecognized at the time, was in a period of transition. In particular, the iron steamship was taking over from wood and sail on international waters, and vessel sizes were increasing. The year 1864 turned out to be the peak for Maritime shipbuilding and, after 1870, it fell off drastically (Saunders, 1939, 3–5). Technological change was not working for the area. Rather iron ships and more advanced machinery favoured the developed countries such as Britain.

The establishment of Canada necessitated a drastic re-orientation from a North Atlantic commercial system to a new continental one but, on balance, most Maritimers felt they could benefit from the new markets to the west. Manufacturing did increase rapidly in the 1870s and 1880s. Acheson (1972, 3) notes that the 1880s were 'characterized by a significant transfer of capital and human resources from the traditional staples into a new manufacturing base which was emerging in response to federal tariff policies'. Unfortunately, world conditions were undermining the prosperity of the traditional sectors. The steamship not only ruined the wooden shipbuilding industry but also crippled many of the smaller ports (Saunders, 1939, 18). The British market for ships and lumber after 1873 weakened, and rather depressed world markets in general made life difficult for the region's exporters. Between 1880 and 1890, population growth was greatly reduced.

The late nineteenth and early twentieth centuries constituted a period of considerable structural change in eastern Canada and have really governed later regional development to a large degree. As noted in Chapter 2, the Maritimers expected to do well but lost out to provinces further west. Under the National Policy, manufacturing did prosper at first and there were notable developments in textiles and iron and steel. To quote Acheson (1972, 14):

The Maritimes by 1885 provided a striking illustration of the success of that policy. With less than one-fifth of the population of the Dominion, the region contained eight of the twenty-three Canadian cotton mills – including seven of the nineteen erected after 1879 – three of five sugar refineries, two of seven rope factories, one of three glass works, both of the Canadian steel mills, and six of the nation's twelve rolling mills.

Problems, however, soon became evident. The region was not

really prepared for the new style of large enterprise. Its tradition was in small, independent business and the area's financial structure was weak (Acheson, 1972, 7). Many operations were established by co-operative ventures of businessmen whose tradition was in shipping and trade, not in manufacturing. Moreover, factories were opened in many small centres and no one metropolis became a source of real strength. In consequence, many new firms lacked financial stability and the recession after 1885 hit them hard. The National Policy had actually encouraged too many producers in some Canadian industries, such as textiles. Reduced demand brought this fact home and powerful Montréal interests determined to buy out competitors in order to control (and reduce) production. The moves started in textiles in 1886 and by 1893 most of the Maritime mills had been taken over. Events in the sugar refining, rope and glass industries were similar (Acheson, 1972, 11–21). The local entrepreneurs were not powerful enough to stop the trend and no regional metropolitan interests had developed. Most of the mergers led not only to loss of control but also to loss of jobs through closures. All in all, the Maritimes could not compete with the strengthened core area, the Montréal-Toronto axis (Archibald, 1971).

The only important resistance to these trends was in iron and steel (Donald, 1915, 194–212). This industry had some real advantages in the area because of coalfields around Springhill and on Cape Breton, and iron ore relatively close on Bell Island, Newfoundland. Existing industry at New Glasgow was stimulated by a protective tariff on iron and steel products in 1887. The tariff encouraged several companies to be set up under local interests, and by 1900 they had re-organized into the Nova Scotia Steel and Coal Company. This company had furnaces, rolling mills and machine shops in New Glasgow, owned coal mines on Cape Breton and iron ore in Newfoundland. The company supplied steel to other manufacturers, especially large car works in Amherst and Saint John. After 1900 the Halifax financial community invested heavily in this company.

Meanwhile, outside business interests set up the Dominion Coal and Dominion Steel companies, based in Sydney where furnaces were established by 1902. Their ownership, though at first partly American, was soon in Montréal and Toronto hands. The Dominion and Nova Scotia interests remained rivals until 1920, when they were consolidated into the British Empire Steel Corporation, and major regional manufacturing finally slipped away from the Maritimers.

Although there was no shortage of local entrepreneurs in the Maritime Provinces in the late nineteenth century, an outstanding feature of the present one is the lack of initiative, especially in the newer industries (those that have been growing fast; electrical products, motor cars, chemicals, for example). Most modern industries are poorly represented and existing plants are mainly branches of outside companies. There have been some outstanding developments in manufacturing, such as the growth of the pulp and paper industry, but in the main the sector has gradually lost ground relatively. One writer (George, 1970, 106–15) has argued that weak entrepreneurship is the key problem but, before coming to any conclusion, we must consider the geographical problems facing east coast firms.

PHYSICAL FACTS

Atlantic Canada is peripheral to the nation and therein lies the cause of many of its problems. Sydney is about 1000 miles away from Toronto, and Newfoundland is even further afield. The distance manifests itself in high costs of transporting goods to and from the major national markets, and more generally in all forms of direct communication. Thus any manufacturer in the region must face substantial distribution costs in Canada or try to break into export markets. After Confederation, the implications of these facts gradually made themselves felt in the economy. Canada's westward spread over the last 100 years has increased the eccentricity of the Atlantic Region. The empty Prairies were settled, and British Columbia and Alberta have become major growth areas. It is hard enough to serve Montréal but every shift westwards has increased the difficulty of marketing.

Such problems could have been overcome given some major comparative advantages, say in key raw material resources. On the whole, unfortunately, the resource base has turned out to be comparatively weak (Black and Maxwell, 1972). Although not particularly high, much of the area is rugged and has poor soils. Good farmland is restricted to Prince Edward Island and a few small areas such as the St John and Annapolis-Cornwallis valleys. Farming did not provide the basis for widespread or large settlement, thus keeping the local market small. Some farm products do form the materials for certain manufacturing industries (e.g. processing vegetables, apple juice, abattoirs). While the fishery is relatively rich, it has been suffering from over-fishing. Fortunately, Canada's 200-mile limit is now reversing this problem (*The Financial Post*, 1978). Fish-processing plants are found all around the coasts of Atlantic Canada, but unfortunately the structure of the industry is not particularly competitive today. There are still too many small operations and even higher catches will not remove the need for rationalization (Copes, 1978).

Forest covers some seventy per cent of the region and provides a basis for saw milling, numerous wood processing industries and some large pulp and paper plants. In many countries, it would be regarded as an excellent resource but in Canada woodland is not in short supply and other parts of the country are better endowed in terms of quantity and quality. The best timber was removed in the nineteenth century and high quality is rare today. Thus the forest resource does not support many high value wood-processing industries but mainly goes to the pulp and paper mills. For a detailed review see Black and Maxwell (1972).

The mining sector has some bright spots. Currently, iron ore production in Labrador on the border with Québec is both large and of good quality (30–60% iron). At the turn of the century, coal on Cape Breton and iron ore on Bell Island (near St John's) promised a bright future for iron and steel, but neither of these resources has proved fully adequate for sustained development (Kerr, 1971). The coalfield is not large compared with those in the Appalachians, mining is expensive because of thin, often steep seams, and the coal has a relatively high sulphur content. In consequence, coal-mining declined steadily until the recent energy problems began to make the area more attractive again. Bell Island ore also posed difficulties because of silica and phosphorous. Production stopped in 1966. Other mineral supplies in Atlantic Canada are relatively small, except for the complex ores of North-Eastern New Brunswick, which yield mainly lead and zinc but also copper, silver, cadmium, antimony and bismuth.

Probably the greatest deficiencies in the region concern energy. The popular twentieth century forms are expensive in the Atlantic Region. There is a shortage of good hydro-electric sites except in Labrador, and a high proportion of electricity is generated thermally. Many of the power stations rely on imported oil, which was not a major problem until the recent sky-rocketing of prices. Today, electricity prices are the highest in Canada. Exploration for petroleum and natural gas off the East Coast has so far not indicated relief in that direction, but there are still hopes for a major find. In the meantime, Atlantic Canada's first nuclear power station is under construction in New Brunswick, coal-mining is being modernized and expanded and the harnessing of Fundy's tidal power looks more and more attractive. A particularly galling fact for Newfoundland is the cheap long-term contract that assures Hydro Québec delivery of most of the hydro-electricity from Churchill Falls, Labrador. Plans for development of Lower Churchill Falls have so far not been worked out, mainly because of inter-provincial difficulties.

TODAY'S ECONOMY

Given the locational and environmental conditions of Atlantic Canada, it is not really surprising that its population and economy have grown slowly, leaving it today as Canada's 'have not' region. From the Second World War until quite recently, there was very high out-migration amounting, for example, to around 150,000 people in the 1961 to 1971 period. Even Newfoundland's high natural increase did not make up for out-migration, so that its population increase amounted to 1.9 per cent annually in the fifties (Canada 2.2%) and 1.1 per cent in the sixties (Canada 1.5%). Rates in the other three provinces were substantially lower, generally under half the national figure (Canada Year Book, 1973, 209).

Population trends reflect the economic situation. While personal income levels have been improving slightly with respect to the Canadian average, they remain at little over 70 per cent on a per capita basis (See Table 2.4). The most dramatic improvements have been in Newfoundland, which had levels under half those in Canada when it joined the country in 1949. Ray and Brewis (1976) showed that these levels are related to lower incomes for similar occupations (p.53), higher unemployment (p. 56) and lower participation rates for both males and females (p. 57), as well as differences in economic structure.

Manufacturing plays a minor role in Atlantic Canada, occupying under five per cent of the country's manufacturing employees and producing only four per cent of value added in manufacture

(Canada, Statistics Canada, 1977). The particularly weak showing in output reflects a manufacturing structure which lacks a substantial element of modern growth industries. There is still a heavy dependence on resource-based industry, particularly food and beverages (over one third of employees), wood processing and pulp and paper. Unfortunately, because of confidentiality restrictions, statistics are poor. Table 3.1 provides 1974 rather than 1975 data because the latter lack even more of the industrial categories than the former. Pulp and paper is important in terms of output as is primary metal (iron and steel). Of the other missing sectors, only transport equipment is sizeable and this unfortunately lacks the modern automobile element and focuses mainly on ships, boats and rail equipment. Recent growth sectors are poorly represented, although there are exceptions, such as Michelin tyres in Nova Scotia.

Even more than Canada as a whole, the Atlantic Region is characterized by small manufacturing firms. The average size of establishment is only about forty employees and the vast majority are small, family concerns. Much of the recent development has been in branch plants of companies from elsewhere, and there seems to be a real shortage of regional entrepreneurs with up-to-date operations capable of future expansion. Thus George's (1970) claim that entrepreneurship is the crucial problem in Nova Scotia has some foundation. The dearth of entrepreneurs has allowed one or two to build up major empires and wield an influence more in line with the nineteenth century norm than that of the late twentieth century. This is particularly true of the mammoth operations of the Irving empire, based in Saint John and on petroleum but extending across the region and into numerous activities. It is interesting to speculate as to what happened to that earlier nineteenth century spirit. Is the region a classic case of Third-world type underdevelopment by powerful outsiders? The mergers and acquisition of the early twentieth century lend some credence to this view, and the problem may have been very deep-seated according to Acheson (1977, 2):

Indeed, most Maritime entrepreneurs were unabashed colonials. They had been raised in a political and social milieu which had emphasized this status and even endowed it with a certain mystique and prestige. To be a junior partner in a relationship whose senior was one of the most universally respected states in the world never had been deemed servility by an elite which gloried in being British.

TABLE 3.1
ATLANTIC PROVINCES:
PRINCIPAL STATISTICS BY INDUSTRY GROUP, 1974

	No. of Establishments	Employees No.	%	Value of Shipments $000	Value Added $000	%
Food and beverage industries	553	26,862	32.2	1,247,540	364,043	23.2
Tobacco products industries	—	—	—	—	—	—
Rubber and plastics product industries	15	*	*	*	*	*
Leather industries	6	*	*	*	*	*
Textile industries	29	1,553	1.8	41,359	16,001	1.0
Knitting Mills	6	*	*	*	*	*
Clothing industries	11	*	*	*	*	*
Wood industries	395	6,962	8.3	202,938	87,056	5.6
Furniture and fixture industries	67	*	*	*	*	*
Paper and allied industries	35	*	*	*	*	*
Printing, Publishing and allied industries	165	3,135	3.7	68,121	49,235	3.1
Primary Metal industries	12	*	*	*	*	*
Metal fabricating industries	111	3,744	4.5	132,552	70,111	4.8
Machinery industries	20	762	0.9	19,616	9,294	0.6
Transportation equipment industries	91	*	*	*	*	*
Electrical products industries	15	2,415	2.9	61,934	33,033	2.1
Non-metallic mineral products industries	87	2,470	3.0	102,521	53,601	3.4
Petroleum and coal products	8	*	*	*	*	*
Chemical and chemical products industries	35	*	*	*	*	*
Miscellaneous manufacturing industries	73	*	*	*	*	*
Total all industries	1,734	83,489	57.4	4,417,759	1,567,795	43.8

* Not available due to confidentiality restrictions.

The fact is, however, that markets are the key to industrial development today. Atlantic Canada with its small population of under 2¼ million, growing on average at a rate well below the national level, just does not provide a lucrative market. The gradual increase in market size has encouraged some new operations, including branch plants of Canadian and foreign companies, but they are mainly small. The region's scattered population and low degree of urbanization makes marketing very expensive. Only four centres have a population of over 100,000 and urban population is well below the usual Canadian percentages (Forward, 1972, 137 –45). As already noted, the area is isolated from the rest of Canada. Export markets hold some promise, especially in Europe, but they will not be established easily.

SPATIAL PATTERNS

While there have always been important sub-regional variations within Atlantic Canada, recent trends seem to have intensified the development of core-periphery distinctions. Indeed Burke and Ireland (1976, 30) argue that in the early 1970s for the first time the core area began to play a major role in the economic leadership of the region. Figure 3.1 shows Burke and Ireland's core, a strip running from Halifax through Moncton to Saint John and Frederic-ton. In many respects this area is close to the national norm – in urbanization, labour force participation, and personal income per capita, for example – while the rest of Atlantic Canada performs very badly (Burke and Ireland, 1976, 28–37). The one sector in which even this core region is relatively weak, however, is manufac-turing. Yet Todd (1977, 51) shows that, apart from resource-oriented industries, manufacturing, in Nova Scotia at least, is quite polarized.

At the eastern end of the corridor is Atlantic Canada's largest urban area, Halifax-Dartmouth, still administered as two cities. Metropolitan Halifax-Dartmouth has its greatest strength in the service sectors – provincial and federal government, education, trade and transport. Its role as a distribution centre for the whole of Atlantic Canada is increasing. Between 1971 and 1974, employment in the service categories rose by 30 per cent (Burke and Ireland, 1976, 35). The main economic advances recently have been in the transport sector. The expansion of container shipping has allowed Halifax to strengthen its position amongst Canada's east coast ports (Wallace, 1975), although the benefits have not greatly affected employment levels. On the waterfront also are the naval dockyards, petroleum refineries and yards for the building and repair of ships and oilrigs. The metropolitan area has some strength in electronics

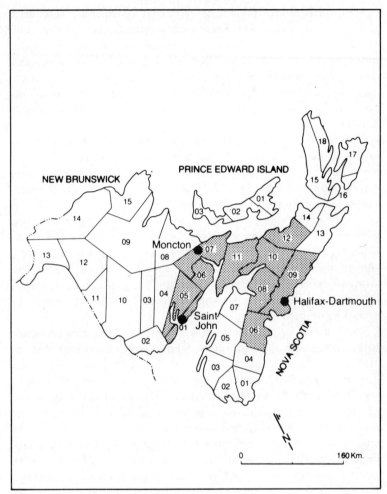

Figure 3.1   Burke and Ireland's Atlantic Core Region.

but otherwise its secondary manufacturing structure is fairly diverse. The early 1970s witnessed broadly based improvements, including automobile assembly (Volvo cars), shipbuilding and electronics, as well as consumer goods for the Atlantic Region's market (Burke and Ireland, 1976, 34). Despite the fact that it is not primarily a manufacturing centre, Halifax-Dartmouth accounts for some 29 per cent of provincial value added with only 14 per cent of the workforce (Canada, Statistics Canada, 1976, 340).

Westwards from Halifax the relatively prosperous core area extends to Moncton, New Brunswick, a metropolitan area of some 85,000 people, which owes its main strength to a strategic transport location. As a result it has become a major wholesaleing and distribution point for the Maritime Provinces. Its urban services, university and transport facilities have encouraged a gradual increase in light manufacturing, geared mainly to the local or regional market.

Between Halifax and Moncton, some small cities such as Truro and Amherst have managed to attract a few new plants and provide a manufacturing base appropriate to their size. Newer developments have mostly been added to older plants, for this is not an area which first saw manufacturing in the 1960s. Coalmining at Springhill and around New Glasgow led to industrial development in the late nineteenth century and some metal-based operations date from the time, e.g. the Trenton railway rolling stock plant. On the whole, though, most earlier industries have long since died out. In the New Glasgow area the Michelin plant and a paper mill are now mainstays of the economy, while Springhill has not managed to attract significant new factories.

South from Moncton there are few towns and almost no manufacturing until one reaches the industrial port city of Saint John. Unlike Halifax, Saint John is not the capital city of its province. Instead government and educational services have concentrated at Fredericton. As a result, Saint John presents a different picture from that of the Nova Scotia capital. It looks like an industrial city and lacks much of the charm of a more diversified place. Home of the Irving empire, it has a pulp and paper mill, oil refinery, shipbuilding and drydock facilities, newspaper, and numerous smaller industries which belong to the family (Hunt and Campbell, 1973). In addition, there is considerable metal processing, as well as food and beverage plants of many types. With around 18 per cent of New Brunswick's manufacturing employment, Saint John accounts for just over a third of the province's value added in manufacturing (Canada, Statistics Canada, 1976, 345). In the last decade, there has been tremendous investment in improving the infrastructure of the city, but the returns in growth of manufacturing employment have not been very marked. The most spectacular project, a metal-working complex, has failed (see below). Saint John's port, also, has not been as successful as that of Halifax in adapting to changing conditions, although it has made some progress recently.

Outside of this narrow area from Halifax to Fredericton, most of Atlantic Canada has severe economic problems. In New Brunswick the hardest-hit area is the Acadian north-east coast, subject of numerous reports and policies (Krueger and Koegler, 1975, 47–62). The north shore has a narrow strip of settlement hugging the coastline and many people make a living by combining small-scale farming, fishing and forestry. Unemployment is very high, incomes very low. Scattered along the coast is the occasional fish processing plant, a few other food or beverage industries, some larger wood and paper operations and a very occasional industry of some other type. Attempts to diversify the economy have largely been unsuccessful because of isolation from both markets and materials. Mining, which has expanded around Bathurst since the early 1960s, has led to a large smelter at Belledune and to some industrial service activities in Bathurst.

Central New Brunswick is rocky, wooded and sparsely populated. Apart from forestry and some wood processing, it offers few opportunities. The Saint John river valley north of Fredericton, however, is more hospitable. It serves as the major routeway to central Canada and thus offers relatively good accessibility. Some farming is also possible. Local potatoes formed the initial base for the McCain frozen food company with a head office at Florenceville. It has since diversified into other frozen products and established plants elsewhere in Canada and overseas. The Saint John Valley has some large wood, pulp and paper operations, for example at Edmundston and the new town of Nackawic. As in most parts of the Maritimes, other industries are mainly small, few and far between.

In much of the Nova Scotian periphery there is a similar situation. In the southern section of the province, the Annapolis valley's farming supports fruit and vegetable processing, woodlands provide material for an occasional plant such as the paper mill at Liverpool, and the coastal settlements have some small boatbuilding and fish-processing firms. Occasional variety is found, with activities such as printing and textiles. Yarmouth, which a decade ago still had a fairly substantial textile sector, has seen it fade away under increasing competition. The one major new bright spot is the large Michelin tyre plant at Bridgewater, which has greatly helped the local economy (Pross, 1975, 5–27).

In the northern half of the province, the situation is quite different for two main reasons. Firstly, there is the problem of a declining industrial area, industrial Cape Breton. Secondly, the Strait of

Canso was a fast-growing industial node in the 1960s and early 1970s. As already noted, coal-mining and iron and steel production were developed around the turn of the century in and around Sydney. A high degree of impurities, and thin, steep seams rendered coal uncompetitive, however, and the coal industry was in decline for many decades, causing severe unemployment. In 1967, the Cape Breton Development Corporation (DEVCO) was established to phase out coalmining and provide alternative job opportunities. Recently, however, high oil costs have led to an up-turn in investment and production. Currently, in fact, the outlook for coal in energy-short Nova Scotia is much better than for steel. Steel at Sydney has always been marginal (Kerr, 1971, 60–2). The private owners (Dominion Steel and Coal Corporation) decided to close their plant in 1968 but it was eventually bought by the provincial government and placed under the direction of a crown corporation (SYSCO) Although the new owners did well for a while and some renovations were made, the basic problems of a very old plant and distance from the Canadian market have not been solved. Recent discussions have focused on the possibilities of a completely new, world-scale complex at Gabarus Bay (Atlantic Provinces Economic Council, 1974) but, as of 1978, the future of this scheme does not look very promising. Meanwhile, industrial Cape Breton has almost entirely failed to attract or hold new manufacturing plants, which could have provided jobs for the unemployed from its basic industries. Despite generous incentives, few firms have come and most of those which did later closed down.

At the other end of Cape Breton Island, the Strait of Canso has been the centre of rapid growth. The building of the causeway to the island in 1954 blocked off the ice flows from the north and created an ice-free harbour, a harbour which was also one of the deepest in eastern North America (Pross, 1975, 30–1). Mainly as a result of the harbour, several large capital intensive plants were located along the Strait (e.g. an oil refinery, power station, heavy water plant, pulp and paper mill) creating considerable planning problems, which are only now being brought under control (Pross, 1975; Watt, 1978). This growth brought back a number of Cape Bretoners to their homeland as well as an influx of managerial and technical experts from elsewhere (Watt, 1978). Plans for further development have not come to fruition, however, and there has been no new manufacturing plant since 1971.

The province of Newfoundland and Labrador has to face the most difficult problems of any of Canada's provinces. Labrador is essentially part of the Canadian North, and faces the harshness of the northern environment. Its scattered coastal settlements rely on water and air transport to keep them in touch with the rest of the world. In the interior, massive resource developments based on iron ore and the Churchill Falls hydro-electric project are localized and isolated. Newfoundland proper also has a relatively harsh environment with cool summers, cold winters, considerable cloud and fog and poor soils.

For centuries, Newfoundland relied on its one rich resource, the fishery. At first, there were only visiting European fishermen, but eventually permanent settlements were established around the coastline, linked only by water. Fish were mainly dried and salted for export, and the fish economy came under the control of a few merchant families based in St John's. The traditional system was essentially feudal, with a merchant supplying foodstuffs, fishing gear and other basic requirements in return for fish. By the early 1930s, the situation had become even more pernicious because the merchants no longer provided adequate support to carry the fishermen through bad times (Neary, 1973, 23–6). Many of the worst elements of this system were removed during the later 1930s.

Meanwhile, from the end of the nineteenth century, some changes had been taking place in the economy. A narrow gauge railway across the island was completed in 1897. Large-scale iron ore mining began on Bell Island in 1895, with production linked to iron and steel manufacturing in Sydney, Nova Scotia. In 1905, a paper mill was started at Grand Falls and this was followed by another at Corner Brook in 1925. Thus, Newfoundland was diversifying and industrializing during the early twentieth century (Neary, 1973, 17–8). Essentially the same trend has continued. The Second World War brought strategic importance with bases at Gander, Torbay (near St John's) and Goose Bay, Labrador. Under Joey Smallwood's post-Confederation regime, diversification was pursued as a major policy thrust. Mr Smallwood particularly emphasized large, capital intensive schemes, many which have since collapsed (e.g. Stephenville liner-board plant, Come-by-Chance oil refinery). It has been a major problem for Newfoundland throughout this period that its projects have been forced to rely on outside capital. With a lack of competitive advantage and a shortage of funds, many developments involved considerable concessions. For example, the building of the railway allowed large concessions to the Reid family, which built it. Currently Newfoundland can obtain power from its Churchill Falls development only by buying it at commercial rates from Québec, for this was part of the deal to get the project off the ground (Harrington, 1976).

While standards of living have improved enormously in Newfoundland (Canada, DREE, 1976, 23–5), *per capita* income is still some 35 per cent below the Canadian average, while the unemployment rate is usually double Canada's. In manufacturing, its base is very restricted. Only 13,000 people work in manufacturing. There are two large, ageing paper plants at Grand Falls and Corner Brook, fish and food processing operations at various centres, and a few other plants mainly in St John's. Despite considerable efforts to attract manufacturers, the limited resource base, small local market and distance from larger markets have proved to be too great to overcome. Add to this a tradition and a way of life that are not particularly conducive to the development of either entrepreneurs or an industrial workforce and it is not difficult to see why manufacturing remains unimportant in the province.

POLICIES AND PROGRAMMES

From a national perspective, Atlantic Canada is clearly the major regional disparity problem. As outlined in Chapter 2, the region has played an important role in the evolution of federal policy designed to aid areas with economic problems. At the same time, each province has also been active in formulating an individual approach to its own particular problems. Since the 1950s, in fact, studies and strategies related to various aspects of regional economic development have appeared and disappeared with bewildering irregularity. The one fact which remains constant is Atlantic Canada's substantial lag behind the rest of the country on most measures of economic prosperity.

Federal Policy

The evolution of federal regional policy has already been described in Chapter 2.[1] The main element for manufacturing was the

[1] This section is based substantially on Walker (1975), with permission of *Regional Studies*.

Area Development Agency. Moreover the policy of the agency in the Atlantic Region was subjected to a thorough evaluation in two studies commissioned by the federal government for Nova Scotia and New Brunswick. A third, for Newfoundland, has never been released. The reports were submitted in 1969 and were completed before the full impact of the programme had been established. Nevertheless, they provide a useful starting point for any review of its results.

In the Nova Scotia study, Comeau (1969) interviewed not only plants that had been supported by the Area Development Agency (58 in number) but also a control group of other plants (54), although not all interviews were fully usable. He followed an input-output approach, estimating capital investment, employment and income. Nova Scotia received about 13 per cent of projects under the ADA scheme, but the total investment formed a smaller percentage, and was in fact below what would be expected on the basis of population. Direct employment created in the supported plants amounted to about 2300 jobs between 1962 and 1967, but almost as many were generated in the control group of plants. Moreover, the investment per job in ADA plants was about $59,000 while that in the control group was about $14,500. There was some improvement in employment percentages for both female and skilled workers. Nevertheless average wages declined slightly, mainly because many jobs were low-income ones. (Average wages in the control group declined even more – 20.5% as opposed to 3.4%.)

Comeau also considered the indirect effects resulting from the input-output structure of the new plants. Most plants were involved with semi-processed goods and marketed their product primarily in the United States. The main items were fish products, pulp and paper products and various textiles, although growth was underway in industrial chemicals and petroleum refining. Most inputs to the ADA plants were from Nova Scotia and, moreover, the proportion of home province materials grew in the 1962–7 period, although remaining smaller than that for the control group.

Calculating for employment in local supply industries, and that generated in the tertiary sector, Comeau considered that 12,361 jobs in Nova Scotia had been created as a result of the ADA programme. Manufacturing employment rose slightly more rapidly than the national average between 1962 and 1967 and unemployment fell more rapidly. The average Nova Scotia per capita income, too, rose from 75.1 per cent of the Canadian figure in 1962 to 77.4 per cent in

1967. A less flattering comparison, however, is a slower growth of incomes in the manufacturing sector taken separately. Comeau considers that development of at most 50–60 per cent of ADA-supported plants could be attributed to the help provided by the programme.

The companion study for New Brunswick by Larsen (1969) took a similar approach. A little over 2500 extra people were employed in the ADA plants in New Brunswick. Most plants were small employers, except for a few resource-based ones. A high proportion of workers were unskilled, especially in the earlier years of the scheme, but wages were higher than for non-aided plants. Larsen noted that a high proportion of the ADA-aided plants were either low-value-adding, resource-based operations or branch plants very close to the distribution stage. He argued that neither category would have a strong impact (the first because of low wages, the second because of low employment). Products on the whole were similar to those already characteristic of the New Brunswick economy, especially those dependent on farming, forestry and fishing (about 67%). This characteristic of the industrial structure encouraged backward linkage within New Brunswick to the primary sector, but there was almost no linkage to other secondary manufacturers in the area. In general the indirect impact was not great.

Both of these studies were inadequate in quality of data obtained, but they do provide many important facts about the operations of the Area Development programme. From their findings and the evaluations of other writers it is possible to summarize the problems that were evident.

As noted in Chapter 2, no consideration was given to the planning of either the structural or the spatial effects of the incentives provided under the ADA programme. In the Atlantic Region existing industries tended to receive the bulk of the support, although it has been argued that modifications to the Atlantic Region's industrial structure are essential. Spatially, the ADA programme tended to encourage decentralization of manufacturing investment (Cannon, 1970, pp. 178–9). In the Atlantic Provinces, a scattering of plants was encouraged by the fact that the only areas not designated were those around the largest urban centres – Halifax-Dartmouth, Saint John-Fredericton. Such a situation was criticized severely within the region (Atlantic Provinces Economic Council, 1968, pp 12–3).

Another difficulty during most of the 1960s was the existence of such a multiplicity of programmes concerned with economic development. Quite apart from provincial policies outlined below, several federal programmes also had a bearing on these matters, as noted in Chapter 2.

This complexity of support programmes did not help manufacturers to make full use of the available aids: it was not easy to find out about them without a very active search. A survey conducted by the author in 1968 of 103 plants which had been built or expanded found that only about 30 per cent of managements knew about relevant programmes (see Walker (1971) for details of the sample used in this study). Smaller, local entrepreneurs who did know about the ADA programme felt that it was designed for larger companies and not concerned with their needs. In general, it would seem that a better information programme would have helped the incentives to be more fully utilized.

The year 1968 saw the federal government's attempt to put its act together in the Department of Regional Economic Expansion (DREE). Incentives to manufacturers were retained under the new 1969 Regional Development Incentives Act but an important change in designated areas left the whole of the region (except Labrador) available for incentives. This has subsequently allowed an emphasis on larger centres such as Halifax and Saint John in contrast to their previous exclusion. A review of the use of incentives for the years 1969–72 suggests that they were having little effect on the region (Atlantic Development Council, 1976). In particular, they did little to change the industrial structure and did not encourage a location in growth centres (pp. 15–16). Another new feature, the Special Areas, did, however, allow such a switch of emphasis. These areas, for which infrastructure grants were available, included Halifax-Dartmouth, Moncton, Saint John and St John's as well as several smaller centres which required help for specific reasons, particularly resettlement schemes in Newfoundland (fig. 3.2).

The new department prepared the way for an overall regional strategy to be pursued in the Atlantic Region but the first attempt to produce one came from another source. In the 1960s the Atlantic Development Board had been requested to prepare a regional development plan. Its successor in the DREE era – the advisory Atlantic Development Council – published its strategy in 1971. The

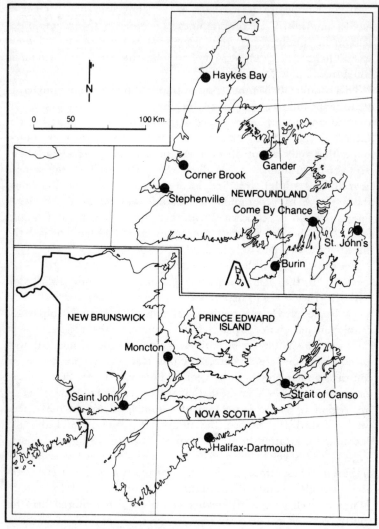

Figure 3.2   Atlantic Provinces: Designated Special Areas.
               Source: D. F. Walker (1975)

core of its proposal was the necessity for the creation of 50,000
manufacturing jobs between 1971 and 1981 in order that 170,000
new regional jobs would become available. Given such achieve-
ments, the region could hope for self-sustaining growth. Amongst
other elements of the strategy were education of both labour and
management. Spatially, growth centres and industrial complexes

were recommended. In addition, the concept of a resource centre, based on resource industries, was supported.

Although the federal government accepted this development strategy, the job targets were not endorsed. Elements of a growth centre strategy have been followed by DREE until very recently. Industrial incentives, however, have applied to the whole region and one of the earliest criticisms of the new department concerned its failure to encourage manufacturing in the largest centres (Atlantic Provinces Economic Council Newsletter, 1973) In addition to the selective support of the 'special areas', however, both Saint John and Halifax-Dartmouth were subject to special help. The most spectacular approach was the attempt to develop an industrial complex in Saint John (Luttrell, 1972). A joint federal-provincial agency, New Brunswick Multiplex Ltd., was established in 1971 and detailed studies led to a suggested complex of inter-related metal industries. Despite thorough research, this project failed at the promotional stage. Sufficient firms were not found to open the required plants. By 1977, Multiplex was clearly a failure and the organization was disbanded. In Halifax-Dartmouth, a lower key approach was used in the form of an investment group designed to encourage local business investment (Metropolitan Area Growth Investment Ltd.), This agency has since broadened its concern to all of mainland Nova Scotia. In manufacturing, therefore, any attempts at effective growth centre policies seem to have been abandoned.

Since 1973, the decentralization of DREE and the signing of general and subsidiary agreements between the federal and provincial governments have brought their development efforts much more closely into line, and so federal policy does not require separate discussion here. The new approach, however, does seem to have reduced the emphasis on overall regional strategy. In 1973 DREE suggested an approach based on a transport corridor (Canada, DREE, 1973, 26–62) but it has not played a noticeable role in subsequent policy. Moreover, despite meetings of the Maritime premiers, suggestions for co-operation on industrial development (Atlantic Development Council, 1971, 7; Atlantic Provinces Economic Council, 1973, 75–93) have been effectively ignored.

Provincial Policies

The four east coast provinces have each evolved their own policies concerning manufacturing. Except in Prince Edward Island, this sector has been considered vital to an improved prosperity. Until very recently, much effort was expended in attempting to attract outside manufacturers to the provinces, often with fairly lucrative financial arrangements. Now, more attention is being given to existing firms and to potential entrepreneurs within the province. On the whole, spatial policies have not been consistently articulated, although New Brunswick pursued a growth centre approach for more than a decade and currently has regional industrial commissions, while Nova Scotia is now encouraging the further expansion of its most successful areas.

In the 1960s and early 1970s the development corporation was the main instrument for attracting industry. Nova Scotia's Industrial Estates Ltd., incorporated in 1957, was the first of these. It is mainly a promotional agency designed to attract and help to finance new secondary manufacturing activity anywhere within Nova Scotia. In its early years, it established two industrial parks at Dartmouth and Stellarton but this policy was not continued (Atlantic Provinces Economic Council Research Centre, 1970, 81–3). This agency has been subjected to a detailed study by George (1974). Despite some major losses in firms such as Clairtone (colour television) and Deuterium (heavy water), George calculates that the agency had brought net benefits of over $120 million dollars to the province by March 1971, although such a return was low as against alternative investments (pp. 111–19). On the other hand, the full benefits of the largest development, Michelin, were not felt by 1971. George argues that Industrial Estates Ltd.'s objectives need to be clarified and, especially, that it needs more sophisticated research in order to identify suitable manufacturing firms for the province (pp. 121–34). He also supports the idea of encouraging smaller firms and developing industrial estates.

In New Brunswick, the New Brunswick Development Corporation was set up with similar but more explicit objectives in 1959 (Atlantic Provinces Economic Council, 1973, 31–4). The Corporation has tended to be more concerned with research than Industrial Estates Ltd. and particularly to stimulate industries using sound economic evaluation. In the 1960s, the growth pole of interrelated industries was pursued as a concept and was used in connection with industrial parks. Thus, near Sackville, the Westmoreland Chemical Park was established. A fisheries-oriented park was planned near St Andrews and a mechanical industries park in Saint

John. The latter eventually blossomed out into the Multiplex Corporation. Incentives were used to influence the location of industry and to encourage sound locations rather than ones in the areas of highest unemployment in the province. In 1967, the Development Corporation received a new manager and enlarged its operation considerably, increasing foreign promotion as well as research on three key·projects – a fish port, a deep water port near Saint John and that which became Multiplex (Atlantic Provinces Economic Council, 1973, 48–52). Despite all this research and expense, these schemes have brought little concrete development to the province, and it would seem that some of the problems were underestimated. In more general promotion, of course, the Corporation has helped many firms.

Prince Edward Island also has a development corporation, Industrial Enterprises Incorporated. It was established in 1965 and modelled on Industrial Estates Ltd. In practice, however, the focus has been different, with an emphasis on assisting local firms (Atlantic Provinces Economic Council Research Centre, 1970, 91–4; Atlantic Provinces Economic Council, 1973, 52–5). In Newfoundland and Labrador, the development corporation (set up only in 1973) was explicitly established to help small businesses with information, management services, and financing (Atlantic Provinces Economic Council, 1973, 55–7). It should be noted, however, that large-scale projects in Newfoundland have traditionally been handled directly by the politicians, especially under Premier Joey Smallwood. Recently the thrust in the two larger provinces has also moved to small, locally owned firms. New Brunswick has closed its development corporation while Industrial Estates Ltd. has been restricted. The days of vast sums of money for large glamorous projects in Atlantic Canada seem to have ended. Instead there is a more realistic appraisal of the problems for secondary manufacturers and a desire to encourage and aid local entrepreneurs.

Most elements of new policy are contained in federal-provincial agreements, illustrating how federal and provincial policies have been brought more closely into line since 1973. Prince Edward Island has been governed by a comprehensive development plan since 1969 under the Fund for Rural Development. Within this broad plan, manufacturing plays a minor role.

In Newfoundland and Labrador, the general development agreement with DREE is concerned with improving employment opportunities. Many sub-agreements involve assessment of the various sectors for economic potential. In addition to its possibilities in the resource sectors (mining, fishing, forestry), the Newfoundland Ocean Research and Development Corporation is being funded 'to stimulate the development of marine technology within the Province and to foster the establishment of marine ice-related industries' (Canada, DREE, 1977, 21). There are still hopes for major oil or gas finds in the area, but in general the range of realistic secondary manufacturing opportunities is small (Davis, 1976). Industrial development support is being concentrated on the less prosperous western side of the island.

Both Nova Scotia and New Brunswick have sub-agreements specifically concerned with industrial development. In Nova Scotia, there are five elements to the strategy. These are:

(1) Opportunity identification, analysis and promotion designed to find and encourage appropriate industries.

(2) Support for local enterprise – especially in management and marketing.

(3) Provision of industrial infrastructure, including serviced land, and industrial parks.

(4) Manpower development.

The fifth element – industrial location – indicates a thrust to encourage growth in the already growing area, – the corridor from Amherst to Halifax. The focus will be on infrastructure, but it is interesting to note that another subsidiary agreement – on Metropolitan Halifax-Dartmouth Area Development – is designed to encourage an increasing metropolitan influence for the capital (Canada, DREE, 1977, 46–9). One objective of the sub-agreement is 'a restructuring of the Halifax-Dartmouth economy towards more highly skilled manufacturing and service activities' (p. 47). Clearly then, Nova Scotia has now committed itself to a distinct spatial strategy of industrial development.

The special problems of Cape Breton are the responsibility of a separate agency, The Cape Breton Development Corporation (DEVCO). Set up in 1967 to wind down the coalmining operations and find alternative jobs, DEVCO has had a singular lack of success in establishing secondary manufacturing in industrial Cape Breton (*Executive*, 1977, 32). As the Sydney steel mill splutters towards extinction, considerable provincial efforts have been given to a new world scale mill (Atlantic Provinces Economic Council, 1974).

New Brunswick's policy is evolving somewhat differently from her neighbour's. With the disbanding of the Development Corporation and of Multiplex Corporation, the provincial development effort is now focused entirely in the Department of Commerce and Development. On the other hand, decentralization has been espoused in the form of regional development commissions under local boards of directors. These commissions are funded under the industrial development sub-agreement and allow considerable scope for sub-regional initiatives. The province itself is not supporting any particular spatial strategy, not even the growth centre policy rather unsuccessfully pursued since the mid-1960s. The sub-agreement (Canada, DREE, 1977, 75–7) stresses industrial infrastructure, development planning and support for manufacturers in the establishment and experimental production stages. Like Nova Scotia, the province is concerned to encourage and help its own entrepreneurs as much as possible.

CONCLUSION

Since Confederation, Canada's east coast provinces have fought a continuous uphill battle to maintain an acceptable standard of living for their inhabitants. The Atlantic Region's economy remains relatively weak and more than a decade of intensive regional policy has had limited effects. Expensive incentive programmes for secondary industry seem to have been rejected as an effective policy tool and easterners currently appear more determined to try to help themselves by encouraging their own businessmen to develop their own ideas. There remain no easy solutions to the basic locational and resource limitations of Atlantic Canada. All that can be said is that the difficulties are now better appreciated.

REFERENCES

Acheson, T. W. (1972), 'The National Policy and the industrialization of the Maritimes, 1880–1919', *Acadiensis*, 1, (Spring), 3–28.

Acheson, T. W. (1977), 'The Maritimes and "Empire Canada"', in D. J. Bercuson (ed.), *Canada and the Burden of Unity*. (Toronto: Macmillan), 87–114.

Archibald, B. (1971), 'Atlantic regional underdevelopment and socialism', in L. LaPierre (ed.), *Essays on the Left*, (Toronto: McClelland and Stewart), 103–20.

Atlantic Development Council (1971), *A Strategy for the Economic Development of the Atlantic Region, 1971–1981*. Fredericton, N.B.

Atlantic Development Council (1976), *Regional Development Incentives Program: Atlantic Region*. Ottawa.

Atlantic Provinces Economic Council (1968), *Second Annual Review*. Halifax.

Atlantic Provinces Economic Council (1973), *Seventh Annual Review*. Halifax.

Atlantic Provinces Economic Council (1974), *Steelmaking in the Atlantic Provinces: A Commentary*. Halifax.

Atlantic Provinces Economic Council Newsletter (1973), 17, 5, (May).

Atlantic Provinces Economic Council Research Centre (1970), *Industrial Development Policies in the Maritime Provinces*. Fredericton: Maritime Union Study.

Black, W. A. and Maxwell, J. W. (1972), 'Resource utilization: change and adaptation', in A. G. Macpherson (ed.), *The Atlantic Provinces*, (Toronto: University of Toronto), 73–136.

Burke, C. D. and Ireland, D. J. (1976), *An Urban/Economic Development Strategy for the Atlantic Region*. Ottawa: Ministry of State for Urban Affairs.

Canada, DREE (1973), *Atlantic Region: Economic Circumstances and Opportunities*. Ottawa.

Canada, DREE (1976), *Climate for Development: Atlantic Region*. Ottawa.

Canada, DREE (1977), *Summaries of Federal-Provincial Agreements and Currently Active Subsidiary Agreements*. Ottawa.

Canada, Statistics Canada (1976), *Market Research Handbook*. Ottawa.

Canada, Statistics Canada (1977), *Manufacturing Industries of Canada 1975*. Ottawa.

Cannon, J. B. (1970), 'An analysis of manufacturing as an instrument of public policy in regional economic development: Canadian Area Development Agency program 1963–1968', Unpublished Ph.D. Dissertation, University of Washington.

Comeau, R. L. (1969), *A Study of the Impact of the Area Development Program in Nova Scotia*. Halifax: Department of Economics, Dalhousie University.

Copes, P. (1978), 'Canada's Atlantic Coast Fisheries: Policy development and the impact of extended jurisdiction', *Canadian Public Policy*, 4, (Spring), 155–71.

Davis, A. (1976), 'Economic Development: Province of Newfoundland and Labrador', Unpublished Economic Development Diploma essay, University of Waterloo.

Donald, W. J. A. (1915), *The Canadian Iron and Steel Industry*. Boston: Houghton Mifflin.

Executive. (1977), 'One orphan plant hobbles along', (April), 32.

The Financial Post (1978), Special Report, 29 April.

Forward, C. N. (1972), 'Cities: Function, Form and Future', in A. Macpherson (ed.), *The Atlantic Provinces*, (Toronto: University of Toronto Press), 137–76.

George, R. E. (1970), *A Leader and a Laggard. Manufacturing Industry in Nova Scotia, Québec and Ontario*. Toronto: University of Toronto Press.

George, R. E. (1974), *The Life and Times of Industrial Estates*. Halifax: Institute of Public Affairs, Dalhousie University.

Harrington, M. (1976), 'Political fuses blown by Churchill Falls power contract', *Financial Post*, 4 Sept.

Hunt, R. and Campbell, R. (1973), 'The man who made New Brunswick a company town', *Saturday Night*, (August), 9–14.

Kerr, D. P. (1971), 'The location of the iron and steel industry in Canada', in R. L. Gentilcore (ed.), *Geographical Approaches to Canadian Problems*, (Toronto: Prentice-Hall of Canada), 59–68.

Krueger, R. R. and Koegler, J. (1975), *Regional Development in Northeast New Brunswick*. Toronto: McClelland and Stewart.

Larsen, H. K. (1969), *A Study of the Economic Impact Generated by A.D.A. Assisted Manufacturing Plants Located in the Province of New Brunswick*. Fredericton, N. B.: Department of Economics, University of New Brunswick.

Luttrell, W. F. (1972), 'Industrial complexes and regional economic development in Canada', in A. Kuklinski (ed.), *Growth Poles and Growth Centres in Regional Planning*, (Paris: Mouton), 243–62.

Neary, P. (ed.) (1973), *The Political Economy of Newfoundland, 1929–1972*. Vancouver: Copp Clark.

Pross, A. P. (1975), *Planning and Development: A Case of Two Nova Scotia Communities*. Halifax: Institute of Public Affairs, Dalhousie University.

Ray, D. M. and Brewis, T. N. (1976), 'The geography of income and its correlates', *Canadian Geographer*, 20, (Spring), 41–71.

Saunders, S. A. (1939), *The Economic History of the Maritime Provinces*. Ottawa: Royal Commission on Dominion-Provincial Relations.

Todd, D. (1977), *Polarization and the Regional Problem. Manufacturing in Nova Scotia, 1960–1973*. Winnipeg: Department of Geography, University of Manitoba.

Walker, D. F. (1971), 'An adaptive framework for the study of industrial location decisions', Unpublished Ph.D. Thesis, University of Toronto.

Walker, D. F. (1975), 'Governmental Influence on manufacturing location: Canadian experience with special reference to the Atlantic Provinces', *Regional Studies*, 9, (August), 203–17.

Wallace, I. (1975), 'Containerization at Canadian ports', *Annals, The Association of American Geographers*, 65, (Sept.), 433–48.

Watt, J. A. (1978), 'The impact of a growth centre on labour migration: the Strait of Canso, Nova Scotia', Unpublished M. A. Thesis, University of Waterloo.

4

Québec

In Chapter 2, Québec was revealed as Canada's second province in both population and manufacturing activity. It shares in the prosperity of Canada's 'Main Street', the narrow strip of country between Windsor and Québec City.[1] At the same time, the province has been experiencing a very slow population growth, high unemployment and relatively low personal income levels in the last two decades. The Québec economy in the mid-1970s is in trouble, and its industrial structure, which includes too high a proportion of slow-growth industries such as textiles and clothing, is a major source of difficulties. Thus a major theme of this chapter is to analyse the way such structural weaknesses have developed and the extent to which policies are operating to remedy them. The other key question for the province concerns the role of Montréal, which dominates the provincial economy but which is faltering in comparison with Toronto. While much needs to be done for the less strong peripheral regions in Québec, Montréal's national and international role cannot be neglected.

QUÉBEC'S INDUSTRIAL STRUCTURE AND STRENGTH

With nearly 31 per cent of Canada's manufacturing employment and 27 per cent of her value added in manufacturing, Québec is clearly in second place to Ontario as an industrial province. The difference between these two percentage figures, however, immediately reveals a productivity problem in the province, for more employees are needed to produce a given output than might be expected. Productivity in manufacturing runs at between 20 and 25 per cent below that of Ontario (Québec, Dept. of Industry and Commerce, 1975, 5), a fact which compromises the province's competitive position, particularly in view of its more peripheral location in the North American market.

A major cause of low productivity is the composition of manufacturing, which can be observed in Table 4.1. Québec has a strong

[1] Yeates (1975) used the name 'Main Street' as the title for a book about this area.

TABLE 4.1
QUÉBEC: PRINCIPAL STATISTICS BY INDUSTRY GROUP, 1975

	No. of Establishments	Employees No.	%	Value of Shipments $000	Value Added $000	%
Food and beverage industries	1,303	57,147	10.7	5,004,279	1,338,911	12.8
Tobacco products industries	17	6,012	1.1	373,403	200,382	1.9
Rubber and plastics product industries	204	13,068	2.5	494,268	218,771	2.1
Leather industries	203	12,757	2.4	278,183	142,757	1.4
Textile industries	376	36,313	6.8	1,317,283	543,192	5.2
Knitting Mills	203	15,204	2.9	429,308	192,059	1.8
Clothing industries	1,472	65,789	12.3	1,619,176	738,837	7.1
Wood industries	916	23,959	4.5	835,762	376,113	3.6
Furniture and fixture industries	704	18,950	3.6	506,826	260,902	2.5
Paper and allied industries	209	44,695	8.4	2,525,114	1,072,017	10.2
Printing, Publishing and allied industries	973	25,098	4.7	894,332	542,281	5.2
Primary Metal industries	88	29,227	5.5	2,282,237	702,209	6.7
Metal fabricating industries	917	39,018	7.3	1,647,622	801,356	7.7
Machinery industries	187	18,871	3.5	749,127	386,252	3.7
Transportation equipment industries	212	31,592	5.9	1,687,960	581,177	5.6
Electrical products industries	184	32,186	6.1	1,384,234	700,091	6.7
Non-metallic mineral products industries	299	15,136	2.8	783,216	407,039	3.9
Petroleum and coal products	24	3,375	0.6	1,791,843	218,364	2.1
Chemical and chemical products industries	298	26,516	5.0	1,785,352	769,464	7.3
Miscellaneous manufacturing industries	586	18,019	3.4	532,462	266,337	2.5
Total all industries	9,375	532,932	100.0	26,921,984	10,458,512	100.0

representation of industries which are growing slowly, such as
leather, textiles, clothing, and food and drink. Moreover, despite a
high level of protection, the first three of these are also experiencing
great difficulties in competition with imports. In contrast, some key
industries, which have been growing fast in North America (iron

and steel, metal fabricating, machinery, electrical, chemicals), are relatively weak. In transport equipment, too, the important car manufacturing sector is quite restricted. Québec's main emphasis is on labour-intensive groups such as textiles and clothing, and those industries closely related to natural resources (wood, pulp and paper, non-ferrous metal refining, food and drink).

It has become conventional to judge the Québec structure in comparison with the more industrialized and more rounded Ontario economy (Dales, 1960; Gilmour and Murricane 1973, 3–4; Fréchette *et al.*, 1975, 81–94). This shows strong over-representation in the two categories referred to above (labour-intensive and resource-based), especially in clothing, tobacco and textiles. Gilmour and Murricane (1973, 5) showed that, in 1968, employment in clothing was three and a half times as great as it should have been, in tobacco over three times as large and in textiles over twice as large. In contrast, rubber, iron and steel, electrical apparatus and transportation equipment were under-represented in Québec by 30 to 45 per cent.

The differential in manufacturing between Ontario and Québec is long-standing, dating from at least the time of Confederation. The actual percentage has varied but, in value added, Québec's position has worsened from 66 per cent of Ontario's in 1870 to 52 per cent in 1968 (Gilmour and Murricane, 1973, 5–6). The characteristics of specialization, however, have varied considerably over the years. For example, Québec's specialization in tobacco products was evident from 1870, the textile industry was more localized in Ontario until 1900 and clothing held a similar position in both provinces until 1910. One conclusion drawn by Gilmour and Murricane is 'that there is no evidence to suggest that their structural differences all originated in one brief time period' (1973, 8).

A certain amount of controversy has developed over the causes of Québec's economic position and industrial structure, with proponents ranging from those taking a purely economic view to those who consider cultural values to be paramount. In a recent book (Durocher and Linteau, 1971) the editors list four factors which summarized the arguments to date – geo-economic, socio-cultural, political, psychological. Certainly a complex mixture of geographical, economic and cultural elements is involved.

Most of the key features of industrial location in central Canada were established in the period 1871 to 1921. It is essential to recognize that, at the time of Confederation and before the major period of industrialization in Canada, Québec's economy was already much smaller than Ontario's: its population was about 74 per cent and value added in manufacturing only 66 per cent of the Ontario total. [1] Moreover, Ontario's prosperous agriculture provided both the base for the more widespread population and the materials for a number of food processing industries. For example, according to the 1871 census, while output of such crops as hay and potatoes was similar in the two provinces, Ontario's production of barley and corn was about five times as great and that of wheat four times. Already, then, a major element in industrial location, the regional market, was tipped in Ontario's favour. In 1900 the situation had changed little, although by 1921 Québec's population had grown to over 80 per cent of Ontario's.

On the market side, also, the West held the future, and with every year the tendency of the North American population centre to shift gradually westwards favoured Ontario. While the Atlantic Provinces suffered most from this trend, Québec's location also became increasingly peripheral and her ability to participate in the opening-up and servicing of the West weakened. Meanwhile, the north-eastern part of the continent grew slowly or stagnated.

Faucher and Lamontagne (1953) argue that the most important feature of the 1866–1911 period for Québec was the switch from an economy based on wood to one based on coal and iron. Southern Ontario, with nearby Appalachian coal and with iron ore that could easily be brought by water from the western edge of Lake Superior, was in a better location to support the iron and steel industry, which provided semi-finished materials for so many other products. While Ontario certainly had an edge in material supply, however, it was not particularly large and the key feature of location in late nineteenth and early twentieth century Central Canada was the market (Walker, 1974, 48–54), including that provided by the existing metal-working industries in the Hamilton-Toronto area. Moreover, the coal requirements for steam engines did not constitute a major locational factor in most industries (Walker, 1974, 65–6).

Nevertheless, at a time when craft industries were being modified

[1] Value added figures in this section are based on a table in Gilmour and Murricane (1973, b).

into modern, factory ones and when new products were being frequently introduced, Ontario did have an advantage over Québec for all the major industrial location factors. Thus for new processes and industries it was usually the logical place to choose, especially for entrepreneurs who lived in neither province. The investors who came from the United States tended to move there and began, in the nineteenth century, a trend which later expanded (see Chapter 2). For many producer goods there was not room at that time for numerous operations, just one or two for the whole of Canada. So Ontario entrenched its position and it has remained the centre for innovation in Canadian manufacturing, even though most new ideas come in from the United States.

As Ontario switched to modern industries, the relative importance of traditional ones declined. In contrast, Québec stressed them more and more, building on sectors which gave comparative advantage through cheap labour (Faucher and Lamontagne, 1953). Unfortunately, the twentieth century has brought increasing competition in such businesses as textiles, leather and clothing from the developing countries of the world, which are now highly competitive. Hence come Québec's current problems, which can only get worse. Indeed, if the free trade views of many Canadian economists prevail, Québec's manufacturing will be very hard hit (see Chapter 1).

Between 1921 and the early 1960s, Québec's manufacturing output 'vis-à-vis' Ontario's held its own quite well without, however, regaining lost ground. The major reason for this seems to be related to one location factor, electricity. The province is well endowed with hydro-electric power, which not only puts it on an even basis with Ontario for most manufacturing, but also provided the opportunity to develop some major power-using industries (Dales, 1957). The most important sites for these were the St Maurice and Saguenay Rivers, while the industries included aluminium refining, chemicals and pulp and paper. The cheap power sites, of course, encouraged early-stage (or primary) manufacturing. On the other hand widespread electricity, cheap oil imports and a growing provincial market helped all secondary industry to develop, and the province picked up some of the modern ones, such as aircraft and electrical products.

During the 1960s, however, the Québec economy began to falter again and a recent textbook entitles a chapter on the years beginning

1961 as 'Le déclin de l'économie du Québec' (Fréchette *et al.*, 1975, 81–95). Between 1962 and 1974 Québec's position relative to Ontario's worsened in terms of most of the important indicators – population growth, net immigration, manufacturing shipments and personal disposable income. As noted in Chapter 2, Québec slipped increasingly into the state of a 'have-not' province. The reasons for this decline seem to be much the same as those cited for earlier periods – the westward movement of the North American market and relatively weak United States' investment. Fréchette *et al.* (1975, 92–3) also argue that some federal government policies hurt Québec, especially the opening of the St Lawrence Seaway (1959), a petroleum policy (1961) which reserved the Ontario market for Canadian oil, and the Canada-USA Auto Pact (1965), which greatly benefited Ontario (see Chapter 1).

It has been argued by several writers that an important cause of Québec's economic difficulties is the character of its French Canadian culture. Harvey (1971), for example, believes that as a result of conquest by the British, the French Canadians have developed an opposition to Anglo-Saxon ideas and methods. Because of their insecurity, they have cut themselves off from North American capitalism. A more widespread view is that the predominant values, especially as projected through the educational system, encouraged a vocation in the priesthood or professions rather than in business (Saint-Germain, 1969).

Milner and Milner (1973) show how Québec for centuries exhibited all the characteristics of a colonial society. In the 1930s, which they consider to represent the culmination of the old system, 'the Church and a small élite of lay people trained by the clergy and directly under their influence controlled almost every non-economic aspect of French Canadian social and cultural life' (pp. 107–8). Education and the media presented a single view of the world and opposition was virtually impossible. A strong French Canadian nationalism was fostered, but a very conservative one, dedicated to traditional and rural ways of life. Capitalism was supported even if some abuses (the fault of Anglo-Saxons) were recognized. Meanwhile, economic control was in fact largely in English Canadian and American hands and foreign ownership was encouraged by limited restrictions and tax breaks. Moreover, an authoritarian approach by clergy and government alike was used to enforce the predominant view and to discourage dissension or such movements as trade unions that seriously attempted to improve the workers' lot or to change the *status quo* in any way.

Given this long-standing cultural situation, it is not surprising that French Canadians have played a minor role as entrepreneurs and even, until recently, as managers (Raynauld, 1974; Gagnon, 1976). Raynauld's (1974) analysis based on 1961 data showed the weakness of Québec manufacturing firms under French Canadian control. By value added, their proportion of control was about 10 per cent, while it rose to 14 per cent in employment. By industry groups, Raynauld showed strongest representation in food, wood industries, leather, printing and metal products. His comparisons with English Canadian and foreign-owned plants showed that French Canadian plants were very much smaller and generally less productive. Traditionally, French Canadian owners have preferred to keep businesses as a family concern rather than expand into a public corporation (Taylor, 1958).

While Québec society has changed considerably since the 1930s (Milner and Milner, 1973), the economic dependence of the Province as well as French Canadian subservience in the boardrooms of Québec have remained. The 'Quiet Revolution' made an enormous contribution in improving individual freedoms, welfare and education, encouraging a flourishing of the arts, and improving the position of the Québecois. Since 1976, the Parti Québecois, dedicated to separation from Canada and to the concept of an independent Québecois nation, has governed the province. Nevertheless, the old ownership patterns remain and the only major new move by the government has been to nationalize asbestos, a product which has always been shipped unfinished to the United States.

Fournier (1976) has examined the role of big business (the hundred largest corporations) in Québec from 1960 to 1974. He shows considerable outside influence but, also, a high degree of interrelationship amongst the firms, especially holding companies such as Argus Corporation, Power Corporation and CPR – Cominco. These companies all have interests in numerous other, often large, ones. As a result, the Québec business élite is 'small in size, tightly knit, socially homogeneous, and largely self-perpetuating' (p. 33). English-speaking managers dominated the scene, especially in finance, but Fournier shows that 'there are no major ideological differences in either general policy or specific legislation between the English and French groups' (p. 38). Thus French Canadians who reach this level in business do so by accepting the prevailing mores. Under previous provincial governments, this élite has had very close association with politicians, and Fournier (p. 79) argues that:

The evidence indicated that the initiative for contacts often came from the ministers themselves and that government courted business perhaps more than business courted government.

While there are still few large French Canadian firms, a change of attitude does seem to have taken place recently. As a result of the educational reform of the 1960s, more students leave school with skills appropriate for the business world, and management education has improved radically. Now one can meet many well-trained young entrepreneurs willing to take risks and wishing to expand. Moreover, changes are taking place in the financing of business, which has been a real problem especially in smaller centres. A new movement of regional financial unions, similar to Credit Unions or 'Caisses Populaires' but geared to investment in local industry and commerce, has expanded rapidly in the last 15 years. The 'Caisses d'Entraide Économiques' are making a marked impact in many areas (L'Entraide Économique, no date). These 'Caisses' are also active in encouraging and educating entrepreneurs.

Behind the growth of the separatist movement in Québec is the feeling that, though such changes are inadequate, they are as much as can be expected under the current political arrangement. The French Canadians lack economic power but the new, more radical nationalists have obtained political power at the provincial level. The key proponents in the separatist argument in Canada are products of the changes in Québec over the last 30 years, who fought together for many of those changes. One group believes the Québecois can do best within Canada. But for another, Bettelheim's slogan is more appropriate:

La première condition du progrès économique et social est l'indépendance politique. (D'Allemagne, 1966, 59).

REGIONAL DISTRIBUTION OF MANUFACTURING WITHIN QUÉBEC

The outstanding feature of industrial location within Québec is the dominance of the Montréal region. Out of the nine administrative regions in the province, this region has roughly 70 per cent of all manufacturing measured either by employment or by value added. The St. Lawrence Lowlands and their extension into the Eastern Townships (Regions 3, 4 and 5) account for another 22 per cent, leaving a very small residue to be shared amongst the vast peripheral areas of the north and east. The distribution in 1961 and its historical evolution are described in detail in Girard (1970). The pattern is not very different today.

The Peripheral Regions

Outside the narrow St Lawrence Lowlands and the Eastern Townships, Québec is mainly rocky and infertile. On the north shore the Canadian Shield stretches to the remote areas of Hudson's Bay, while in the south-east an extension of the Appalachians is not much more hospitable except on the coast. These areas do, however, have considerable resources in vast forests, water and hydro-electric power, minerals and, in a more restricted area, fish. Population is sparse and manufacturing generally closely tied to the resource base.

Eastern Québec is still very weakly developed. Despite the fact that the Lower St Lawrence-Gaspé Peninsula has more farming than most of the periphery, it is not a good farming area. As in many similar parts of Atlantic Canada, the farmers frequently supplement their income by fishing or cutting wood. The fishing industry is still run mainly along traditional lines. In fact the whole way of life is reminiscent of the past and, while the picturesqueness of the area attracts tourists, this region has the lowest average incomes in the province. Value added in manufacturing is also the lowest for any provincial region. The most important industrial groups, accounting for about three-quarters of output, are food and drink and wood processing.

On the North Shore (below Québec), manufacturing produces a similar total output but the area is quite different. Relatively isolated and late to be developed, this area has recently benefited from continuous resource development, especially in connection with the iron ore mines on the Labrador-Québec border. As a result, Sept Iles and Port Cartier have grown rapidly and are picking up some consumer industries. The area's manufacturing, though, is dominated by large, scattered pulp and paper plants and early-stage processing of metals.

The latter two categories in fact predominate across northern Québec and are oriented mainly to the export market. The most

important manufacturing region is Saguenay-Lac St Jean, which
has many pulp and paper operations and two aluminium smelters
belonging to the Aluminum Company of Canada (Alcan). The
attraction for these smelters is not the ores, which must be imported,
but vast cheap supplies of hydro-electricity at Alma and Arvida as
well as tide water location for ore imports. Further west, wood and
paper industries play a more important role than metals. Because of
its location near the growing national capital area, the Outaouais
region may be expected to build up its consumer industries and
perhaps some modern growth ones as well, but so far it has not
progressed far in this direction.

On the whole, the prospects for significant changes in the
peripheral regions are not great. Some of the plants are ageing and
modernization can be expected. Perhaps a few paper plants will
close as a result of inability to compete with more modern and
efficient operations elsewhere. Other operations will no doubt come
on stream to use resources more completely (e.g. a new pulp plant
being built at St Félicien, designed to use wood more rationally by
processing chips from sawmills after the best wood has been sawn;
another example in the same Lac St Jean area is a blueberry
processing and wine plant, using a major local resource). As
population grows some consumer industries will no doubt develop,
especially in centres like Chicoutimi or Sept Iles. Apart from this,
however, small population, isolation from other markets and a
limited supply of skilled labour all mitigate against manufacturing
except perhaps very close to Ottawa.

Québec City

The Québec metropolitan area[1] provides about half of the manufacturing jobs in the administrative region. The region as a whole is
characterized by small to medium-sized industries, with a strong
concentration in the food and beverage and paper groups. Apart
from paper manufactures, the region's industries export little out of
Canada, and for many groups the local and regional market is very
important (food and beverage, printing and publishing, machinery,
metal products). The industrial structure remains very traditional
(Québec, Ministère de L'Industrie et du Commerce, 1973, 9–23).

The Québec metropolitan area reflects many of the same features.
It is, of course, primarily a political, educational and service centre

rather than a manufacturing one. A large section of the city's secondary employment is, therefore, in consumer goods industries, especially food and beverages, leather products, textiles and printing and publishing. Printing and publishing derives its importance from the demands of the provincial government and Laval University, which generate a good business. Two other important sectors are paper and shipbuilding, the latter concentrated at a large yard on the south shore at Lauzon. Also on the south shore is the Golden Eagle oil refinery opened in 1971.

Québec City lacks modern exporting plants and considerable promotional efforts in the last few years have failed to make major inroads into the problem. It has been argued that some of the existing operations are highly vulnerable, as, for example, the shipyard, in which employment fluctuates widely at short notice (Hulbert, 1975, 39–41). Moreover, textiles and leather are facing difficulties everywhere in the province.[2]

There has been a tendency to decentralize from the city proper to industrial parks and zones in more peripheral locations. The south shore has received new plants in the last ten years, but the Québec Urban Community is now developing a large park to the west of the agglomeration in St. Augustin. Political problems make development difficult because the south shore municipalities do not belong to the Urban Community. Current attention seems to be focusing on the port, which provides the city with one of its major locational advantages. The climate, however, seems to be against industrial development in comparison with efforts to promote tourism and encourage tertiary and quaternary growth. Given the disadvantage posed by the distance of North American markets, a minimal requirement for industrial growth would seem to be a supporting environment for businessmen to work in.

Trois-Rivières

The administrative region of Trois-Rivières includes not only the agglomeration itself and nearby Shawinigan (known in combination as La Mauricie) but also substantial areas to the north and on the south shore across the St Lawrence. In scale of manufacturing, this region is roughly equivalent to that of the Québec one, although

[1] Québec Urban Community plus several south shore municipalities.
[2] See Seifried (1972) on the leather shoe industry.

currently slightly less important.[1] South of the river, the textile and clothing industries predominate, and the existence of one or two large operations in these vulnerable industries is a threat to many of the small towns and cities. Other industries in the area are also mainly traditional – food and furniture especially – and the tendency has been to lose population rather than to attract other firms. North of the Mauricie, on the Shield, manufacturing is largely restricted to wood processing and pulp and paper plants, with La Tuque particularly notable.

The population centre of this region is divided into two sections separated by about 20 miles. At the confluence of the St Maurice and the St Lawrence is 'metropolitan' Trois-Rivières with a population of about 120,000. Further north, located at the major hydroelectric power site on the St Maurice, is Shawinigan – Grand Mère, home of another 56,000 people. Although this was the site of Canada's first iron works in the eighteenth century (Donald, 1915, 47–8), the Mauricie is very much a product of twentieth century hydro-electricity. Power supply has attracted large plants for aluminium smelting and processing, chemicals and pulp and paper. Trois-Rivières, although dominated by the pulp and paper industry, has considerable employment in textiles and clothing, metal products and electrical products. Of late, manufacturing has been stagnating in the Mauricie because of ageing plants and a failure to break away sufficiently from slow growth industries.

While the more northerly Shawinigan-Grand Mère may find it difficult to adapt, Trois-Rivières should be in a good position to strengthen its position in manufacturing. It no longer suffers from the inadequate road network, which plagued the north shore until recently, but is now linked by motorway to Montréal. A bridge over the St Lawrence, too, was completed in 1967, this being part of the Trans-Québec Autoroute, which will eventually run south to the United States border at Rock Island. Thus, with its port and rail connections, Trois-Rivières is well integrated into the wider space-economy. To this can be added a long industrial history which has produced an interest in manufacturing and a suitable labour force, and the existence of well serviced land. Thus the key ingredients for expansion seem to be present. The city could also benefit from the Bécancours Industrial Park on the south shore. This park is being

[1] 1973 statistics show Trois-Rivières Region with 8.8 per cent provincial employment and 7.9 per cent value added. The Québec Region had 9.5 per cent and 8.7 per cent.

developed by the Québec Ministry of Industry and Commerce for large plants. It could provide opportunities for the supply of materials and for sub-contract work.

Sherbrooke

South of the Trois-Rivières Region are the Eastern Townships, which were originally settled by English-speaking immigrants and where English is still more prevalent than in other parts of rural Québec. It is a relatively small region and the dimensions of manufacturing industry correspond, output being less than half that of the Trois-Rivières region. Outside Sherbrooke, there are a few centres specializing mostly in pulp and paper or textiles. Asbestos is mined at Asbestos (as well as further east at Thetford Mines) and some processing takes place there. In general, however, resources in the area are unimportant.

The Sherbrooke agglomeration, with about 110,000 people, is an attractive city with well developed tertiary, administrative and educational functions. While its textile and clothing industries are very important, Sherbrooke also has considerable strength in steel and engineering as well as some food processing. The city is linked by motorway to Montréal but has perhaps been hampered by the fact that several other centres along the same route are nearer to the metropolis. Certainly, Sherbrooke's manufacturing sector has not been very dynamic of late. Nonetheless it possesses some key factors for growth – good transport, an industrial tradition, attractive living conditions and services (including two universities), a large modern industrial park and closeness to the United States border for exporting purposes.

Montréal

Montréal[1] dominates Québec manufacturing, accounting for over half of the manufacturing employees in the province. In fact over two-thirds of them are found in the Montréal administrative region. It is not surprising, therefore, that its industrial structure resembles that of the province as a whole, the main differences being less primary manufacturing and more modern growth industries. Montréal's major employer is the clothing industry and over one quarter

[1] Unless otherwise stated, 'Montréal' refers to the Montréal Urban Community.

of its manufacturing employment is in textiles, knitting mills and clothing. Shipments of women's clothing have the largest value of any industry, while men's clothing ranks fourth. Amongst other important employers are food and beverages (over 10 per cent), metal fabricating, electrical products and chemicals. In transport equipment, the aircraft and aircraft parts industry plays a major role but its position tends to fluctuate greatly. Although Montréal's industrial structure is reasonably diverse, it has a high proportion of slow-growth industries and has failed to adapt its industry adequately to current market conditions (Chung, 1974, 327).

From the perspective of Québec, Montréal's economy seems to be strong: it has even been argued that the metropolis has a stifling effect on other areas. Recently, however, it is the fragility of the economy in comparison with other major North American cities that has received the attention of researchers. Higgins *et al.* (1970, 54–7) placed great emphasis on this point. They argued that the Montréal metropolitan region, in comparison with its major North American competitors, was relatively small both in size and especially in population, that the city lacked the strong ring of complementary centres that characterized Toronto (e.g. Oshawa, Hamilton, Kitchener-Waterloo, etc.) and that it is further from important American cities than Toronto. More recently, the slow growth of employment, relative decline of Montréal as a financial market and drastic decline of head offices located there have been documented (Chung, 1974, 327–8). Chung, however, also notes the historic character of Montréal's vulnerability:

> L'histoire économique de Montréal depuis 1930 peut se caractériser, d'une part, par sa vulnérabilité attribuable à sa dépendance vis-à-vis d'un marché canadien dominé de plus en plus par la région de Toronto et, d'autre part, par son incapacité de modifier sa structure industrielle (p.330).

These points are echoed by Leveillée (1977a), who agrees that Toronto's relative growth began in the 1930s. Since 1945, Montréal has increasingly become a satellite, losing its position quite rapidly in both finance and manufacturing and only competing seriously in commerce (p. 29). The reason for this change, Léveillée argues, is the increasing integration of the Canadian economy into a wider North American one and the fact that Americans have been responsible for so much economic growth in Canada since the Second World War. This trend, combined with a westward shift of dynamism on the continent has weakened Montréal's location. In manufacturing, especially, there is little autonomous control in Montréal.

Intra-Urban Patterns

The current industrial areas of Montréal are shown on Figure 4.1. Most early manufacturing developed along the river and the Lachine Canal, which provided water power. The waterfront is still important for some port-using industries, such as flour milling and sugar refining (Beauregard, 1959; Manzagol, 1972, 132). Along the Lachine Canal, which is no longer in use, some important factories remain (e.g. Northern Telecom and Dosco). On the waterfront to the east is the single most important petroleum refinery area in Canada. Its supplies, however, come not by water but by pipelines from the United States and since 1975, from western Canada. The waterfront within Montréal is built up and is not an area of recent industrial growth. In fact, many of the plants are quite old.

During the late nineteenth and early twentieth centuries, manufacturing spread away from the waterfront mainly along the rail lines. Within Montréal, the relationship of the two can still be clearly seen especially along the belt line that encircles Mount Royal. In contrast to the diverse character and scattered location of these plants, the shoe and garment area around the St Lawrence Boulevard and Bleury formed (as it still does) a concentrated and specialized district. Here are numerous firms, many of them small, in a well-integrated complex, forming Canada's major clothing district. Many of the buildings are several stories high and relatively old. This area has always depended primarily on cheap, female labour, often making use of immigrants. The industry has gradually spread outwards, mainly along the St Lawrence Boulevard, but is still highly concentrated.

The post-war era has seen a considerable decentralization of manufacturing in the Montréal area. Such suburbanization is typical of most North American cities, reflecting on the one hand inadequate conditions and lack of space in the older areas, and other, cheap land and growing populations in the suburbs. Figure 4.1 shows the zones and industrial parks, illustrating a strong highway orientation, especially in those industrial parks which are still under development: the Trans-Canada highway is lined by

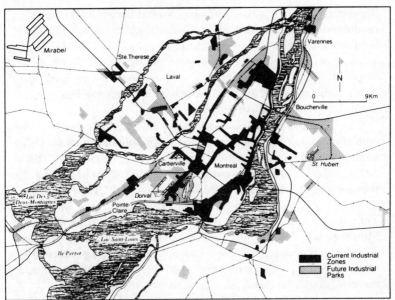

Figure 4.1   Montreal's Industrial Areas.
              Source: C. Manzagol (1972)

industrial areas along most of its length. Development in the west
includes more modern light industry involving many branch plants
of English Canadian and United States firms (Manzagol, 1972,
133). It has not been tested but this location pattern seems to be
related to ease of access to major external markets and to the
English-speaking residential areas of the West End, (Leveillée,
1977a, 30). Dorval Airport is no doubt an additional factor in its
favour. There is still plenty of industrial space available on Montréal
Island and the various municipalities compete for industry, using
serviced industrial parks as one tool.[1]

The process of decentralization has, however, spread further,
mainly by the location of new industries in some of the existing
centres within fifty kilometres or so of downtown Montréal. Most of
these developments are not distinguished by any particularly un-
usual features. On the south shore to the east of the city, however, an
area of heavy industry is building up. At Varennes, petrochemical
plants are linked to refining at Montréal East over the river.

[1] For details of manufacturing in each municipality see Montréal Urban Community
(1974).

Between Varennes and Sorel are several large metal working (mainly steel) plants and other chemical operations, while Sorel itself has a well-established shipyard (Manzagol, 1972, 133). With a location on the St Lawrence, east of the main population nodes (westerly winds prevail), the Varennes-Contrecoeur-Sorel strip seems well placed for further growth as a centre for heavy, often somewhat noxious industry.

A study of goods linkages in the Montréal area has provided some indication of interrelationships in the metropolitan economy. Using a sample of all types of manufacturing industry, Brooks *et al.* (1973) distinguished between the centre (roughly the City of Montréal) the suburbs (approximately the rest of the Montréal Urban Community), and the periphery (up to 55 kilometres from central Montréal). They found that the average percentage of sales to metropolitan Montréal was 34.4, while purchases amounted to 39.3 per cent. Their major finding, however, was the strong linkages of smaller establishments (1–25 employees) to Montréal (44%) as well as to the province (a further 25%). In contrast, the group with 26–100 employees had 38 per cent of linkage with Montréal (55% with Québec in total), while that with over 100 workers had 28 per cent with Montréal (only 47% with Québec in total). Interestingly, Brooks *et al.* found that, in general, suburban rather than peripheral plants were the least integrated into the local and regional economy. A later paper by Gilmour and Murricane (1975) related these findings to the type of industry. In this, they contrasted centre and suburb, showing the former to possess most of the labour-intensive industries (clothing, textiles, leather, printing and publishing, etc.) and a large number of small plants. These centre-dominant industries were shown to have higher percentages of linkage with Montréal than the type of manufacturing which is more typical of the suburbs.

INDUSTRIAL DEVELOPMENT POLICY

In the 1960s and 1970s, the Province of Québec's industrial development policy has expanded and widened to the point where it is probably the most fully developed of any in Canada. As elsewhere in the country, Québec's policy includes both sectoral and spatial elements. It is primarily the responsibility of the Department of Industry and Commerce, although all planning must receive the confirmation of the planning and development bureau, L'Office de Planification et de Développement du Québec usually referred to as the OPDQ. The role of the OPDQ and its predecessor, Le Conseil d'Orientation Économique, is described in L'Office de Planification et de Développement du Québec (1973). The OPDQ essentially is concerned with regional balance in the province, the linking of planning and development and the encouragement of inter-departmental co-operation.

Programmes in the 1960s in Québec were primarily support programmes. Various aids to management were provided to help, for example, with exporting, expansion or the development of new products. Early in the decade an important step was taken by the Department of Industry and Commerce to encourage the use of these services. In 1960, the Ministry began to appoint regional representatives, who were located around the province and were responsible for particular areas. These representatives were influential not only in stimulating manufacturers but also in encouraging municipalities to become involved in industrial development. At that time there were few industrial parks or industrial commissioners. A key element in encouraging municipalities to become involved in developing industrial land was the Industrial Funds Act of 1961, which enabled them to establish funds for parks and buildings.[1] As a result, many municipalities have set up such funds and nearly one hundred have established industrial parks.

Meanwhile the Department was also active in prospecting across the world for investment, and interested manufacturers were passed on to the regional representatives in relevant parts of the province. Already in the 1960s, however, it was recognized that the Province could not rely entirely on outside investment. A General Investment Corporation was set up in 1962 to encourage the participation of the Québecois in their own economic development. Subsequently (in 1972), the provincial government took all the shares in the Corporation. The objective, however, has remained the same and the corporation has set up companies and taken equity in others. Another major initiative was the establishment of a provincially owned iron and steel company (SIDBEC) in 1968.

Despite all of these programmes, Québec's policy in the 1960s did not adequately correspond to its major economic problems – weak industrial structure, regional dominance by Montréal and

[1] Power to finance construction was retracted in 1968.

Montréal's loss of ground nationally. The Department in fact stated:
  In the early 60's government involvement in the industrial sector
  was mainly aimed at the short term creation of jobs, particularly
  in the less economically favoured regions of Québec. In the light
  of studies which brought out the most serious deficiencies in
  Québec's industrial sector, it appeared necessary to exercise
  greater selectivity in such involvement in order to more efficiently
  contribute to the transformation and modernization of the industrial structure. (1975, 20)
Selectivity of industrial sectors has now become the practice. Two
thrusts are followed:
(1) The consolidation and modernization of some of the traditional
or existing sectors, such as sawmills and some food and beverage
groups. Steel is receiving special attention, through a 1974–8
expansion plan for SIDBEC and through consideration of a new
mill.
(2) Development of modern industries. Detailed studies have been
completed on aluminium, petrochemical and pulp and paper complexes.
The promotional aspect of the Department has also followed the
path to selectivity. A study conducted by the Fantus company,
begun in 1971, identified sectors which appeared to have good
prospects in the Province, and current policy is to attract firms
which can work in these sectors.
   This whole approach is fully in line with studies by the Department of Regional Economic Expansion (1973 and 1976), the most
recent of which indicated possibilities in specific sectors which could
help establish a lasting dynamism in Québec's manufacturing
(1976, 21). It suggested food processing, forest industries, petrochemicals, iron and steel, aeronautical industries, asbestos products,
aluminium and transport equipment for special attention. The
General Development Agreement between Québec and the Department of Régional Economic Expansion echoes the Québec department's objective of consolidating older industries and establishing
modern ones (Canada, DREE, 1977a). So far, though, the only
sub-agreement along these lines concerns the expansion of SIDBEC
at Contrecoeur. The operation of the Québec Industrial Development Corporation, established in 1971, is clearly geared to these
ends as well. It provides financial support to firms in industries
which have prospects of continuous growth and encourages amal-

gamations which will improve efficiency. Ten mergers, for example, were assisted in 1974–5. (Québec Department of Industry and Commerce, 1975, 31).

At the same time, the general support programmes for all manufacturers everywhere in the province are not being neglected but rather have expanded. These programmes are geared especially to small and medium-sized firms, partly in recognition of the fact that most French-speaking entrepreneurs operate in such firms. A considerable effort to improve management in these firms is essential, and the Department provides help in training and information, aid to exports, financial support (through the Development Corporation), research and development and the formation of groups of enterprises. The latter function, begun in 1974, is designed to provide specialist help to small firms through an organization in which they co-operate, the Québec Group of Enterprises Inc. The regional service of the department which is largely responsible for encouraging the use of these programmes, has been expanded. In 1966, the province was divided into ten administrative regions and many of these are sub-divided into sub-regions. Departmental delegates are located in all of these, so that the services really are close to the users.

As a logical follow-up to the Industrial Funds Act, the province has moved to encourage municipalities to become involved in industrial development by appointing industrial commissioners. As late as 1972, there were only about ten such commissioners in the province. The Department of Industry and Commerce therefore began a programme of financial incentives, offering 50 per cent of an industrial commission's cost, up to a maximum of $30,000. Fifty-seven commissions had been set by 1976, many of them supported by a group of small municipalities rather than just one town. This of course has brought local authorities more into the development picture. At the same time, the province retains a great influence: for example, industrial commissioners must be approved by a selection committee, on which the province has two out of five members.[1] If a non-approved commissioner is appointed, no grant is available. Control is also exercised by the province in the matter of industrial parks. These receive support only if approved after a provincial study. The province had also provided a guidebook for good

[1] Two come from the municipality, one from the Québec Industrial Commissioners Association.

industrial park development (Québec, Ministère de l'Industrie et du Commerce, 1974), but unfortunately its control in this area is less complete. Municipalities have power over zoning and in consequence, many of the province's industrial parks are less attractive than they might be.

If there was a weakness in the policies developed by the mid-1970s in Québec, it related to spatial priorities and especially to the role of Montréal. Despite all the evidence that Montréal is declining in relation to its North American competitors, a clear-cut programme in its support does not yet exist. Admittedly, Montréal benefits from all the programmes, which apply province-wide, and it is likely to be the chief beneficiary of efforts to modernize the province's industrial sector. But will this be enough? Higgins *et al.* (1970) showed that Montréal is the only real development pole in the province and that only from this metropolis could beneficial influences be expected to flow out to improve the whole of Québec. Other centres just do not have notable spread effects.

The strategy supported by Higgins *et al.* (1970, 135–52), would favour Montréal by encouraging developmental activities and strengthening its competitive position. Some specific suggestions were made later by DREE, for whom the Higgins *et al.* study was conducted. DREE (1973, 82) proposed to strengthen 'the area's role in manufacturing, transportation, communications, finance and sophisticated business services'. In the manufacturing sector, the Department hoped for development of a large steel mill in the Contrecoeur area with considerable expansion of the steel-using industries in Montréal and nearby towns. It also indicated distinct possibilities for expansion in electrical products and transport equipment, while petrochemical development based on the East Montréal refineries was encouraged. Suggestions were made for older industries in Montréal as well. It was proposed that the textile industry move towards the high-priced end of the market, stressing quality and design. These ideas do not find expression in DREE's 1976 report on Québec and do not figure directly in the General Development Agreement with the province.

Other elements of a spatial strategy suggested in the period 1970 to 1973 were the more organized decentralization of manufacturing around Montréal and the stimulation of a few large growth centres. Both elements derive from the Higgins *et al.* (1970) study. In connection with the first, it was agreed that decentralization had in the past been rather dispersed and that efforts should be made to form a few centres which could provide specialized services. DREE (1973, 95) listed Sorel, Ste. Hyacinthe, Granby, Saint-Jean, Valleyfield, Saint-Jérome, Joliette and Mirabel International Airport. The latter has become the focus of a provincial plan involving an integrated industrial and transport package (*Financial Times of Canada*, 1975, 50–65). As for the expansion of other growth centres, Sherbrooke and Trois-Rivières-Shawinigan were suggested because it was thought they could benefit through close ties to Montréal. Québec City, with half a million inhabitants, a port and a very well developed tertiary sector, was a third suggestion. Lastly, Sept-Iles-Port Cartier, much smaller but in a growing frontier area, was expected to continue its expansion based on resource developments in its hinterland.

Underlying the lack of decision concerning spatial strategy were some distinct differences on policy objectives. Léveillée (1977b) shows how the Higgins *et al.* proposals were supported by the federal government as a means of linking the province more firmly into the east-west development corridor running to Toronto and Windsor. The provincial government, however, especially in the 1960s, was concerned to spread the benefits more widely in Québec and wished to encourage a north-south axis from Sherbrooke through Trois-Rivières to Chicoutimi. The differences were brought out in discussions concerning the site of the new international airport. The Mirabel site to the north-west of Montréal was championed by the federal government in opposition to the provincial government's south-eastern proposal. Provincial desires for a greater spread of income and development were also related to the fact that, outside Montréal, there are few anglophobes. The problem with an anti-Montréal policy, however, was the large number of French Canadian entrepreneurs operating in the city. They could not be neglected. Thus there was a conflict within provincial government circles.

It would seem that more direct measures will be needed at the provincial scale if growth centres are to fulfill the suggested roles. The industrial park and industrial commission programmes to date have been applied much more widely and most support services are available everywhere. There is a movement, however, to remove some smaller parks and to develop large regional parks. One of these is in the early stages of development in Sherbrooke. Theoretically, infrastructure policy could be used to foster growth centres, and this is an approach that should be used. But special attention is also required at Québec, Trois-Rivières-Shawinigan and Sherbrooke. All have active industrial development programmes but face distinct problems. In Québec, the Urban Municipality does not include the South Shore and municipal rivalries make for a difficult planning situation. Moreover, there is a strong anti-industrial development lobby in the area. The setting up of the Société Interport de Québec in 1974 is an example of direct measures. It is designed as a port-connected industrial complex for the city. Sherbrooke and Trois-Rivières both require help to adapt an ageing industrial structure and to build up some competitive new ventures.

During 1977, a number of policies were introduced by the new Parti Québecois government. In the main, however, they follow the earlier-established lines quite closely. The new government is less ready to allow its older industries to be phased out and is attempting to secure a long-term future for textiles, clothing and footwear. This will involve improvement in productivity as well as trying to persuade the federal government to look at trade barriers against imports (*Financial Times of Canada*, 1977). Two new programmes introduced in August 1977 provide new sources of support for manufacturers (Québec, Ministère de l'Industrie et du Commerce, no date). The first helps small and medium-sized firms (200 or fewer employees, net assets under $7.5 million) to modernize, expand or engage in research. The second is designed for all non-primary manufacturers outside metropolitan Montréal, providing somewhat better support for firms in the more distant peripheral areas. Both of these programmes consist of support via tax relief rather than outright grants. Despite these measures favourable to small business, traditional sectors and peripheral regions, the new government has reiterated its desire to welcome foreign investors as well.

In spatial strategy, a more selective approach is noticeable, perhaps partly because of the influence of the federal government. DREE has made the Montréal Region a special area and will provide support for certain manufacturing industries with prospects of expansion and development. These include specified operations in the food and beverage, metal fabricating, machinery, transport equipment, electrical product, chemical and miscellaneous industrial groups. Grants of up to 25 per cent of the capital costs of a new facility and 20 per cent for modernizations are allowable (Canada,

DREE, 1977b). A renewed subsidiary agreement on industrial infrastructure (Canada, DREE, 1978) provides considerable support to selected centres in the Montréal Region to enable them to become more attractive to manufacturers. This agreement provides funds to other centres in the province as well, being 'aimed at providing the prerequisites for sustained industrial growth and for creating productive employment, improving the standard of living, reinforcing the industrial structure in Québec regional centres and promoting development in the Saguenay-Lac Saint-Jean, Abitibi-Témiscamingue, Eastern Québec and North Shore regions' (p.3).

CONCLUSIONS

The weakness of Québec's industrial structure is now fully recognized and provincial policy is geared to modernizing older industries and expanding modern sectors. Special efforts are being made to increase the role of Québecois businessmen and encourage their more active role in the economy. There is a strong provincial lead in industrial development, which has encouraged the establishment of industrial commissions and industrial parks across Québec. Policy concerning Montréal, however, remains somewhat ambiguous with the federal government still seemingly more concerned about the city's relative economic decline than is the province.

Big question marks hang over the province as a result of the election of the Parti Québecois in 1976. The provincial government is committed to separation and will hold a referendum on the topic in 1980. The current climate of uncertainty is making the business community, especially English Canadian and American elements, edgy. Separation would probably lead ultimately to some form of common market arrangement with the rest of Canada or the United States (Tremblay, 1970) but in the meantime it is difficult to make sound judgements about investment. On the other hand, the Parti Québecois has so far been fairly conservative on the economic front. Nationalization has been only of asbestos and is not threatened for other sectors, and investment from outside is welcomed. Until this matter is cleared up, however, the Québec economy could well remain in some difficulty and all the evidence suggests that jobs are being moved out of the province at an unsatisfactorily high rate (*Financial Post*, 1977).

128   CANADA'S INDUSTRIAL SPACE-ECONOMY

REFERENCES

Beauregard, L. (1959), 'Géographie manufacturière de Montréal', *Cahiers de Géographie de Québec*, 6, (Jan. – March), 275–94.

Brooks, S. *et al.*, (1973) 'The spatial linkages of manufacturing in Montréal and its surroundings', *Cahiers de Géographie de Québec*, 17, (April), 107–22.

Canada, DREE, (Department of Regional Economic Expansion) (1973), *Québec: Economic Circumstances and Opportunities*. Ottawa.

Canada, DREE, (1976), *Perspectives de Développment: La Région du Québec*. Ottawa.

Canada, DREE, (1977a), *Summary of Federal-Provincial General Development Agreements and Currently Active Subsidiary Agreements*. Ottawa.

Canada, DREE, (1977b), *Industrial Incentives Program: Montréal Special Area. Questions and Answers*. Ottawa.

Canada, DREE, (1978), *News Release. Ottawa and Québec Have Agreed on Intensive Industrial Development up to 1983*. Ottawa.

Chung, J.H. (1974), 'La nature du déclin économique de la région de Montréal', *L'Actualité Économique*, 50, (juillet-septembre), 326–41.

Dales, J.H. (1957), *Hydroelectricity and Industrial Development, Québec 1898 –1940*. Cambridge, Mass.: Harvard University Press.

Dales, J.H. (1960), 'A comparison of manufacturing industry in Québec and Ontario, 1952', in Mason Wade (ed.), *Canadian Dualism*, (Toronto: University of Toronto Press), 203–21.

D'Allemagne, A. (1966), *Le Colonialisme au Québec*. Montréal: Les Editions R-B.

Donald, W.J.A. (1915), *The Canadian Iron and Steel Industry*, Boston: Houghton Mifflin.

Durocher, René and Linteau, Paul-André (1971), *Le retard du Québec et l'infériorité économique des Canadiens français*. Trois-Rivières: Editions du Boréal Express.

L'Entraide Economique (no date), *L'Entraide Economique: instrument de développement de l'économie regionale*. Alma: L'Entraide Économique.

Faucher, Albert and Lamontagne, Maurice (1953), 'History of industrial development', in Jean C. Falardeau (ed.), *Essais sur le Québec contemporain*, (Québec: Les Presses Universitaires Laval), 23–37.

Financial Post (1977), 'Moves out of Québec build to an exodus', (13 August), 1.

Financial Times of Canada (1975), *Mirabel*, Special edition of Perspective on Money. Don Mills, Ontario: *Financial Times of Canada*.

Financial Times of Canada(1977), 'Québec seeks more protection for ailing sectors', (12 Sept.), 10.

Fournier, P. (1976), *The Québec Establishment*. Montréal: Black Rose Books.

Fréchette, P. *et al.* (1975), *L'économie du Québec*. Montréal: Les éditions HRW.

Gagnon, L. (1976), 'La participation des Québecois à leur économie', in R. Tremblay (ed.), *L'économie québécoise: histoire, développement, politiques*, (Montréal: Les Presses de l'Université du Québec), 361–78.

Gilmour, J.M. and Murricane, K. (1973), 'Structural divergence in Canada's manufacturing belt', *Canadian Geographer*(Spring), 1–18.

Gilmour, J.M. and Murricane, K. (1975), 'Industrial type and dependence on the Montréal economy', *Cahiers de Géographie de Québec*, 19, (September), 353–60.

Girard, Jacques (1970), *Géographie de l'Industrie Manufacturière du Québec*. Québec: Ministère de l'Industrie et du Commerce.

Harvey, Pierre (1971), 'Pourquoi le Québec et les Canadiens francais occupent-ils une place inférieure sur le plan économique?', in R. Durocher and P.A. Linteau, (1971), 113–27.

Higgins, B. (1972), 'Growth pole policy in Canada', in N. Hansen (ed.), *Growth Centers in Regional Economic Development*, (New York: Free Press), 204–28.

Higgins, B. *et all*. (1970), *Les orientations du développement économique régional dans la province de Québec*. Ottawa: Department of Regional Economic Expansion.

Hulbert, F. (1975), *Le Développement et l'Aménagement Industriel du Territoire dans la Région du Québec*. Québec: Université Laval, Département de Géographie.

Léveillée, J. (1977a), 'Contextes socio-économiques, configuration des classes sociales et enjeux structurels de l'agglomération montréalaise – 1945–1976', *Urban Forum*, (Spring), 26–36.

Léveillée, J. (1977b), 'Les stratégies urbaines fédérales, et québécoises en rapport avec enjeux structurels montréalais', *Urban Forum*, (June-July), 26–36.

Manzagol, C. (1972), 'Manufacturing industry in Montréal', in L. Beauregard (ed.), *Montréal: Field Guide*, (Montréal: Les Presses de L'Université de Montréal), 125–35.

Milner, H. and Milner, S.H. (1973), *The Decolonization of Québec*. Toronto: McClelland and Stewart.

Montréal Urban Community (1974), *Directory of Industrial Parks*. Montréal: Economic Development Office.

L'Office de Planification et de Développement du Québec (1973), 'L'Office de Planification et de Développement du Québec', in G. Gagnon and L. Martin (eds.), *Québec 1960–1980: La Crise du Développement*, (Montréal: Hurtubise HMH), 175–92.

Québec, Department of Industry and Commerce (1975), *Comparative Analysis of Productivity in Québec's Manufacturing Sector*. Québec City: Department of Industry and Commerce, Communications Division.

Québec, Department of Industry and Commerce (1975), *MIC in Action:Report of Activities 1974/75*. Québec City.

Québec, Ministère de l'Industrie et du Commerce (1973), *L'Industrie Manufacturière la Région Administrative de Québec*. Québec City.

Québec, Ministère de l'Industrie et du Commerce (1974), *Guide de Développement des Parcs Industriel*. Québec City.

Québec, Ministère de l'Industrie et du Commerce (no date), *Fiscal Incentives to Industrial Development*. Québec.

Raynauld, André (1974), *La propriété des entreprises au Québec: les années 60*. Montréal: Les Presses de l'Université de Montréal.

Saint-Germain (1969), 'La société québécoise et la vie économique: quelques échos de la décennie de la "grande ambivalence", 1920–1929', in R.

Comeau (ed.), *Economie québecoise*, (Montréal: Les Presses de l'Université du Québec).

Seifried, Neil R. (1972), 'Locational change in the Canadian leather footwear industry', *Canadian Geographer*, 16, (Winter), 209–322.

Taylor, N.W. (1958), 'A Study of French-Canadians as Industrial Entrepreneurs', Unpublished Ph.D. Dissertation, Yale University.

Tremblay, R. (1970), *Indépendence et Marché Commun Québec – Etats – Unis*. Montréal: Editions du Jour.

Walker, David F. (1974), 'Energy and industrial location in Southern Ontario, 1871–1921', in D.F. Walker and J.H. Bater (eds.), *Industrial Development in Southern Ontario*, (Waterloo: University of Waterloo, Department of Geography), 41–68.

Yeates, Maurice (1975), *Main Street*. Toronto: Macmillan of Canada.

5

Ontario

Ontario is unquestionably the strong province in the Canadian confederation. As pointed out in Chapter 2, about thirty six per cent of Canada's population lives in the province while its percentage of value added in manufacturing is a massive fifty-two. Ontario is a rich province with high income levels and relatively low unemployment, with a wealth and diversity of resources and a highly developed urban structure. Nevertheless there are some challenges. The province has its own pattern of well-marked regional disparities with problems arising in the vast northern area and, to a lesser extent, in eastern Ontario. Regional policy is, in fact, relatively well articulated although its degree of success does not seem to have been very great so far. The high level of foreign ownership in the manufacturing and resource sectors is also the cause of much concern. In fact considerable attention has been given to the character and quality of economic development in the last decade. The basic attractiveness of southern Ontario to businessmen has allowed many communities to insist on the improvements that they desire, and environmental and community groups have been pressing for even higher standards to be enforced.

INDUSTRIAL HISTORY

The development of Ontario's industrial space-economy, particularly the locational aspects, has been examined more thoroughly than is the case for other provinces. In the early years the province grew in line with the rest of the country, that is on the basis of export staples. Permanent settlement spread inland from a number of places along the St Lawrence and Great Lakes. It was usually associated with timber at first, followed by farming (figure 5.1). Many parts of southern Ontario proved to be attractive to farmers and formed the backbone of a permanent urban pattern there (Spelt, 1972, 55–100). By the time of Confederation, about 50 per cent of employment in southern Ontario was still in the primary sector although it was already declining (Gilmour, 1972, 27).

131

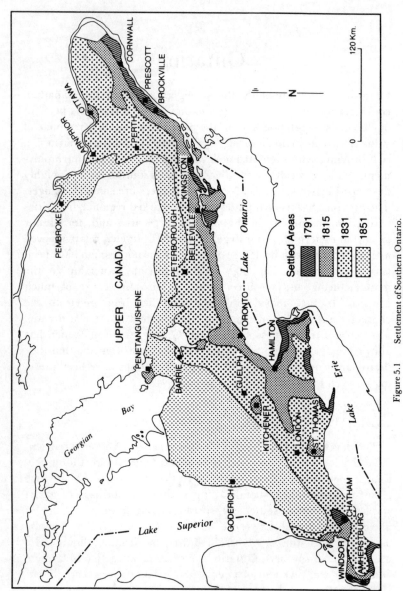

Figure 5.1   Settlement of Southern Ontario.
Source: J. M. Gilmour (1972)

The period 1851 to 1891 has been studied in considerable detail by Gilmour (1972). It was in the latter two decades of this period that changes associated with the 'industrial revolution' affected Ontario, although the increase in the proportion of employment in manufacturing did not, in fact, change very much (20.2% in 1851, 20.3% in 1871, 21.8% in 1891 in southern Ontario). Employment lost in the primary sector was mainly picked up by tertiary activities such as trade and transport. The manufacturing sector was dominated by the consumer goods industries, which catered for the small but growing population. Such items as food and drink, clothing, footwear and household goods provided nearly 50 per cent of manufacturing employment even in 1891 (Gilmour, 1972, 27). Their relative importance declined about 12 percentage points from 1851 to 1891 and was balanced mainly by the growth of early-stage primary manufacturing (i.e. initial processing of materials). Primary manufacturing represented an increase in the degree of processing of the staples which continued to be an important money-earner. The expansion of such activities as saw-milling was greatly aided by improvements in transport, which facilitated shipments to the market (Walker, 1971b, 16–24).

The development of producer goods should be stressed because they provide the wherewithal for other manufacturers and represent a more mature element in the economy. By 1891, despite relative as well as absolute growth over the years, however, Ontario was still not particularly strong in this department (Gilmour, 1972, 34). Although some of the new methods of production had affected the province by this time and factories using steam power had replaced many craft operations (Walker, 1971a), the more fundamental shift in type of production had barely begun. Of great importance in this respect was the establishment of a modern primary iron and steel industry in Hamilton and later at Sault Ste. Marie (Walker, 1974, 50–4). From the late 1890s, this industry provided key materials to a wide and growing number of producer goods industries. By 1910, Ontario's current structure was recognizable.

These structural modifications and expansions of manufacturing had important locational effects. In the early years, most of the manufacturing in southern Ontario was dispersed in rough conformity to population. Industries were usually small, craft operations which had little difficulty in finding water power sites of adequate size. Gilmour (1972, 48–52) has shown that primary manufacturing tended to be of most importance in newly settled areas and consequently moved gradually northwards from the St Lawrence-Great Lakes axis over the years. The relationships, however, were not perfect and some early settled areas retained their emphasis on primary manufacturing. On the other hand, the Toronto region and the area from the Niagara Peninsula through to Brant and Waterloo counties were, by 1891, already exhibiting a lead in industrial maturity with a higher proportion of secondary manufacturing, especially producer goods.

It is clear that a trend towards spatial concentration of manufacturing was underway by 1891. It is a feature of the southern Ontario economy that has remained to this day. Gilmour (1972, 86–120) outlines a number of theoretical reasons for such concentration. He notes that the dispersed activity could not be expected to last. It was associated with small markets, small scale production and a specialization on consumer goods and primary manufacturing. A more advanced stage of technology would inevitably bring larger scale production at fewer sites; a growing population and market would encourage such larger scale production; urbanization would lead to certain places offering both a large market and agglomeration economies; transport improvements would reduce freight costs and lessen the need for raw material orientation, and a rise in the proportion of producer goods would encourage the development of a few large manufacturing centres. This process of spatial concentration could be expected to operate by eliminating many of the small early firms through competition, and by restricting the location of new firms to a smaller area. Gilmour shows how these processes operated in Ontario from 1851 to 1891 to increase continuously the domination of Toronto and a few other places to the west of the capital city.

After 1891 the same trend continued. There are major problems with data sources (Gilmour, 1966; Bland 1970, 14), but figure 5.2 provides a picture of regional trends to 1911. Unfortunately, census boundaries cause some discontinuities and irregularities but the increasing dominance of the area from Toronto around the western end of Lake Ontario can be seen. In addition to Toronto itself with its diverse production, the area contains Hamilton, which became the country's major iron, steel and metalworking complex in the early twentieth century. In addition, many smaller centres in the Niagara Peninsula possessed thriving industries (Watson, 1945).

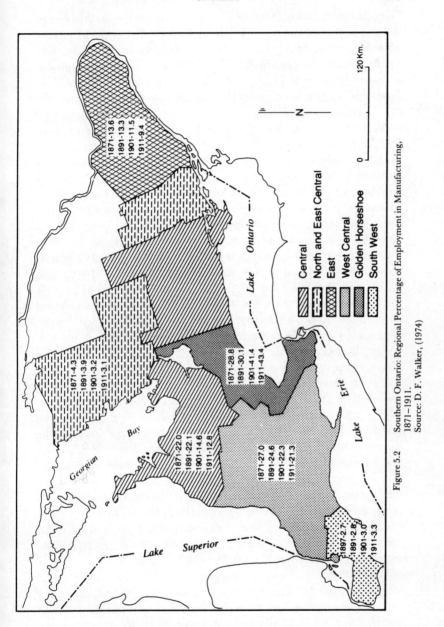

Figure 5.2 Southern Ontario: Regional Percentage of Employment in Manufacturing, 1871–1911.

Source: D. F. Walker, (1974)

Outside this 'Golden Horseshoe', there was relative decline except in the south-west, where Windsor expanded. The regional picture does hide important growth points, especially in the Galt, Kitchener, Brantford area. Bland (1970, 131) has mapped net shifts on a county basis from 1881 to 1932 but unfortunately this could be done only by number of factories and not by employment. Still, the downward shift in the majority of counties was demonstrated, and contrasted with massive gains in Toronto and large ones in Hamilton.

On the whole, then, it seems fair to assume that the forces outlined by Gilmour as providing spatial concentration operated well beyond the period that he studied and through the profound structural changes that modified the Ontario economy in the early twentieth century. It was indeed an era of great change as factories based on steam power first replaced the craft industries at the end of the nineteenth century, steam was then itself very quickly replaced by electricity for most uses by the end of the First World War, and the overall level of production rose rapidly (Walker, 1971a). It might have been expected that electricity would encourage dispersal of industry, and indeed the crusade for publicly-owned hydro-electricity was led by industrialists in smaller municipalities who wished to secure cheap power (Nelles, 1974, 237–55). In reality, however, the relatively even price structure across southern Ontario just neutralized power as a locational factor rather than having a major effect (Walker, 1971a). As a result of changing conditions, many small companies went out of business and mergers and takeovers were common. In agricultural machinery, for example, the result was a concentration in three centres, Toronto, Brantford and Hamilton (Walker, 1974, 58–61), while in brewing Toronto and London became dominant (Gilmour, 1972, 153–67). At the same time, most of the newer industries chose locations in the Golden Horseshoe or nearby. For example, the large heavy chemical factory of Canadian Industries Limited was located in Hamilton while the secondary chemical industry (except fertilizers) was highly concentrated in Toronto (Bland, 1970, 195–7).

During this transitional period Ontario also became more aware of its northlands. The spread of settlement pushed the forest industries further and further north, railbuilding to the West opened up the transport links and more and more evidence of rich mineral reserves came to light. Because it owned the land and granted the rights to mine or to cut timber, the provincial government was intimately involved with resource development. The interrelationships between a government concerned to promote development, and businessmen aiming at rich profits are too complex to discuss here but have been explored in detail for the period up to the Second World War by Nelles (1974). Apart from supplies of timber and minerals as raw materials to southern Ontario industries, the main effect on manufacturing was the establishment of a number of northern manufacturing centres. Most of these were one-industry towns based on smelting, pulp and paper or other forest industries.

ONTARIO'S INDUSTRIAL STRUCTURE

Since the 1920s, Ontario's economy has seen many ups and downs but many aspects of the province's space-economy have remained relatively stable. Population has grown considerably, reaching over 7.7 million in 1976, and the tendency for concentration into urban areas has continued. The urban population rose from 73 per cent of the total in 1951 to 82 per cent in 1976. The main element of growth in urban areas and especially in the central parts of southern Ontario has been migration. Meanwhile, although rural population is now fairly stable as a whole, northern and eastern Ontario are still losing much of their natural increase through out-migration (Ontario, TEIGA, 1976, 10–1).

In the post-war years, manufacturing has not been a particularly dynamic sector for employment. In common with that of most western countries, it is the tertiary sector that has grown fastest. In fact manufacturing's share of total provincial output is expected to decline in the future (Ontario, TEIGA, 1976, 13). The province does, however, have a reasonable proportion of modern growth industries. Table 5.1 shows quite high figures for transport (mainly a strong automobile industry), electrical products, chemicals and the metal groups. In contrast, Canada's problem industries (leather, textiles and clothing) do not play a major role, even though they are very important to some communities. Thus, although many of the problems of Canadian manufacturing outlined in Chapter 1 certainly affect the province, Ontario's industrial structure is relatively healthy.

A problem that has received considerable prominence in the last decade has been that of foreign ownership. Ontario has been the

TABLE 5.1
ONTARIO: PRINCIPAL STATISTICS BY INDUSTRY GROUP, 1975

	No. of Establishments	Employees No.	%	Value of Shipments $000	Value Added $000	%
Food and beverage industries'	1,550	86,508	10.2	7,538,147	2,396,684	11.9
Tobacco products industries	10	3,416	0.4	481,818	166,463	0.8
Rubber and plastics product industries	401	33,723	4.0	1,622,233	708,809	3.5
Leather industries	161	12,631	1.5	344,202	154,397	0.8
Textile industries	385	30,330	3.6	1,153,740	493,817	2.4
Knitting Mills	84	7,349	0.9	164,789	79,877	0.4
Clothing industries	435	22,360	2.6	543,611	272,874	1.4
Wood industries	726	19,284	2.3	675,501	306,896	1.5
Furniture and fixture industries	785	23,890	2.8	718,596	360,067	1.8
Paper and allied industries	302	45,178	5.3	2,291,122	999,360	5.0
Printing, Publishing and allied industries	1,588	47,429	5.6	1,526,149	966,884	4.8
Primary Metal industries	201	70,254	8.2	4,019,006	1,731,470	8.6
Metal fabricating industries	2,070	86,457	10.2	3,951,599	1,894,319	9.4
Machinery industries	606	56,260	6.6	3,083,881	1,341,405	6.7
Transportation equipment industries	392	100,695	11.8	12,857,054	3,164,233	15.7
Electrical products industries	487	83,065	9.8	4,023,524	1,755,326	8.7
Non-metallic mineral products industries	489	27,618	3.2	1,374,388	713,372	3.6
Petroleum and coal products	31	9,269	1.1	1,761,851	267,917	1.3
Chemical and chemical products industries	538	44,405	5.2	3,594,240	1,550,572	7.7
Miscellaneous manufacturing industries	1,004	40,170	4.7	1,630,479	798,190	4.0
Total all industries	12,245	850,291	100.0	53,355,887	20,122,934	100.0

main beneficiary of high tariff walls designed to encourage foreigners to develop manufacturing plants in Canada, but the kind of economy that has resulted is no longer considered an unmixed blessing. Difficulties in this area are not confined to manufacturing but extend to all aspects of Ontario's economy. A select committee of the legislative assembly has been examining the subject and commissioned a study by consultants that was completed in 1974 (Ontario, Legislative Assembly, 1974). The consultants attempted to assess differences in corporate behaviour between Canadian and non-Canadian companies. They examined six industries in detail; advertising, architecture and engineering consulting, automotive parts, electronics, forest-based industries and mining. Only three of these, of course, are in the manufacturing sector.

The report stressed the fact that foreign ownership in Ontario was highly concentrated in large manufacturing corporations (Ontario, Legislative Assembly, 1974, 198–225). Many managers felt that it was very difficult for smaller Canadian companies to break into the market against such competition. Employees felt that there is too much United States investment in Canada, but they also considered that Canadian companies were conservative and less willing to take risks. Job satisfaction was not noticeably different according to ownership type. Community leaders and the public at large did not wish to see more large foreign-owned companies in their communities. In summarizing their findings on corporate behaviour, the report found two main differencies: first, 'a tendency for foreign controlled firms to buy more components, machinery and/or services from foreign sources as well as frequently being less autonomous on key decisions' (p. 207), secondly, a specialization by foreign firms on certain lines to the virtual exclusion of Canadian firms. Many of the other findings of the committee related to long-term effects of foreign ownership and are similar to the problems reviewed in Chapter 1.

All in all, the foreign ownership question in Ontario is a reflection of the province's locational attraction. It is near to very large United States markets, close to the head offices of U.S. firms and, therefore, attractive as a base for them to serve Canadian markets, has rich and varied resources and a diverse and growing supply of labour. Unfortunately, there never seem to have been enough indigenous entrepreneurs to seize all of the profitable opportunities. Instead the risks, and the subsequent benefits, have in large measure gone to outsiders.

THE SPATIAL PATTERN

The main elements of the spatial pattern of manufacturing in Ontario have tended to follow the trends established at the turn of the century. Changes have been gradual and the forces of spatial

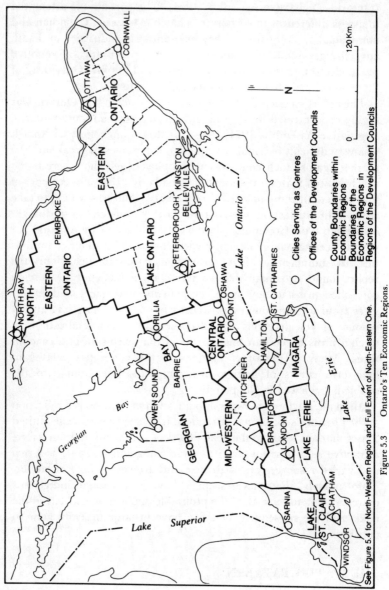

Figure 5.3   Ontario's Ten Economic Regions.

concentration continue to be strong. During the 1960s and until recently, provincial spatial analysis was conducted on the basis of ten regions. Figure 5.3 shows the economic regions into which Ontario is divided.

Wong (1969, 45–55) examined the degree of manufacturing specialization of these regions in 1961. Using the coefficient of specialization (Isard, 1960, 270–9), Wong found that the two northern regions were the most specialized, followed by the St Clair region around Windsor. At the other end of the scale was Central Ontario around Toronto. The remaining regions had fairly similar scores. Wong also looked at the extent to which the major industrial groups were localized in a few regions in Ontario. Primary metal was the most highly localized with an index of over fifty (Isard, 1960, 251–4), followed by the wood processing industries. Both of these industries are associated with their resource base, and especially found in the north. Amongst the other groups, there was a steady progression from textiles and clothing (indices in the low thirties) to the most widespread, food and beverages and metal fabrication.

The components of locational change in Ontario for the years 1961 to 1966 have been analysed in considerable detail by Collins (1972). His study was based upon the returns that are made annually by every establishment for the Census of Manufacturers and involved manipulation of the source data at Statistics Canada rather than the use of its published materials. It is not likely that the situation today is drastically different from that observed by Collins. In the period 1961 to 1966, the dominant provincial trend was a loss of establishments in the city of Toronto and large gains in the Toronto suburbs and the fringe areas[1] beyond them (p.80). The city lost 11 per cent of its plants but the suburbs increased theirs by 42 per cent and the fringes grew even faster at 65 per cent. Outside the Metropolitan Toronto areas, the changes were quite small except for growth in the Kitchener-Cambridge-Guelph triangle.

These changes could be the result either of the difference between new plants (i.e. new to Ontario) and those which go out of business in the province, or of migrations within Ontario. Births and deaths are almost balanced in the city of Toronto, but the suburbs have many new plants and few losses, while further out in the fringes the

[1] Fringe areas include the townships of Toronto, Vaughan, Markham, Chinguacousy and Pickering with their towns.

birth/death differential is even greater (p.85). Outside the Metropolitan Toronto area, only Waterloo, Barrie, Burlington and Oakville had birth rates higher than the provincial average. Thus, while
new activity is still focused on Metropolitan Toronto, it is now
taking place in the suburbs. In plant size, the suburbs gained small
operations while many of the city of Toronto's losses were relatively
large. In the fringe areas, gains from larger plants helped employment growth but elsewhere in Ontario employment grew only in a
few large centres (Hamilton, Windsor, Ottawa and London) (p. 89).

Relocations within Ontario from 1961 to 1966 mainly reflected a
trend to suburbanization in the Toronto area (p. 93–100). About 20
per cent of Toronto's suburban employment increase (7,600 new
jobs) resulted from plants moving out from Toronto. There was also
some movement from the older to the newer suburbs, mainly
benefiting Etobicoke, Scarborough and North York. Dispersal from
Toronto to places further afield involved over 2,000 jobs and fifty
plants but was largely confined within a 50 mile radius of Toronto.
Moreover, over half as many employees were involved in plants
which moved in the opposite direction, into Metropolitan Toronto.
Other forms of relocation (mainly between other urban centres)
were not very important. They generally involved movements to
larger centres, especially Windsor, Hamilton-Burlington and Kitchener-Waterloo.

Collins (p. 89–90) also noted that expansion of plants 'in situ'
provided about 85 per cent of all manufacturing employment growth
in Ontario during his study period. Similar patterns were found in
Toronto as for other elements – slow growth in the city, much faster
in the suburbs and faster still in the fringe areas. A few isolated
centres grew as fast as, or faster than, the fringe areas – for example,
Woodstock and Aurora.

Among location factors that operate within Ontario, the market is
a powerful influence on manufacturing. Kerr and Spelt (1960)
measured this factor in terms of market potential, or a place's
accessibility to all other places.[1] They included the market (measured by wholesale sales) in southern Ontario and southern Québec
cities. Market potential proved to be high near to Montréal and
Toronto but fell off rapidly away from the metropolitan centres
leaving most of the rest of southern Ontario in fairly similar
positions. Ray's later (1965) study, however, shows a strong ridge of

[1] Gravity models and market potential are well described in Isard (1960, 493–568).

high market potential south-westwards from Toronto to Hamilton and London. He used an empirically derived distance exponent of 1.42 and replaced wholesale sales with retail sales as a measurement of the mass variable. Ray's measures of market potential conform with the location of manufacturing quite well and, in fact, statistically explain three quarters of the spatial variation in southern Ontario(p.145).

Of course, actual transport costs could distort the accessibility of various cities. Trucking rates in Ontario are quite complex and are based on specific journeys rather than distance. Despite the massive freight manuals, however, a clear pattern arises, one favouring the larger centres. Toronto has the best variety of service and usually has lower rates per ton mile than other centres. In general then, transport costs reinforce market potential.

Supply of materials does not seem to be a crucial locational factor for most industries in southern Ontario. In a few instances a location near the material is vital, for example the processing of fruit in the Niagara area or of vegetables in other parts of south-west Ontario. For other firms location at a good importing position is required, such as petrochemicals at Sarnia, where the pipeline comes in from the West, or sugar refining on the Toronto harbour front. Most of southern Ontario's industry, however, does not lose much weight in process and its materials are not heavy or expensive relative to the product. While reduced material handling cost is an attraction, it is often a minor financial element. Thus, for example, many metal-using and machinery industries cluster in Hamilton around the steel producers but they are also common in many other centres farther away. In any case, many of Ontario's industries use numerous materials and components and, therefore, cannot locate near to all supplies. The automobile industry is an excellent example. On the other hand, in northern Ontario, material supply is (or was) the key element in the location of the major metal smelting, pulp and paper and wood industries. Their location has formed the basis of the urban centres in which, later, some small consumer industries developed.

Another Weberian locational factor, labour, is frequently prominent in studies which have examined industry in various parts of the province. Rusling (1974, 157–60), for example, showed that it was important for all major plants locating in Cambridge between 1960 and 1970. In some cases, availability of skilled metal workers was crucial, in others a pool of unskilled, female labour. Kerr and Spelt (1960) looked at rates in the 1950s and found that, in southern Ontario, the east and Georgian Bay areas had low costs for skilled labour, while in Niagara-Hamilton and the extreme south-west around Windsor they were higher than in Toronto. In most parts of southern Ontario, rates for semi-skilled workers were higher than in Toronto but lower for labourers. Kerr and Spelt (p. 21) also looked at strike and lock-out records, which identified certain unsatisfactory centres (Windsor, St Catharines, Oshawa, Chatham, Kitchener, Hamilton).

With his concept of economic shadow, Ray (1965) has focused on the element of foreign ownership as a locational factor in Ontario. The starting point for his work was the recognition by Kerr and Spelt (1960, 21) that market accessibility and labour factors could not explain why eastern Ontario lagged behind the south-west in manufacturing. Ray's model of economic shadow included three elements: interactance decay, sectoral affinity and sectoral penetration (pp. 89–110). Interactance decay indicates that the likelihood of a branch plant's being established in Ontario is inversely proportional to the distance from the head office of the parent company. Thus, for example, one would expect far more plants owned by Detroit companies than those based in Los Angeles. The second element, sectoral affinity, indicates that branches will be located in the sector of Ontario between the head office and the major market, Toronto, and is based on the concept of intervening opportunity. Thus Peterborough is unlikely to obtain a Chicago plant because severe competition from Toronto intervenes. Sectoral penetration, the last element of economic shadow, allows for the close connections of plants located immediately on either side of the border. It indicates that the further away the parent from the international boundary the further into Ontario will be the branch plant. Ray defined his three elements in such a way that they could be tested statistically and went on to show their validity for southern Ontario. Economic shadow operates differently from market potential and especially helps to explain the attraction of the area west of Toronto which lies between the metropolitan area and the major United States manufacturing areas (p. 142).

In a less model-oriented and more historically based study, Blackbourn (1969, 50) showed that the early location of American plants in Ontario was mainly at the border, especially in Windsor.

These plants gradually located further inland but the lack of them in eastern Ontario was evident in 1913. It was between 1913 and 1930 that Toronto became particularly attractive and since then it has steadily increased in comparison to the border areas. The period 1930 to 1962 also saw more dispersion of American-owned plants so that their distribution is becoming increasingly similar to Canadian ones. He also showed that new plants established between 1952 and 1966 by non-American foreign owners had similar locations to the American ones, both strongly concentrated in Toronto (p. 75).

Blackbourn's questionnaire survey revealed a number of interesting aspects of foreign-owned plants. He showed, for example that quite a high proportion of plants in southwestern Ontario (excluding the Windsor area) were taken over from other companies rather than established by the parent (pp. 103–5). In locations chosen by the parent, the south-west was less important (15% of total in Blackbourn's survey as opposed to 26% of those taken over). Most of this difference is taken up by Metropolitan Toronto. Blackbourn concludes that the locational attraction of southwestern Ontario is overemphasized by studies using a simple count of American-owned plants. In locational factors, Blackbourn (pp. 122–35) found that American owners stressed those elements which might be expected for any manufacturer, especially markets, labour, availability of materials, transport facilities and plant costs. Distance to the parent was important to 44 per cent of respondents and was especially prominent among those in the Windsor area. The factor of material shipment was also particularly important in Windsor but equally so in Metropolitan Toronto (pp. 111–72). Blackbourn found that distance did not influence the percentage of materials received from parent plants and, therefore, that interaction models of the type used by Ray are inappropriate (p. 113).

Too little is known about the operation of branch plants to agree with this conclusion. In an examination of a particular group of industries (metal-working and machinery) in Hamilton and midwestern Ontario (Guelph, Cambridge, Brantford, Kitchener-Waterloo), the linkage patterns of Canadian and foreign-owned plants were fairly similar (Bater and Walker, 1974b). There was a distinct tendency for Canadian firms to buy more of their materials locally but the two groups were not significantly different in terms of supplies from foreign countries. In marketing, the foreign-owned plants did tend to export more. Some interesting results were found when distance was combined with plant size. For the Hamilton data, value of material linkage (over a year) was predicted, in a multiple correlation analysis using distance and employment, with a coefficient of 0.57 for foreign plants and 0.80 for Canadian ones (Bater and Walker, 1974a). From the regression coefficients it was found that for Canadian operations almost all the variation was related to plant size, whereas distance and plant size operated about equally for the foreign-owned plants. Market linkages were less well explained by this analysis. On the whole, it must be concluded that the operation of the foreign-owned companies in Ontario and its effect on the provincial space-economy is still imperfectly understood.

THE FIVE PLANNING REGIONS

Since 1972, the Ontario government has been using five large regions for the purpose of regional planning and development. The discussion of regional manufacturing conditions will, therefore, follow the provincial scheme, although central Ontario requires considerable subdivision. Figure 5.4 shows the new regions, which represent a collapsing of the ten former economic regions of figure 5.3. Central Ontario dominates the picture in both population and manufacturing, and has been increasing its strength in the post-war years.

Central Ontario

Central Ontario is essentially the nodal region focused strongly on Metropolitan Toronto. The outlying areas certainly have a great deal of independent character but nevertheless business ties with Toronto are considerable and there is even daily commuting to the metropolis. The region is the heart of Ontario's and Canada's industrial space-economy containing over 70 per cent of the province's manufacturing (measured by employees or value added) and most of the country's head offices.

METROPOLITAN TORONTO

It has already been observed that trends associated with Toronto form the major elements in locational change in Ontario. The

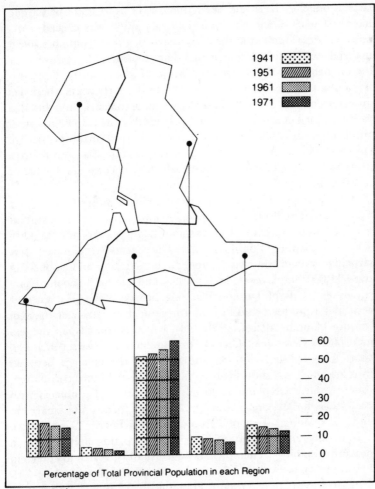

Figure 5.4 Ontario: Population Change By Region, 1941–1971.
Source: Ontario, TEIGA (1976)

metropolitan area and surrounding counties represent the key point of attraction for new industries, relocations and expansions. At the same time, the City of Toronto proper, at the heart of the agglomeration, is losing manufacturing employment.

Manufacturing in its modern form grew up in Toronto mainly around the harbour and along the rail lines. This influence can still be seen in the present locational pattern of industry in the older parts of the city (Kerr and Spelt, 1965, 131). Kerr and Spelt argue that the choice of the city as a political capital was crucial to its industrial development in the early years (p. 76). Toronto became a financial and political centre that had considerable control over developments in the north and west of the country and also developed a rich market of its own. From the early years, there has always been great diversity in the city's industrial structure and this tradition has continued to the present-day metropolitan area. Another 'traditional' element is the small to medium size of Toronto's plants. A key twentieth century feature has been metro's attraction for foreign-owned plants, which has been a notable factor in its recent growth (see discussion above).

The city proper lost manufacturing employment in the 1950s and 1960s at an annual rate of nearly 4,000 jobs a year, but it is still an important industrial area, having some 82,000 workers in 1971 (City of Toronto Planning Board, 1974, 2). The central part of the city has particular strength in two groups; paper, printing and publishing (over 11,000 employees), and textiles and clothing (about 8,000 employees) (City of Toronto Planning Board, 1971b, 13). Further west, metal products and food and beverages are stronger (City of Toronto Planning Board, 1971a, 14), which is true also of the less important eastern areas (City of Toronto Planning Board, 1973, 14). Apart from textiles, clothing and printing, the linkages between firms are small and most firms do not need to be in the central area. Many, in fact, are planning to relocate because of problems with congestion for trucking and parking, or inadequate space in outdated buildings (City of Toronto Planning Board, 1974, 11–12). It is mainly a few large, often fairly old, plants that provide a measure of stability. Their owners have usually invested too much in their sites to be willing to abandon them completely.

In 1974 the City of Toronto Planning Board issued a discussion paper, which stressed the need for retaining some industry. It was argued that if manufacturing were allowed to disappear completely it would result in the breakdown of some of the inner city working class areas that were associated with industrial job opportunities. Further, it was stressed that some industries really needed a city location because of the market, a central location, specialized services and the availability of cheap (especially female or immigrant) labour. More recently, some of these assertions have been examined in more detail.

In one paper, the Board considered the attraction of the city for industry (City of Toronto Planning Board, 1976). Two of the central city's main industries were looked at in some detail with the aid of a linkage analysis by Mock (1976). Both the garment and the printing and publishing industries require fast, often face-to-face contact. Mock's study compared the linkages of plants in a downtown area (between Avenue and Bathurst and Queen and Front) with plants located elsewhere in Metropolitan Toronto. In the garment industry, ordering of supplies of materials from visiting salesmen is important both for checking the unstandardized materials and for obtaining fast delivery. The garment district also has many showrooms, which attract out-of-town buyers. Further, sub-contracting is more common in this downtown area. These features all make a location outside the main garment district less attractive, especially for small firms. In the printing industry, the important downtown linkages are on the marketing side. Close contact is not always essential but helps for fast service and face-to-face contact to discuss unstandardized jobs (City of Toronto Planning Board, 1976, 10–11).

The remainder of this 1976 study by the Planning Board looks at some other advantages of the city for the garment and printing industries (pp. 15–19). For the garment industry, cheap space in older buildings and accessible labour (mainly female) are cited as major attractions. For printing, however, such elements are not usually crucial. Workers mostly live in the suburbs and cheap rent is less important. Thus the industry is much more widespread within metro (47% of Metropolitan Toronto's employment in printing was in the city in 1971 as contrasted to 87% for apparel) and is tending to become less city-oriented. Only one other manufacturing sector was identified as being city-oriented, the jewellery industry, which has similar characteristics to the garment trade. Other firms, however, are oriented to the port, mainly because of imported materials (e.g. sugar refining).

Quite a lot of firms in the City of Toronto lack some of the typical features that encourage a location there (City of Toronto, 1976, 22–3). Many of these are large and could not move easily because of existing capital investment. The most common type is in the food and beverage industry, ranging from packing plants to distilleries. Others (for example, many metal-working firms), however, could rationally be located anywhere in metro Toronto but currently see no advantage in making a move.

A second study paper by the Board (City of Toronto Planning

Board, 1975) examined the effects of industrial relocation by city firms to the suburbs. This reflected a concern expressed in its 1974 paper that people suffered as a result of relocations. Management and employees of eight firms, which moved between 1972 and 1974, were interviewed. The firms generally benefited from increased space and single-storey buildings as result of the move. The proportion of workers taken from one site to the other varied, but generally the lower income workers moved less readily (pp. 24–5). On average, employees who had worked at both sites had longer trip times to work at the new one. It was the lowest-paid workers who suffered most (a 16–minute average increase) while those earning over $9,000 *per annum* actually reduced their journey time. In the suburbs, fewer workers used public transit, and the poorer service may well be responsible for the longer trip times of the lowest-paid ones (p. 41). The fact that a relatively higher proportion of them live in the city is also a factor (p. 42). Despite some difficulties, however, most workers were satisfied (pp. 49–50). Thus relocation does not seem to have posed severe problems.

The difficulties of plants in the city of Toronto provided much of the basis for developments in the suburbs. Kerr and Spelt's (1958, 13–4) analysis showed that two-thirds of suburban firms had previous locations in the city. This is a natural form of fringe expansion (Wood 1974) and still continues. As already noted, however, the suburbs have become the major focus of growth in Metropolitan Toronto and attract new firms and plants from outside the area. Collins showed that from 1961 to 1966 only about 20 per cent of new suburban plants were relocations from the city, although no doubt there were some branch plant developments as well. Suburban growth is very diversified, mainly in small to medium-sized plants, and includes a relatively high proportion of growth industries. Many foreign subsidiaries are included and they seem to be attracted to the west end, possibly by the airport, which allows easy executive contact. Suburban growth has mainly been in planned industrial areas.

HAMILTON

Hamilton is Canada's major steel centre and its industrial fortunes are very much bound up with the two giant primary iron and steel companies, Steel Company of Canada Limited (STELCO) and the Dominion Foundry and Steel Company (DOFASCO), which employ about a third of the manufacturing workforce. Industry is concentrated in the city proper, especially around the harbour, but recently the major growth has been out in the suburbs, especially in Burlington and Saltfleet.

The city was of minor importance until after the building of the first railway, the Great Western, in 1853, which stimulated a boom in population and industry. During the nineteenth century, its accessibility by water and rail and its closeness to the main areas of population (and market) growth encouraged manufacturing. When coal became the key industrial energy source Hamilton was very well placed to receive supplies cheaply from Pennsylvania and later it was equally well located to benefit from Niagara electricity as soon as that came on stream after 1898. In the critical years, as well, Hamilton seemed to be able to produce or attract the kind of entrepreneur who could make the most of available opportunities (Middleton, 1978). From the early years, metal-working and metal-using industries (for example, foundries, agricultural and other machinery) were important in Hamilton. The development of primary iron and steel in 1896 complemented that early structure and in turn set in motion a cumulative process of expansion in the whole metal-working sector, a process still in existence (Bater and Walker, 1971b, 5–6).

Today, Hamilton's metal-working complex is still located around the harbour, apart from a few, mainly small, operations in the suburbs. Primary metals employ about 35 per cent of the manufacturing labour force while metal fabricating and machinery take up a further 22 per cent (Bater and Walker, 1971b, 7–10). Only one other manufacturing group, electrical products, employs as much as ten per cent, although there are many small plants in the food and beverage industry. Within metal-working itself, there is a major size contrast between the two giants and a very large number of small operations, many of which have been started recently by former employees in the larger companies. Both of the big companies have purchased land for expansion on the north shore of Lake Erie and there are some fears that development there may have a deleterious effect on Hamilton. So far, however, renovations and expansions have continued in the city and only STELCO is developing a new site, at Nanticoke.

The primary metal industry in Hamilton is Canadian-owned and geared to supplying the Canadian market. In fact, over 80 per cent of its output went to Ontario in 1969 and less than three per cent was exported. On the other hand, the industry relied quite heavily on imported materials, especially coal and iron ore from the United States. Just about 50 per cent of materials by value came from outside Canada. In contrast, the metal-working and machinery groups seem to be strongly influenced by supplies from the primary sector. About 56 per cent by value of their materials in 1969 came from within the Hamilton area and well over 80 per cent from Ontario as a whole. The markets of these secondary sectors are much more widespread, with about 28 per cent of products going to Canadian provinces outside Ontario and nearly 20 per cent being shipped to the United States. The latter are mainly but not exclusively shipped by United States' subsidiaries (Bater and Walker, 1971b, 23–30).

The City of Hamilton has been stagnating in manufacturing employment for some time. Some older industries have gone out of business and there is an acute shortage of new industrial land. Developments have mainly taken place in suburban municipalities such as Burlington and Saltfleet. In these areas, most plants are small or medium in size and are housed in industrial parks or districts. While more diversity is found than in Hamilton, metal-working and machinery are still relatively strong and quite a number of the new entrepreneurs are local (Walker and Bater, 1972, Arathoon, 1974).

The Niagara Peninsula

East of Hamilton between Lakes Ontario and Erie is another early-settled area of the province, the Niagara Peninsula. This is one of Canada's major border areas inasmuch as, with Windsor, it forms a key route into the United States industrial heartland. As such it attracted nineteenth century settlers from the south and has more than its fair share of U.S. branch plants. An early start has brought some current problems of ageing industries, and the area has not been very attractive to new operations in the last twenty years. Moreover, land use conflicts pose severe problems because this is a prime tender fruits area and has considerable charm for tourists. The Peninsula is now under a Regional Municipality, which should in theory help to solve some of its planning problems by reducing municipal conflicts.

Manufacturing industry in the Niagara Peninsula has recently been the subject of a comprehensive study (Jackson and White, 1971). In 1970, not far off half of the manufacturing labour force of over 47,000 was employed in the motor vehicle parts and accessories or the primary metals industry. Also significant in scale were paper, metal fabricating, food and beverage and non-metallic minerals industries. The Niagara Peninsula, then, tends to be specialized in its industrial structure. Even more is this the case for some of its cities. St Catharines-Thorold, the largest centre of manufacturing, has over 55 per cent of its employment in transport equipment and another 14 per cent in paper. Welland has over 50 per cent in iron and steel, steel pipe and tubes, and iron foundries. The smaller employment of Port Colborne is nearly 70 per cent in two primary metals industries (nickel and iron). Of the four largest employment centres in the peninsula only Niagara Falls has some reasonable diversity in industrial structure but even there three groups (food and beverage, non-metallic minerals, chemicals) account for over 60 per cent of manufacturing employment. This kind of structure reflects the importance of a few large operations such as four plants in St Catharines-Thorold which employ almost 60 per cent of all industrial workers (Jackson and White, 1971, 102) or the three employing a similar percentage in Welland (pp. 151–2).

Quite why such a structure has developed is not entirely clear. With a strategic position and good transport facilities, the Niagara Peninsula might be expected to attract a great diversity of activities. What seems to have happened is that a number of large-scale activities were attracted and these have discouraged smaller ones. Cheap hydro-electric power from Niagara was an extremely important attraction for power-intensive industries in the early part of the twentieth century, although equalization of rates in 1960 removed this locational advantage. Thus a number of abrasive manufacturers, chemical firms and specialized metal operations moved into the area. Some large plants were attracted by the Welland Canal for power, water and/or transport. The paper industry is one good example, while Port Colborne's iron works also fits into this category. Many of these large plants have always paid relatively high wages, pushing labour costs up to uncompetitive levels (Jackson and White, 1971, 70–75). In consequence, smaller entrepreneurs have found if difficult, though not impossible, to establish themselves. As if to prove that it could be done, the largest plant in St Catharines grew from local initiatives, though General Motors took it over in 1929.

While the Niagara Peninsula is highly accessible to the United States and has attracted many branch plants of American firms, it is not as well placed to serve the Canadian market as some centres further in from the border. This has probably encouraged stagnation, especially in the south away from the Queen Elizabeth Way. The area does not compensate in materials, which, apart from fruits and vegetables, are almost non-existent. Thus elements of a mature industrial economy (high wages, old plants, some problems of pollution) are difficult to overcome.

MIDWESTERN ONTARIO

To the west of the Toronto area, Ontario's economy has also been quite dynamic in the post-war period. One of the fastest-growing areas has been that around Kitchener. The area enclosed by Guelph, Kitchener-Waterloo and Cambridge is sometimes referred to as the 'Golden Triangle'. Along with Brantford, this part of the province has shown strength as a manufacturing area since the early years of settlement. Its inhabitants, especially those with a German background, have included many successful entrepreneurs, while the general location in southwest Ontario has proved to be very favourable. The area employs about eleven per cent of Ontario's manufacturing work force.

The industrial structure of this area is fairly diverse, though more so in some cities than others. About one-third of employment is in the metal and machinery industries, another 14 per cent in electrical products. The rest is quite well spread out amongst other groups, the most important being food and beverages, textiles and clothing, rubber goods, leather and chemical products (Parker, 1976, 9). The midwestern Ontario area, then, has strong representation in both growth industries and stagnant or declining ones. During the 1960s very few industrial groups actually declined in employment (rubber was one) but relatively there were problems for textiles and clothing, food and beverages and wood industries (Bater and Walker, 1971a, 149). Between 1970 and 1975, most of these groups registered absolute declines (Parker, 1976, 9). In contrast, there has been fast growth in metals and machinery, electrical and chemical products. The expansion of transport equipment (mainly automobile parts) in the 1960s has levelled off more recently.

Kitchener-Waterloo has both the largest employment and the most diverse industrial structure (Bater and Walker, 1971a, 150). Here some local entrepreneurs have established successful national-scale companies, as, for example, Schneiders in meat-packing and Electrohome in home appliances. At the same time, the city has been attractive to the international companies such as Uniroyal and B. F. Goodrich in tyres and Budd Automotive in car frames. Most firms in the twin cities, however, are small and locally-owned. Kitchener developed industrial parks to the south of the city centre in the 1960s but has been short of industrial land for a few years so that recent expansion has been in the north end of Waterloo or, more often, in Cambridge or Guelph.

Cambridge is a much more specialized centre than Kitchener-Waterloo. It still concentrates heavily on two sectors, which have formed the backbone of the local economy since the late nineteenth century, these being metals and machinery (over 43% of manufacturing employment) and textiles and clothing (nearly 15%). The latter sector is gradually losing importance, suffering as does the whole industry in Canada, from the difficulty of competing against much cheaper products from the Far East. Cambridge's industry has been expanding and gradually diversifying in the last decade (Parker, 1976, 13). Both Guelph and Brantford also have strong specializations in metals and machinery, each with well over one third of manufacturing employment in these categories. Guelph has, in addition, an important electrical products sector which, however, has declined in the early 1970s (Bater and Walker, 1971a, 152–3, Parker, 1976, 15–16).

Apart from local differences related to availability of land and services, the centres offer similar locational advantages. A study by Rusling (1974) investigated the factors influencing plants locating in Cambridge between 1960 and 1970. He showed that market accessibility was almost always a key advantage, manufacturers being impressed with the ability to serve a large market easily. He found that the attraction of the area as a place to live in was also important for many firms, especially the smaller ones. There were some differences amongst the industrial groups in that raw material supplies were most important for some industries (e.g. metal fabrication, food and beverages) while labour elements were prominent for machinery establishments. Rusling's interviews with Cambridge firms established before 1960 showed that they also appreciated the city's advantages of market accessibility, labour and material availability. General satisfaction with the area is also indicated by firms which needed to relocate from older buildings in the city: nearly all of them moved to other sites within Cambridge. In general, midwestern Ontario is close enough to Toronto to benefit from many of the metropolitan advantages but at the same time provides cheaper land and a less hectic living and working environment.

Southwestern Ontario

Southwestern Ontario is mainly rural and contains many rich farming areas. The southern section benefits not only from good soils but also a relatively mild climate which encourages corn, tobacco, vegetables and fruits to grow well. A fairly dense settlement pattern has, therefore, built up but there is no large metropolis, London (270,400) and Windsor (247,600) being the largest centres. With a population of about one and a quarter million, southwestern Ontario ranks just ahead of eastern Ontario in this respect.

Although manufacturing industry is located in isolated urban centres and there is no large industrial core, employment in manufacturing matches population. Each stands at just over 15 per cent of the provincial total. Value added in manufacturing is actually a little higher than this (17%). Except in Grey and Bruce counties, most towns and cities have a number of small firms plus one or two larger branch plants of major corporations. Grey and Bruce in the north are further away from the province's economic centre and find it more difficult to attract and hold new operations: many towns in these counties rely on older industries such as furniture and textiles. This region of Ontario benefits from its location between Toronto and many major industrial cities of the United States manufacturing belt. It is thus well placed both for material supply and product shipment either to the American or to the Canadian market. The importance of the automobile industry is a reflection of this location. It is by far the major employer in the region and many of the important machinery and metal fabricating plants supply it either directly or indirectly. Other growth industries such as electrical products and chemicals are well represented. The other major manufacturing employer is the food and beverage industry, which benefits from the richness of local farm output.

Of the two large cities in southwestern Ontario, Windsor is the more important manufacturing centre. Its proximity to Detroit was a stimulus to growth even as early as the mid-nineteenth century, when Hiram Walker, the founder of the large distilling company, moved across and set up a grain business (Blackbourn, 1969, 137). This pattern continued during the nineteenth century. After 1910, Detroit automobile manufacturers, especially Ford, expanded rapidly in Windsor and the city gradually became increasingly an automobile city. The industry's high wages and industrial militancy drove most other industries out (Blackbourn, 149). With the ageing of plants and the movement of Ford's assembly operation to Oakville in 1953, Windsor had a difficult time well into the sixties, although things have been much more stable since. The metropolitan area is still dominated by the automobile industry, which accounts for well over half of value added and employment in manufacturing. Amongst the others, only food and beverages make a noticeable contribution.

London, with its strong services and well-established university, is much less an industrial city than Windsor but its manufacturing workforce is only a few thousand fewer. Its major industrial group is food and beverages, reflecting the surrounding farmland. The industrial structure is fairly diverse with metal fabricating, machinery and electrical products all quite well represented. The plants are not closely linked but rather connected to Toronto (Houston, 1973, 65). Manufacturing is tending to move to the southern section of the city near to Highway 401 (Odell, 1975), and Ford opened a major car plant a little further south at Talbotville in 1968.

The smaller centre of Sarnia plays a very important role as the location of Canada's major petrochemical complex. The 'Chemical Valley' runs southward from the city for some fourteen miles and includes massive investment in 'a truly awesome series of multi-million dollar petrochemical plants' (Sarnia and District Commercial and Industrial Development Commission, 1977). Production includes refinery products, synthetic rubbers, caustic soda, plastics, fertilizers, ammonia, chlorine, fibre glass and numerous other chemical products of many types. Diverse petrochemical production has developed mainly since the Second World War when the federal government decided to build a plant for the production of synthetic rubber. For this purpose, Polymer Corporation was incorporated in 1942. Several private companies were associated with its management in the war years and production began in 1943. After the war Polymer was able to establish export markets and many of the associated companies expanded and diversified (Ford, 1976, 11–2).

The choice of Sarnia for Polymer's site was not a capricious one. As a result of oil production in and around Petrolia and Oil Springs since the 1850s, a refining industry had been established in Petrolia and Sarnia. Sarnia's first refinery was built in 1871. Following mergers and takeovers, Imperial Oil became the dominant company by 1900. It made Sarnia its headquarters and its refinery and expertise provided the main reason for Polymer's location in 1942. Large local salt supplies and the plentiful water supply are additional advantages for chemical plants (Ford, 1976, 1–12).

Discovery of oil in Alberta in 1947 provided further security for Sarnia's post-war expansion. Pipeline connections at first to Superior, Wisconsin and later directly to Sarnia provided an assured raw material. The 1950s saw a resultant opening of refineries by Sun Oil and Canadian Oil as well as numerous chemical plants. Recently a world-scale ethylene plant has opened. This, Petrosar, is jointly owned by some of the other companies in Sarnia as well as the Canadian Development Corporation. Its products will provide materials for many chemical plants, illustrating the high degree of industrial linkage that is found in Sarnia.

Eastern Ontario

The Eastern Ontario Planning Region contains the nation's capital, Ottawa, but is nevertheless a relatively poor region. Situated between Toronto and Montréal yet isolated from their main spheres of influence, the region exhibits all the characteristics of the intermetropolitan periphery (Friedmann, 1966, 35–7). Essentially such areas have a weak economy requiring federal support, are losing population through out-migration of the most productive members, and have suffered socially through declining services. The extent to which eastern Ontario fits the description is explored by Staple (1975).

There is a strong contrast between the capital area, with its growth and wealth, and the rest of eastern Ontario. Ottawa's development has not spread prosperity far beyond its boundaries, probably because its strength is in the political and administrative rather than economic sphere. Moreover, the capital's manufacturing is quite limited for a place of its size. It mainly concentrates on some high value-added items such as electrical, scientific and professional equipment, and on printing and publishing (Staple, 1975, 22).

The rest of eastern Ontario has a large share of slow growth industries and there are many old plants, reflecting the industrial development of an earlier era, when the area was more prosperous. New industries are also represented, however, and the main groups are food and beverages, electrical products, textiles, metals, machinery and chemicals. The main spatial concentration is in the line of cities along the St Lawrence and Lake Ontario, which benefit from good accessibility via road, rail and water. It is interesting that branch plant control in the region is predominantly from Montréal rather than Toronto (Staple, 1975, 93). In fact, the eastern part of the region is oriented to Montréal in many respects.

Eastern Ontario's manufacturing sector is remarkably small for its population. Nearly 14 per cent of Ontario's population provides only 7.5 per cent of manufacturing employees and 6.8 per cent of value added. As early plants have aged or firms have gone out of business, replacement has been limited and the region has fallen behind. It lacks resources and, given industry's propensity to market orientation, suffers from an intermediate location between the two major Canadian metropolises. Cheap land, pleasant living conditions and good accessibility, however, may work in favour of the communities stretched along the transport corridor of the south. Nothing can change the fact, however, that the Canadian market is moving gradually westwards, and the political turmoil in Québec does not enhance eastern Ontario as a manufacturing location.

Northeastern Ontario

Northeastern Ontario has a narrow economic base with a high degree of dependence on forestry and mining, and on manufacturing industries that are closely related to these two primary sectors. With a little over four per cent of provincial manufacturing workers (slightly less of value added), the region's position in this sector is weak relatively to its seven per cent share of the population.

Moreover it has been very difficult to expand or diversify in the face of a small population and isolation from other markets.

The region has excellent mineral resources, including supplies of nickel, copper, iron ore, lead, zinc and uranium (Ontario, Department of Treasury and Economics, 1971, 95–103). As a result, over half of the manufacturing workforce is involved in processing of metals and the two largest centres, Sudbury and Sault Ste. Marie owe their growth to this sector. Sudbury is mainly associated with nickel whereas Sault Ste. Marie, Canada's second steel city, is dominated by the operations of Algoma Steel. There is little processing beyond smelting and refining, and the Ontario government would like to increase processing in the north-east (Ontario, TEIGA, 1976, xiii). Hodge and Wong (1972) have examined the possibility of developing a metal-based complex in the area. They looked both at industries which supply the existing refining industries and those which use their products to a high degree. A comparative cost analysis suggested that northeastern Ontario could support a copper and brass mill, a wire and cable plant, one or two non-ferrous foundries, and a cement factory.

The forest-based manufacturing industries are less important to the area, supplying some three-fifths by value of the output of the primary metal sector. There are several large pulp and paper mills, which ship mainly to the United States market and have fairly stable production. Many of these are now quite old and they are not very competitive with British Columbia mills. Moreover they pose problems because of high pollution levels, causing a conflict between the twin desires of a clean environment and an expansion of jobs (Ontario Economic Council, 1976, 27). Wood processing is mainly carried out in smaller units and is therefore more dispersed. Its major problem is the smallness of the local market (Ontario Economic Council, 1976, 28).

Other manufacturing in the north-east is quite restricted. It is mainly geared to the local market and operates on a small scale. Food and beverage industries are most important, with the majority of plants confined to larger centres.

Although many northern centres are not very far from southern Ontario or United States markets, northern Ontario is highly peripheral in character, finding it difficult to compete in anything other than its resources. Its scattered population makes regional consumer industries difficult to establish and isolated production centres are often not very attractive to workers, so that labour difficulties are not uncommon. A harsh climate discourages population expansion despite a rugged beauty that appeals to a minority of people. The north is probably also hampered by lack of local control over its economy as well as by transport rates which are frequently held to be discriminatory (Ontario Economic Council, 1976, 14).

Northwestern Ontario

What is true for northeastern Ontario applies with greater force in the north-west. This area is even more isolated from the richest north American markets and, apart from a few larger cities, its population is widely scattered in small centres. Northwestern Ontario has less mineral wealth than the north-east and has failed to establish smelting and refining. Its minerals generally go through a beneficiation process and that is all. Thus the manufacturing sector largely consists of pulp and paper (about twice the value added of the north-east) and wood processing (less than half as important as in the north-east). These have been fairly static recently, having similar characteristics to those in the north-east (Ontario, Department of Treasury and Economics, 1970, 7–19).

Transport to western Canada does provide some business in this region, especially at Thunder Bay, which is an important transshipment point to the Great Lakes system. Also, as the largest city, Thunder Bay benefits from some of the small consumer industries. Still, in total, the north-west accounts for only about 1.6 per cent of Ontario's manufacturing activity.

POLICY

At a provincial level, manufacturing industry in Ontario is mainly the concern of the Ministry of Industry and Tourism, which administers an extensive variety of services. As in Québec, however, a different ministry is responsible for spatial planning and overall regional strategy. For over a decade, regional development has received considerable attention in Ontario and is now mainly the responsibility of the Ministry of Treasury, Economics and Intergovernmental Affairs (TEIGA), through its Regional Planning Branch. As befits Canada's most industrialized province, local authorities and development groups also have a long history of involvement in matters of industrial development. This shows itself in a high degree of independence from provincial officials which can pose problems for overall provincial objectives.

Industrial services in Ontario take a similar form to those in other provinces but are particularly well-developed. Their objective is to encourage both expansion of existing companies and the establishment of new ones (Ontario, Ministry of Industry and Tourism, no date c, 3). Specialists are available to help improve technology and productivity, research is undertaken, and information is provided about new opportunities. A trade group concentrates on the marketing aspect with a focus on overseas markets. Ontario's services are in many ways geared to the small businessman, and field offices in the province provide them close at hand. The industrial development branch is also designed to help municipalities and will provide advice on such topics as the planning of industrial parks. In addition, it helps manufacturers from overseas who wish to locate in Ontario. This service includes fairly complete guidance on plant location involving provision of data and discussion with consultants.

In the main, the work of the Ministry of Industry and Tourism is concerned with the overall economic health of the province and its services are available everywhere. Regional strategy is the concern of TEIGA, which is not to say that Industry and Tourism is uninvolved. It does in fact keep closely in touch and tries to make sure that industry's requirements are looked after. During the early 1960s, Ontario became quite concerned about regional disparities, as well as disorderly growth, which threatened environmental quality in some parts of the province. This led, in 1966, to a major policy statement by the prime minister, initiating the 'Design for Development' (Ontario, 1966). The Ontario government recognized its responsibility to provide the 'best possible environment' and 'the creation and maintenance of an atmosphere which will encourage economic growth and development throughout the province' (p. 3). The idea of comprehensive planning was accepted, involving a major effort to co-ordinate the impact of the numerous provincial ministries and agencies that affect regional development. To accomplish such co-ordination a Committee of Cabinet and an assisting Departmental Advisory Committee (composed of civil servants) were set up. In addition, the Regional Development Branch was to develop a major regional research programme. Outside the governmental structure, Regional Development Councils were to be funded in order to encourage local involvement from individuals and municipalities. Ten regions were recognized for the purpose of this programme (fig. 5.3) and a commitment was made to encourage the ministries to work towards the administrative use of these regions rather than alternatives.

In the wake of this policy statement, the most obvious result was a stepping-up of research designed to provide essential analysis to aid in regional development and the establishment of strategies for the ten regions. A detailed description of events to 1970 is provided by Thoman (1971), the first director of the Regional Development Branch. A fact-finding, or analytic, stage was to be followed by policy recommendations (Thoman, 1971, 69–73). By 1971, an analysis of several regions and two policy papers, on Northwestern Ontario (Ontario, Dept. of Treasury and Economics, 1970) and the Toronto-Centred Region (Ontario, 1970) had been published. The work was completed with substantial help and comment within the relevant regions via the Regional Economic Councils. Since that time, however, such publications have ceased.

In 1972, Design for Development, Phase Three (Ontario, 1972) modified the programme. The ten economic regions were reduced to five planning regions (see fig. 5.4), which obviously removed the need to publish studies on the basis of the former ten regions. In a sense, this reflected the earlier publication on the Toronto-Centred Region, which had in fact cut across no less than five of the economic regions and clearly suggested that they had limitations as administrative units. In 1976, the Ontario government published a revised set of policy objectives as follows:

(1) To reduce disparities among the various regions of Ontario in prosperity and access to services; and to achieve a more even distribution of growth across the province;

(2) To correct, using regional economic and social development, specific problems in the several regions, such as those arising from too narrow an economic base; to encourage each region to realize its optimum economic potential; where necessary to broaden the range of employment opportunities in regions and localities; and to maintain a minimum standard of convenience and amenity throughout all regions by improving the level of services and access to recreation where necessary;

(3) To protect and husband the natural resources of the province; and to ensure good management of the rural and forest environments;

(4) To encourage planning for the distribution of population growth

and urban development so as to ensure that the people of the province will be served by an efficient urban system; to avoid the problems of excessively rapid urban growth; and to achieve healthy, attractive urban communities.

(Ontario, TEIGA, 1976, 27–8)

Three policy and programme areas have been defined to meet these objectives – economic development, rural and resource management, and settlement and urban development. The focus of economic development policy is on the stimulation of northern and eastern Ontario, where jobs are relatively few and restricted in range, and many centres are too dependent on one industry (pp. 27–32). Policy will concentrate on developing the area's resources, diversifying mainly by further resource processing rather than by expanding other types of manufacturing. Industry will be encouraged to cluster in larger centres and local entrepreneurs will be helped. Ontario's agreements with the Department of Regional Economic Expansion reflect this concern for the north and east, being concerned exclusively with these parts of the province (Canada, DREE, 1975).

The revised policy enunciated in 1976 also takes a province-wide approach to the urban system, with the twin objectives of improving the delivery of services and achieving more balanced urban growth across the province (Ontario, TEIGA, 1976, 41–50). This appears to be an extension of approaches developed earlier. The Northwestern strategy (Ontario, Dept. of Treasury and Economics, 1970), for example, included various levels of growth centre while that for the Toronto-Centred Region (Ontario, 1970) was concerned with reducing pressures on the western Lake Ontario lakeshore. An important element of the concept is to strengthen centres other than Toronto: to this end a number of preferred centres have been designated (fig. 5.5). There are four major regional centres (Thunder Bay, London, Kingston and Ottawa) with one to follow in northeastern Ontario, plus several sub-regional ones. These are to be developed as service centres. The policy statement also mentions economic growth but indicates that not all centres (even Regional Centres) will be given special treatment in this respect. It is made clear that the overall strategy for southern Ontario has not been agreed upon (p. 49).

Clearly, to the extent that such provincial policies are im-

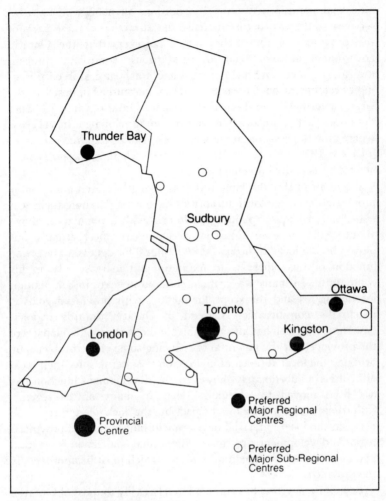

Figure 5.5   Urban System Concept For Ontario.
              Source: Ontario, TEIGA (1976)

plemented, they will have considerable bearing upon the location of
manufacturing in Ontario. Northern and eastern Ontario are
already being favoured by the agreements with DREE (involving
both services and direct grants to manufacturers), loan policies
under provincial development corporations[1], and the provincial

[1]See Ontario, Ministry of Industry and Tourism pamphlets (no date a) and (no date
b).

industrial parks programme. In addition, all policies to improve
services and infrastructure increase the attraction of these parts of
the province. It should be noted, however, that the Ontario
government has not been prepared to use controls to prevent
industrial growth and has not even had much success in encouraging development on the eastern side of Toronto as opposed to the
west. Nevertheless, in discussing southern Ontario, the 1976 paper
does note that 'more stringent controls on development in the areas
where growth pressures are now greatest' will be required (Ontario,
TEIGA, 1976, 49). It remains to be seen whether, in fact, such a
statement is really implemented.

While all of this thinking and re-thinking has been going on at
provincial level, the local authorities have been pursuing their own
policies. Most municipalities in Ontario with a population above
about 20,000 have an industrial development officer, usually employed by the local authority (see Chapter 8 for details). The prime
function of this officer is to maintain and increase jobs in his
community. In many ways, then, communities are in competition
for businesses and the scope for conflict with provincial goals is
potentially considerable. A trend in Ontario towards regional
government, which has affected many of the more populated parts of
the province, has the potential of reducing some of the problems by
bringing the local authorities in a region together to solve their local
difficulties. Unfortunately, however, the development function has
not been moved to a regional level in many of the regions.
Co-ordination is not being helped by the lack of a direct link
between the local industrial development officer and the provincial
regional development strategists. The formal connection is via local
planners through the medium of plans, which must be approved by
the province.

Economic progress has come relatively easily to most of Ontario.
In periods of economic growth, a high degree of independence
amongst authorities concerned with industrial development has
worked well. Given Canada's relatively weak competitive situation
at the present time, however, a more concerted effort will be needed.
In particular, the weak interaction between provincial and local
government authorities should be remedied and the jealousies which
hinder a province-wide approach to economic development be
overcome.

REFERENCES

Arathoon, D. N. (1974), 'Evaluating the economic impact of an industrial development programme: an application to Saltfleet Township', in D. F. Walker and J. H. Bater (1974), 231–90.

Bater, J. H. and Walker, D. F. (1971a), 'The industrial structure of Midwestern Ontario', in A. G. McLellan (ed.) *The Waterloo County Area: Selected Essays*. (Waterloo: University of Waterloo, Department of Geography), 147–57.

Bater J. H. and Walker , D. F. (1971b), *The Linkage Study of the Hamilton Metal Industries*. Hamilton: Hamilton Planning Department, Hamilton Chamber of Commerce and Hamilton Economic Development Commission.

Bater J. H. and Walker, D. F. (1974a), 'Aspects of industrial linkage: the example of the Hamilton metal-working complex', *Révue de géographie de Montréal*, 28, 3, 233–43.

Bater J. H. and Walker, D. F. (1974b), 'Foreign ownership and industrial linkage', in D. F. Walker and J. H. Bater (1974), 101–25.

Blackbourn, A. (1969), 'Locational patterns of American-owned industry in Southern Ontario', Unpublished Ph.D. Dissertation, University of Toronto.

Bland, W. (1970), 'The changing locational pattern of manufacturing in Southern Ontario from 1881 to 1932', Unpublished Ph.D. Dissertation, University of Indiana.

Canada, DREE, (Department of Regional Economic Expansion) (1975), *Summaries of General Development Agreements and Subsidiary Agreements, Federal-Provincial*. Ottawa.

Collins, L. (1972) *Industrial Migration in Ontario*. Ottawa: Statistics Canada.

Ford, R. W. (1976), *A History of the Chemical Industry in Lambton County*. Revised Edition, Sarnia: R. W. Ford.

Friedmann, J. (1966), *Regional Development Policy: A Case Study of Venezuela*. Cambridge, Mass.: M.I.T. Press

Gilmour, J. M. (1966), 'A joint anarchy of confidentiality and definitional change', *Canadian Geographer*, 10, 1, 40–8.

Gilmour, J. M. (1972), *Spatial Evolution of Manufacturing: Southern Ontario, 1851–1891*. Toronto: University of Toronto Press.

Hodge, G. and Wong, C.C. (1972), 'Adapting industrial complex analysis to the realities of regional data', *Papers, Regional Science Association*, 145–66.

Houston, S. R. (1973), 'Analysis of intracity industrial location: London, Ontario', Unpublished B.A. Essay, University of Western Ontario.

Isard, W. (1960) *Methods of Regional Analysis: An Introduction to Regional Science*. Cambridge, Mass: M.I.T. Press.

Jackson, J. and White, L. (1971), *The Industrial Structure of the Niagara Peninsula*. St Catharines: Brock University, Department of Geography.

Kerr, D. and Spelt, J. (1958) 'Manufacturing in suburban Toronto', *Canadian Geographer*, 12, 11–9.

Kerr, D. and Spelt, J. (1960), 'Some aspects of industrial location in Southern Ontario', *Canadian Geographer*, 15, 12–25.

Kerr, D. and Spelt, J. (1965), *The Changing Face of Toronto*. Ottawa: Queen's Printer.

Middleton, D. J. (1978), 'Industrial entrepreneurship in Hamilton, 1871 –1911', Unpublished B.E.S. Essay, University of Waterloo.

Mock, D. R. (1976), *Economic Linkages of the 'Communication Oriented' Industries in Metropolitan Toronto*. Toronto: City of Toronto Planning Board.

Nelles, H. V. (1974), *The Politics of Development: Forest, Mines and Hydro –electric Power in Ontario, 1849–1941*. Toronto: Macmillan.

Odell, Diane (1975), 'Suburbanization of industry: A case study of London' Ontario', Unpublished B.E.S. Honours Essay, University of Waterloo.

Ontario (1966), *Design for Development: Statement by the Prime Minister of the Province of Ontario on Regional Development Policy*. Toronto.

Ontario (1970), *Design for Development: The Toronto-Centred Region*. Toronto.

Ontario (1972), *Design for Development: Phase Three*. Toronto.

Ontario, Department of Treasury and Economics (1970), *Design for Development: Northwestern Region. Phase 2: Policy Recommendations*. Toronto.

Ontario, Department of Treasury and Economics (1971), *Design for Development: Northeastern Ontario Development Region. Analysis: Phase 1*. Toronto.

Ontario, Legislative Assembly (1974), *Foreign Ownership: Corporate Behaviour and Public Attitudes. Overview Report*. Toronto: Select Committee on Economic and Cultural Nationalism of the Legislative Assembly.

Ontario, Ministry of Industry and Tourism (no date a), *Financial Services Programs Administered by the Eastern Ontario Development Corporation*. Toronto.

Ontario, Ministry of Industry and Tourism (no date b), *Financial Services Programs Administered by the Northern Ontario Development Corporation*. Toronto.

Ontario, Ministry of Industry and Tourism (no date c), *Ministry Services*. Toronto.

Ontario, TEIGA (Ministry of Treasury, Economics and Intergovernmental Affairs) (1976) *Design for Development: Ontario's Future Trends and Options*. Toronto.

Ontario, TEIGA, (1976), *Design for Development. Northeastern Ontario. A Proposed Planning and Development Strategy*. Toronto: Regional Planning Branch.

Ontario Economic Council (1976), *Northern Ontario Development: Issues and Alternatives*. Toronto.

Parker, H. A. (1976),'Services linkages of selected metal-working firms in Cambridge, Ontario', Unpublished M. A. Thesis, University of Waterloo.

Ray, D. M. (1965), *Market Potential and Economic Shadow*. Chicago: University of Chicago, Department of Geography.

Rusling, J. R. (1974), 'Factors influencing the location of manufacturing activity in Cambridge, Ontario, in D. F. Walker and J. H. Bater (1974), 145–66.

Sarnia and District Commercial and Industrial Development Commission (1977), *The Industries of Canada's Chemical Valley*. Sarnia.

Spelt, J. (1972), *Urban Development in South-Central Ontario*. Toronto: McClelland and Stewart.

Staple, M. G. (1975), 'The extent and intensity of metropolitan influence in Eastern Ontario', Unpublished M.A. Thesis, University of Waterloo.

Thoman, R. S. (1971), *Design for Development in Ontario: The Initiation of a Regional Planning Program*. Toronto: Allister Typesetting and Graphics.

Toronto, City of, Planning Board (1971a), *Report on Industry 1: Survey of the Western Area*. Toronto.

Toronto, City of, Planning Board (1971b), *Report on Industry 2: Survey of the Central Area*. Toronto.

Toronto, City of, Planning Board (1973), *Report on Industry 3: Northern and Eastern Areas*. Toronto.

Toronto, City of, Planning Board (1974), *A Place for Industry*. Toronto.

Toronto, City of, Planning Board (1975), *Industrial Relocation and its Impact on Employees*. Toronto.

Toronto, City of, Planning Board (1976), *The City's Attractiveness for Industry*. Toronto.

Walker, D. F. (1971a), 'The energy sources of manufacturing industry in Southern Ontario, 1871–1921', *Ontario Geography*, 6, 56–66.

Walker D. F. (1971b), 'Transportation of coal into Southern Ontario, 1871–1921', *Ontario History*, 63, 15–30.

Walker, D. F. (1974), 'Energy and industrial location in Southern Ontario, 1871–1921', in D. F. Walker and J. H. Bater (1974), 41–68.

Walker, D. F. and Bater J. H. (1972), 'Industrial development planning: the example of Saltfleet Township', *Plan Canada*, 11, 3, 217–27.

Walker D. F. and Bater, J. H. (1974), *Industrial Development in Southern Ontario*. Waterloo: University of Waterloo, Department of Geography.

Watson, J. W. (1945), 'Geography of the Niagara Peninsula', Unpublished Ph.D. Dissertation, University of Toronto.

Wong, C. C. (1969), 'The spatial structure of manufacturing industries in Ontario', *Ontario Geography*, 4, 45–55.

Wood, P. A. (1974), 'Urban manufacturing: A view from the fringe', in James H. Johnson (ed.) *Suburban Growth*(London: John Wiley), 129–54.

6

The Prairie Provinces

One hundred years ago, Canada's Prairie Provinces – Manitoba, Saskatchewan and Alberta – were virtually uninhabited by the white man. There were a few settlers in the east, but, apart from the fact that many animals had been drastically reduced by fur traders, this vast territory was still in an almost entirely natural state (Nelson, 1972, 38–43). Agricultural settlement on a large scale took place only after completion of the first transcontinental railway in 1886, a great deal of experimentation on crops and farm management (designed to counteract the short growing season and low precipitation), reduced freight rates on grain to Liverpool and the stemming of a long decline in wheat prices after 1897 (Proudfoot, 1972, 52–3). The early twentieth century was a period of great expansion, with population rising from 419,512 in 1901 to 1,328,121 in 1911 and nearly 2 million in 1921. Such recent development took place mainly under the direction of federal government policy within the context of an already industrialized Ontario and Québec. The dependency relationships built up early in the century are a source of great concern today, being at the heart of all discussion and controversy about western economic development.

The three Prairie provinces have their own individual characteristics. In the east, Manitoba's head start on settlement was accompanied by Winnipeg's establishment as a major transport and service centre for the whole of the West. While it has now lost some of its territory and suffered under competition from Calgary and Edmonton (Burghardt, 1971), Winnipeg retains a more diverse manufacturing base than other Prairie cities and Manitoba has a higher proportion of its workers in manufacturing than do the other provinces. Saskatchewan, the most rural of the provinces, is still highly dependent on wheat. Its population has been declining absolutely since the mid-1960s and out-migration remains considerable. Unlike Saskatchewan and Manitoba, which are below the Canadian average in income levels, Alberta is one of the country's richest provinces. Petroleum and natural gas have almost revolutionized the Albertan economy since 1947, when the Leduc field was found. Moreover, the province is also rich in coal so that energy resources should assure Alberta's prosperity for many years. It has 89 per cent of Canada's proved crude oil reserves, 80 per cent of natural gas and about 28 per cent of coal (Alberta, Dept. of Business Development and Tourism, 1975, 73–4). In consequence, population has been growing rapidly and the major cities, Edmonton and Calgary, have been expanded and transformed by the new prosperity.

Despite these differences, however, the three provinces have much in common. They share the Prairie region with its vast potential for agriculture; each has a forested northern area with a large native population; all three are effectively landlocked for most of the year (despite Hudson's Bay); they are a long way from those population centres which constitute large markets and rely on common transport connections to reach them; settlement is sparse. Moreover, the historical development of the West was completed at much the same time and by the same process across the whole region. Lastly, there are many kinship relationships in the Prairies, especially between Manitoba and Saskatchewan residents and relations who have moved westwards to Alberta over the years. Today, these common features manifest themselves in similar complaints, hopes and policies in all three provinces.

Economically, the Prairie provinces are vulnerable because of an excessive dependence on primary products. The fortunes of wheat affect the whole economy perceptibly, especially in Saskatchewan. While the base has now widened - to more varied crops, metals, potash, oil and natural gas, and coal – these primary products are still sold mainly in world markets, which are subject to severe cyclical trends. One review concludes:

Yet, while the pace of growth and change has been extensive, the basic elements of the economy have remained the same. The west is still a region heavily dependent on resource development, on primary processing, on trade with other regions and other countries and on the importing of its basic items for industry and people. It exports most of its grain, oil and gas, ore and wood and imports most of its machinery, clothes, appliances and transportation vehicles.

(Canada, DREE, 1973a, 18)

The obverse of the importance of the primary activities on the

Canadian Prairies is the weakness of the manufacturing sector. The secondary sector is only half as important as in Canada as a whole (Barr, 1972, 70), which means that many manufactured goods are imported into the region. As the West developed relatively late, Ontario and Québec manufacturers established a hold on western markets which they have retained to the present day. Prairie manufacturing has mainly been stimulated by resource development. While growth in regional demand has encouraged manufacturing and branch plant development in some sectors, the range and scale of activities remain small.

Although the Prairie region is still highly dependent on primary activities, it can no longer be characterized as farm-based and rural. Since the 1930s, radical changes have taken place as a result of increased mining, oil and gas development and farm mechanization. Rural-urban migration has been considerable, leading to a fast growth of the cities (except for Winnipeg, the five largest all at least doubled in population from 1941 to 1971). Very rapid growth of Calgary and Edmonton as a result of Alberta's mineral developments means that Winnipeg's earlier dominant position is now challenged. Calgary and Edmonton grew respectively from 93,000 and 98,000 in 1941 to 458,000 and 543,000 in 1976, while Winnipeg moved from 300,000 to roughly 571,000 in the same period.

A recent study of freight flows illustrates the economic structure of the Prairies very well. Thompson (1977) examined both rail and truck movements, using data from a one per cent sample taken in 1971 for rail, and the results of a one-week analysis of trucks in May, 1973. The data were not perfect but are adequate to show the overall picture. Thompson factor-analysed the data on tonnages, using flows between seventeen cities plus those to the east and west but not to the United States. Rail carried about 55 per cent of all freight and showed a relatively simple three-factor pattern, illustrated in figure 6.1. Movements were predominantly out from the region, with the west coast (especially Vancouver) a more important destination than the east. The figure shows clearly that the Prairies are largely carved up into two supply zones. Thompson suggests that the region does 'not constitute a functionally integrated unit or a single system of towns but represents two peripheral areas joined to the east and west respectively' (p.154).

Road transport provides the intra-regional connections. In fact, much of its business is transacted within provincial boundaries

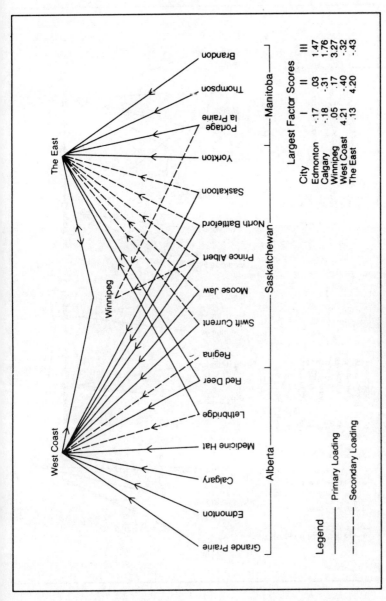

Largest Factor Scores

City	I	II	III
Edmonton	-.17	.03	1.47
Calgary	-.18	-.31	1.76
Winnipeg	.05	.17	3.27
West Coast	4.21	-.40	-.32
The East	.13	4.20	-.43

Legend

—— Primary Loading

---- Secondary Loading

Figure 6.1   Degraph of Rail Tonnage Flows in the Prairies.
Source: R. R. Thompson (1977)

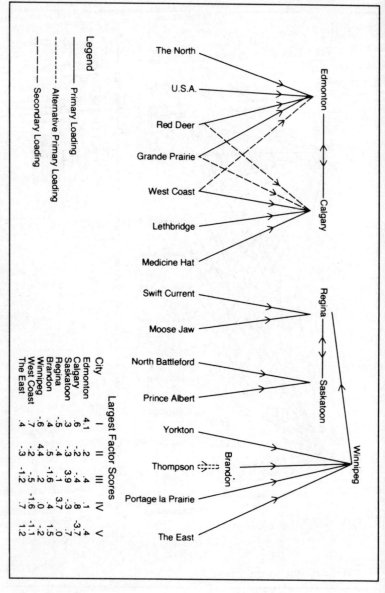

Figure 6.2   Degraph of Road Tonnage Flows in the Prairies.
Source: R. R. Thompson (1977)

(Thompson, 1977, 158). The diagram of flows for road tonnages provides a complete contrast to that for rail (figure 6.2), so that Thompson in this case argues, 'the Prairies do not constitute a single functional unit, but rather, consists of three separate functional units divided by the provincial boundaries' (p.162). Thompson's study included a more complex multidimensional diadic factor analysis of the main flow movements for particular commodities. The simpler cases outlined here, however, present the main elements of the freight pattern and illustrate the most important elements of the region's spatial interactions.

MANUFACTURING IN THE PRAIRIES

Manufacturing employment in the region has been expanding for several decades. In 1975, the 139,000 total represented an increase of about 50 per cent over 1961. Value added by manufacturing industry rose almost four times in the same period. This growth, however, has done little to strengthen the Prairies' role in manufacturing in Canada, which stands at eight per cent of employment and value added as compared to nearly 17 per cent of population. In addition, diversification has remained very limited.

Table 6.1 shows the continued importance of the food and beverage group to the Prairie Provinces. In fact, of the twenty most important industries (three and four digit categories of the SIC), no fewer than one half are within the food and beverage group. In value added, slaughtering and meat processing is by far the most important, followed by dairy products.

Given the importance of primary activities in the Prairie Provinces, it is not surprising that so much manufacturing is closely related to the resource base. From the earliest years, agriculture has provided raw materials so that butter and cheese were both processed by 1880, flour milling was the first significant industry in Manitoba in 1882–3, livestock were slaughtered and processed locally in the early years of the settlement and, as new crops were added, processing usually followed (Appana, 1975, 38–45). Similarly, mining led to oil refining and petrochemicals, mainly in Alberta, and to processing of metals at such centres as Lynn Lake, Flin Flon and Thompson on the Canadian Shield in northern Saskatchewan and northern Manitoba. The timber resources of the north encouraged sawmilling from the early twentieth century. While the first

TABLE 6.1
PRAIRIE PROVINCES:
PRINCIPAL STATISTICS BY INDUSTRY GROUP, 1975

	No. of Establishments	Employees No.	%	Value of Shipments $000	Value Added $000	%
Food and beverage industries	866	32,310	23.3	3,309,585	760,649	24.0
Tobacco products industries	—	—	—	—	—	—
Rubber and plastics product industries	72	*	*	*	*	*
Leather industries	32	*	*	*	*	*
Textile industries	77	1,815	1.3	60,760	26,458	0.8
Knitting Mills	6	*	*	*	*	*
Clothing industries	133	*	*	*	*	*
Wood industries	308	9,164	6.6	415,397	159,642	5.0
Furniture and fixture industries	218	3,736	2.7	117,023	56,964	1.8
Paper and allied industries	52	*	*	*	*	*
Printing, Publishing and allied industries	530	10,364	7.5	291,895	191,728	6.0
Primary Metal industries	44	*'	*	*	*	*
Metal fabricating industries	415	12,752	9.2	618,842	303,246	9.6
Machinery industries	157	10,623	7.7	471,488	204,791	6.5
Transportation equipment industries	127	10,536	7.6	422,207	182,479	5.8
Electrical products industries	53	4,459	3.2	188,002	84,802	2.7
Non-metallic mineral products industries	187	6,600	4.8	377,130	217,384	6.9
Petroleum and coal products	30	*	*	*	*	*
Chemical and chemical products industries	87	4,413	3.2	421,532	181,468	5.7
Miscellaneous manufacturing industries	295	3,378	2.4	77,384	46,515	1.5
Total all industries	3,689	138,901	78.5	9,274,839	3,173,929	76.3

* Not available due to confidentiality restrictions.

newsprint mill was opened in 1927 at Pine Falls, Manitoba (Appana, 1975, 55), it is only recently that pulp and paper has expanded at such centres as The Pas, Manitoba, Prince Albert, Saskatchewan, and Hinton and Grande Prairie, Alberta. A long period of maturation reduces the value of the timber in the northern climate and hindered earlier exploitation. In summary, then, the materials supplied by the primary sector have clearly been an important influence on the location of manufacturing in the Prairies.

The demands of the primary sector have also encouraged manufacturing. Implements and fertilizers for farms, and steel pipe and building equipment for the oil industry are probably the best examples of this type of linkage. The supply of capital equipment to the resource sector constitutes a major theme in Prairie manufacturing, and one which will continue to hold attention. Quite apart from the need for construction materials and mobile homes (for construction workers), a wide range of metal and machinery products is required and there are numerous specialized demands connected to oil and gas exploration and production. It is the latter sector and the pipelines which accompany it which promise a continuous, sustained demand for a long time to come.

Many consumer industries are, or have been, linked to resource developments as well as being encouraged by the general growth of western markets. Winnipeg's apparel industry, for example, initially provided work clothes. It soon diversified and continued to expand until the 1950s (Hastie, 1974, 131–4). Mobile and modular homes, which are vital to the construction business, also are built for normal housing requirements and for the tourist trade (McEwen, 1976). On balance, though, the limited size of western Canadian markets is still considered to be a major problem for manufacturing development. It means that, commonly, distant markets must be penetrated for successful operation. Exceptionally, this has been accomplished: for example, aerospace and aircraft components and buses in Manitoba (Appana, 1975, 63; Kuz, 1974, 71),[1] specialized mining apparatus in Alberta and mobile homes in Alberta. Apart from resource-based products, however, the examples are few and far between. Lack of success is blamed on freight rates by many Westerners. The topic constitutes one of the major arguments with central Canada and Ottawa. It is generally considered that rates are set to encourage raw materials to move east with as little processing as possible.

In the past, western complaints have often been shrugged off but some recent studies have established the validity of the case on transport. The Hall Commission on Grain Handling and Transportation examined the charge that freight rates discriminated against

[1] These industries are currently facing severe problems.

the West in a very detailed study of four industries – flour milling, rapeseed crushing, livestock production and processing, and malting. In each case, the Commission found extra charges for western producers and/or special benefits that encouraged the raw material to move east. Strong conclusions included:

> An analysis of freight structures confirms that the prairie provinces have been victimized by disciminatory freight rates from the beginning. (Canada, Grain Handling and Transportation Commission, 1977, 273)

and

> The transportation system which was developed to open the West has served well but some of the policies associated with transportation have permitted the system to continue to drain the West of employment and development opportunities. (pp. 274–5)

Another report, by the Economic Council of Canada (1977, 199 –200), also supports the view that the rate structure artificially lowers the level of manufacturing by setting very low rates from the Prairies on raw materials as compared to manufactured goods. It seems likely that some changes will be made in the near future given the weight of the evidence and the strength of the political pressure on this issue.

Even without discrimination the considerable distance to markets will have to be faced. A study covering a range of manufacturing activities has attempted to estimate the extra transport costs involved in a Prairie as opposed to an eastern Canadian location (M.P.S. Associates Ltd., 1975). Thirteen industries in four categories were considered, in line with suggestions for potential growth by Canada's Department of Regional Economic Expansion in 1973. These categories were:

(1) Increased processing of primary materials
(2) Materials and equipment for the resource industries
(3) More sophisticated products
(4) Transportation, distribution and service functions.

The results of comparisons of representative locations in central Canada and the Prairies showed that for food industries, transport costs were lower in the Prairies because of the cost of material inputs. Cost of shipments were higher for Prairie manufacturers (p. 54). For other products, however, costs in the Prairies were considerably higher on both materials and outputs (pp. 55–9). On average over all industries, transport costs were some 26 per cent lower in central Canada. In non-charge (quality of service) elements (such as reliability, equipment, materials handling, variety of modes), larger Prairie centres are well endowed (pp. 85–96). Nevertheless the report concluded, 'It is evident that for many industries there is a transportation cost penalty in locating industries in the Prairies versus central Canada – particularly if they wish to serve more than a local market' (p. 109). Even in serving local markets, the cost of transporting materials in most cases more than outweighs the savings on shipments.

It is clear then that the Prairie Provinces do face some major locational disadvantages in manufacturing. It could be argued that Alberta's strength in energy will prove a major attraction but, given the cost of energy relative to other production costs and the ease with which it can be transported, it is not likely that much manufacturing will locate at energy sources. Alberta is even finding it difficult to develop the petrochemical industry in the way that was thought possible only five years ago.

Strangely enough, in a region where manufacturing is relatively unimportant, the labour situation has also become difficult in the Prairies. With so many well-paid opportunities in the primary sector, manufacturers frequently find labour in short supply and expensive. Even in 1978, with high unemployment levels across Canada, the labour market is tight in Alberta. Shortages of skilled labour across the Prairies are expected to become quite severe in the near future, especially if immigration is reduced by federal policy (Bill C24). Further, the limited manufacturing tradition in the region means that many special skills are lacking. All in all, 'industrial expansion presently underway and planned for the region (including British Columbia) over the next decade will place severe strains upon the western Canadian labour market' (Canada, DREE, 1976, 25).

Finally, two other concerns have relevance to the manufacturing sector across the region. It is frequently complained that financial institutions make it more difficult to obtain capital in the Prairies than in Ontario and Québec. In fact, the eastern-owned banks have often been accused of draining capital from the region (*Financial Times of Canada*, 1973). Since finance became a political issue in the early 1970s, some improvements seem to have been made, but the region still lacks institutions that can supply venture capital (Canada, DREE, 1976, 27). Just as regionally-controlled financial institutions are limited, so too are entrepreneurs and Prairie-owned manufacturing companies. Economic control by the West over its own affairs is limited by these ownership patterns but they are proving hard to break. There are some important western companies but, apart from the case of food-processing, most of them are only of local significance and tend to be concentrated in the few sectors in which Prairies manufacturing is strong. The difficulty is in finding entrepreneurs to play a role in diversification. All three provincial governments, however, have taken equity positions in a number of manufacturing operations and this is one response to the limitations of the local private sector. The other, as will be noted below, is to provide special services and encouragements for the local entrepreneur.

Manitoba

As noted above, Manitoba was the first area of the Prairies to be settled. Winnipeg's businessmen were extremely aggressive in establishing its pre-eminence in the pre-World War I years (Artibise, 1975, 60–125). They made sure that rail developments gave Winnipeg a nodal position by about 1890 and allowed it to expand as a gateway to the Prairies from the east (Burghardt, 1971, 273–6). Also obtained were certain rate concessions, which strengthened this position. These covered both goods shipped from Winnipeg (15% discount on shipments to the west in 1886) and items coming from the east (1890). In 1897, rates were arranged in such a way that Winnipeg wholesalers would not pay higher rates than if goods were shipped directly to western points from the east (Bellan, 1958, 92–3, 135–7). As a result, Winnipeg's wholesaleing and distribution functions gained tremendous strength and manufacturing was also stimulated.

An early start has allowed Manitoba to build a more diverse manufacturing base than the other Prairie provinces. It is no longer the largest, having been overtaken by Alberta's in value added around 1955 and employment around 1967 (Appana, 1975, 72). Manufacturing in the province is in fact growing slowly and becoming relatively less important. Winnipeg with over 43,000 employees retains its position as the largest manufacturing centre in the Prairies but it is being challenged by Edmonton and Calgary. By western standards, however, Manitoba can still boast of variety.

The food and beverage group employs about one-fifth of Manitoba's manufacturing workers and creates a slightly higher proportion of provincial value added. It has been important from the first and many items are shipped out of the province (Bellan, 1958, 19–52; Manitoba, Department of Industry and Commerce, 1977, 14). The largest industry in this group is slaughtering and meat packing but there is a wide variety of products based on farm output. At one time, Manitoba was able to draw its materials from all over the Prairies but as processing developed further west, supplies became more restricted (Parliament, 1974, 31–2). They still come from Saskatchewan but reductions from that source can be expected as a result of efforts to increase the manufacturing sector there. Manitoba will be forced to rely on its own resources so that food and beverage industries will probably remain fairly stable in the future.

Metal and machinery groups in combination are slightly more important to Manitoba than food and beverages, producing a little over a quarter of the value added in manufacturing. Primary metal industries consist of the processing of Manitoba's metal ores, which are then mainly exported. Metal fabricating and machinery industries, however, are largely geared to the provincial and regional market. Materials (semi-processed metals) must usually be brought in from Ontario. Transport equipment is also largely metal-based and was initiated to supply local markets, particularly the railroads (Appana, 1975, 47). This group, which employs over 10 per cent of Manitoba's manufacturing workers, has succeeded in penetrating export markets with aircraft components and buses (Manitoba, Dept. of Industry and Commerce, 1977, 18).

Manitoba has also developed a significant clothing industry. In this respect, Winnipeg ranks third in Canada behind Montréal and Toronto. Textiles and clothing employ about 16 per cent of the province's manufacturing employees but account for only some eight per cent of value added. The industry started in the 1870s and expanded in the twentieth century. Since about 1951, partly as a result of Canada's difficulty in competing with imports, there has been instability. In addition, labour has been in short supply and has become more expensive (Hastie, 1974, 131–9). The industry, however, has rationalized. Firms have become larger, considerable modernization has taken place and there has been a modification of product emphasis. About 85 per cent of total production is shipped outside the province, not just to the West but also to other Canadian provinces and to the United States (Manitoba, Dept. of Industry and Commerce, 1977, 14–6).

Other groups which add to the range of industrial activities to a significant degree are printing and publishing, non-metallic mineral products, electrical products, chemicals and furniture.

SPATIAL PATTERN

Within Manitoba, Winnipeg dominates manufacturing to a higher degree than it does population: two-thirds of manufacturing employment is in the capital (Manitoba, 1973, 121). Apart from food and beverages, primary metals, wood processing and pulp and paper, most industrial groups are largely confined to the metropolitan area. In order of importance, Winnipeg's major industries include food and beverages, clothing, printing and publishing, metal fabricating and transport equipment. Thus there is good balance between durables and non-durables, consumer and producer goods. As the West developed in the twentieth century, Winnipeg's strategic gateway location diminished in importance, leading to a drastic decline in wholesaleing and distribution from the 1920s (Burghardt, 1971, 273–6). In manufacturing, however, the city has retained considerable strength. It still has more than the manufacturing employment of Edmonton and Calgary combined. Nevertheless the challenge from further west is stepping up and Winnipeg's sector is growing slowly.

The larger industrial areas within Winnipeg are shown on figure 6.3. An older central area (1) just north of the downtown core was once the base for the garment industry as well as wholesaleing and other light manufacturing. It has been declining, however, and the large garment firms have moved out to Lord Selkirk (5). East of the Red River, an extensive industrial area (2) includes the packing houses of St. Boniface, the rail shops of Transcona, farm machinery, heavy and light metal works and bus manufacturing. This area is well served by rail and includes a fairly new industrial park, which is still not much utilized. Around the airport (3) is the aerospace industry as well as an extensive wholesaleing area with some metal goods. Fort Garry (4) similarly has wholesaleing, metal and light products although just to the west (6) is a heavy industrial area concentrating on such items as cement and lime. Lastly a small area in Kildonan (7) has light industry including mini-computers. All in

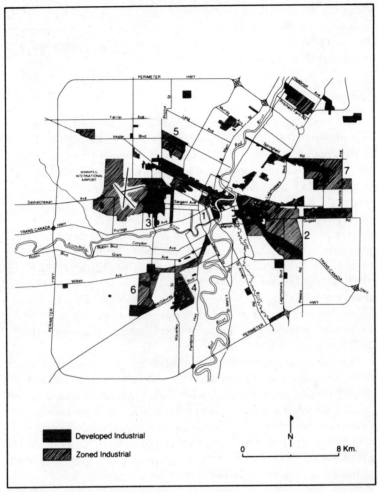

Figure 6.3   Winnipeg's Industrial Areas.
Source: Winnipeg Economic Development Board; Economic Development Map of the City of Winnipeg, 1973

all, Winnipeg's industry is reasonably spread across the metropolis rather than being overly concentrated in one sector.

Apart from the processing of provincial resources, little manufacturing exists outside Winnipeg. The historical development of the province, the transport pattern and the large size of the metropolitan area relative to other cities all help to explain this fact. Most other places are confined to a narrow range of activities such as smelting of

nickel at Thompson or copper, zinc and lead at Flin Flon, forest
industries at The Pas, or food processing and farm implements in
the southern cities. Even the second largest place, Brandon, has
found it difficult to diversify.

Saskatchewan

The total number of manufacturing workers in Saskatchewan is
only about 18,000. The province is the epitome of the popular image
of the Prairies: a land of vast numbers of farms and farmers, with a
large rural population and many small towns and villages. Although
it is Canada's most agricultural province, mechanization has reduced the number of farms and encouraged a rural exodus of very
large proportions. In fact, migration has not only been to Saskatchewan's two largest cities, Regina and Saskatoon, but right out of the
province. Provincial population declined from the mid-1930s
through to 1951 and again in the late 1960s and early 1970s. In
1971, for the first time, Saskatchewan's population was more urban
than rural but the economy was still 'principally resource-based,
highly capital intensive' and dependent 'in large measure on its
mainstay – agriculture – for future performance' (Canada, DREE,
1973b, 3).

Not surprisingly, the food and beverage processing industries
form the major manufacturing sector, with almost one-third of both
employees and value added. A fairly wide range of activities is found
in this sector, including meat-packing, dairies, flour-milling and
breweries. All other groups are quite small and relatively unimportant except for steel. The Interprovincial Steel and Pipe Corporation
(IPSCO) in Regina uses scrap to produce skelp, pipe and some
plate. It is western Canada's largest steel producer, has plants in
Alberta, and is expected to expand under a joint Federal-Provincial
subsidiary agreement. If pipeline developments take place, IPSCO
stands to benefit substantially. Although there are some important
ties to other Prairie Provinces, there is little linkage between
manufacturing industries within Saskatchewan. Either they process
raw materials and ship directly to the market, or they import
materials to make finished products such as clothing or farm
machinery.

The early 1970s have seen some definite improvements as a result
mainly of the development of numerous, small, often locally-owned

plants. Between 1971 and 1975, manufacturing accounted for a quarter of the increase in the Saskatchewan labour force. The major gains were in wood products, agricultural implements, clothing, transport equipment and electrical products (Saskatchewan Department of Industry and Commerce, no date, 7–8).

Buckley's (1965) analysis of manufacturing in Saskatchewan is still largely applicable today. She examined twelve specific industries in some detail. Despite the agricultural character of the province, she noted the limited range of products available for the food processing industry, the irregularity of supply because of part-time farming, and the lack of a guaranteed quality of output as a result of small producers (pp. 55–6). Other materials for manufacturing were very limited in range (p. 57). As a result of a long period of underdevelopment, Saskatchewan lacked suppliers and industrial service operations (p.60), and people's attitudes were generally not geared to industrial development (p.60). Attitudes have changed somewhat in the last decade but Buckley's other points are still valid. Moreover, she notes the short supply of local entrepreneurs and the fact that branch plant developments frequently work against Saskatchewan's interests (pp.58–9). These conclusions were based on a study of only industries which seemed to have real potential in the province. More generally, she reflected that:

> the small market, the limited range of raw materials, the long haul to eastern markets and from eastern suppliers: all these must be set against the more favourable conditions in most other regions. (p.18)

Spatial Pattern

The manufacturing sector is concentrated mainly in the two largest centres. Both of them have strong trade and service functions. Regina is the provincial capital. It has the steel plant, the employment in which is usually about 1400, several food and beverage firms, and a variety of small and medium-sized operations in many sectors. Saskatoon, the university centre, is dominated by food and beverages. Located there are several quite large plants in this sector, producing items based on milk, flour and grains, and meat. The largest of the other sectors (by employment) in Saskatoon are textiles and printing. The city benefits from potash mining in the neighbourhood and could soon be the location of a uranium refinery based on the output of northern Saskatchewan's mines. It gained quite a high proportion of the province's manufacturing growth in the 1960s and developments in the 1970s have aided diversification. Its manufacturing sector, however, is still distinctly smaller than Regina's. A recent report argues that development should aid the city and that chemical industries have definite prospects. The main problems concern shortages of entrepreneurs and skilled labour (Underwood McLellan and Associates Ltd. and Jellicoe Resources Associates Ltd., 1975, xviii–xxii).

Alberta

Rapid growth of manufacturing in Alberta since the Second World War has given it the largest sector amongst the Prairie Provinces, with a value added about half as large again as that of Manitoba. Relative to total provincial output, however, manufacturing plays a smaller role in Alberta than in Manitoba. Until the Leduc oil discovery, the province relied heavily on its farm sector, and manufacturing was dominated by food processing. Other industries were geared to provincial demands – construction materials, metal products, farm machinery, for example – and were small in scale. The requirements of the oil and gas sector and the fast population growth consequent upon its development have provided the stimulus for the advances of the last thirty years. Events in the north are expected to maintain a similar expansionary climate in the future.

Despite all the recent changes, Alberta remains quite dependent on the food and beverage industries. They employ about one quarter of manufacturing workers and produce only a fractionally smaller proportion of value added. Alberta's large area of agricultural land (almost 30% of Canada's) and varied farm production provide a solid material base for these industries, of which slaughtering and meat packing is the most important, followed by dairies and the production of animal feed (Alberta, Dept. of Business Development and Tourism, 1975, 35). New products are added as farm production is modified: rapeseed crushing, for example, has developed recently. Although some products (e.g. beer, baked goods) are shipped to local markets, about one-third of production moves out of Alberta (Barr and Fairbairn, 1976, 47). Metal and machinery industries form the second major group in Alberta, accounting for about one-fifth of employment and value added. This group, along with transport equipment, is the one with the most significant linkages to other manufacturers in the province (Barr and Fairbairn, 1976, 59). Many of the final products, however, are geared to the oil and gas industry either directly or through construction. Pipe, for example, is a major product and pumps are important. Rapid growth has taken place since 1947 (Crowston, 1971, 20). Nevertheless, little steel is produced in Alberta and the basic ingredients for the sector must still be imported into the Prairies. The Alberta government has invested in Regina-based IPSCO, which has plants in the province. Current discussions indicate that considerable expansion may take place in the steel industry in Saskatchewan and Alberta, especially now that the $10 billion Alaska Highway pipeline has been accepted. The project is under the control of the Calgary-based Foothills group.

Other industrial groups are less important in Alberta. Oil refining, which perhaps could be expected to be large, is very capital-intensive and employs relatively small numbers of people. In value added in manufacturing, it is rather less important than printing and publishing. The chemical sector, much of which is based on petroleum, employs less than five per cent of the manufacturing work force but produces around eight per cent of value added. Petrochemicals, however, is a sector in which there is considerable current activity. The Alberta government has made great efforts to encourage further processing of petroleum and natural gas in the province. As a result, construction is under way following an agreement announced in September 1975 (Alberta, 1975). A world-scale ethylene plant with an annual capacity of 1.2 billion pounds, is being built at Joffre, near Red Deer, by Alberta Gas Ethylene Ltd., in which the government indirectly has shares. Ethylene will be produced from ethane and is expected to form the base material for many plastic and chemical products in Alberta. Plants are also being built by Dome Petroleum and Alberta Gas Trunk to extract ethane from natural gas at Cochrane, Edmonton and Empress. Meanwhile, Dow Chemical has agreed to take at least 700 million pounds of the ethylene output annually for production of such items as vinyl chloride monomer, styrene and ethylene oxide. Dow is, therefore, involved in a $400 million building project in Edmonton. A large benzene plant is also expected soon (*Business Life*, 1977, 15–17). All in all, the role of chemicals in the Albertan manufacturing economy can be expected to expand significantly. A high proportion of output currently is exported from the province but new developments will increase the extent to which the semi-finished products of one plant move to another within Alberta for further processing. Barr and Fairbairn (1976, 52) show that many base chemicals are in fact imported into the province at present and that linkages are weak. Moreover, few Alberta manufacturers buy materials from the petrochemical industry (Barr and Fairbairn 1976, 56–7).

Amongst other manufacturing groups, the wood-processing industries are quite a large employer with over 10 per cent of the manufacturing work force and almost 15 per cent of value added. The industry benefits from the continuous demands of construction. Pulp and paper is relatively new to the province, the first plant at Hinton having been opened in 1956 (Ironside, 1970). Slow maturation of trees in the northern, forested areas of the province, however, necessitates very large catchment areas for a mill and restricts the scope for expansion. Another group largely oriented to provincial construction, non-metallic minerals, also has substantial sales and accounts for about 8 per cent of value added.

Barr and Fairbairn (1976, 61–2), on the basis of their linkage study of over 500 manufacturers, note that Alberta's manufacturers still rely heavily on outside supplies for industrial sub-components and manufactured items. In fact, 'An important segment of Alberta's manufacturing economy is related to the final stages of various national and international production chains', (p. 61). In other words, most of the processing takes place elsewhere and a small final stage is carried out in Alberta. There is only 'a weakly-developed regional industrial complex', (p.62). As already observed, the most characteristic Albertan industries process the province's resources, frequently to only a semi-processed stage. The limitations of the manufacturing sector, however, do not mean that an Alberta environment is viewed negatively by industrialists. In fact, most manufacturers (at least in Edmonton and Calgary) have positive views, although many are concerned about labour shortages (Barr and Fairbairn, 1977, 17).

Spatial Pattern

As in the other Prairie provinces, metropolitan areas play a dominant role in manufacturing in Alberta. Edmonton and Calgary account for over two-thirds of output (Alberta, 1975, 39). Both cities have been growing rapidly, attracting immigrants from both rural Alberta and elsewhere. Edmonton has always been larger and its metropolitan area in 1976 had a population of 543,000 as compared to Calgary's 458,000. Although Calgary and Edmonton have much in common, the latter has more public functions, being the seat of provincial government and the location of the main provincial university. Calgary has become an important head office centre, the third largest in Canada, as a result of its being the seat of the petroleum industry (Zieber, 1975).

Edmonton had some 24,500 manufacturing workers in 1974, of whom about a quarter were in food and beverage industries. Other important employers were primary metals, metal fabricating and clothing, though the latter is in decline. In value added, the non-metallic minerals group ranks second, ahead of metal fabricating, while petroleum products and chemicals are both important. It should be noted that the major refinery complex and the heavier chemical industries are outside the city proper in Strathcona and Fort Saskatchewan. Further developments are expected in the north-east, where land is available and the prevailing winds carry pollution away from the main built-up area.

Lee (1963) has traced the development of Edmonton's industry. Already by 1914, processing of farm products for the national market was important, while other activities (such as metal fabricating and printing) served the local market and northern Alberta (p. 24). This structure remained until the Second World War. The war itself encouraged a faster manufacturing growth but structural change awaited the 1947 oil and gas discoveries. These resulted in activities using petroleum and gas as materials, starting with the first refinery in 1948 and such companies as CIL making polyethylene resin and Canadian Chemical Industries (cellulose acetate) in 1953 (pp. 34–7). Rapid growth of market-oriented industry was also encouraged. Today's industries reflect the three complexes identified by Lee in 1963 (pp. 40–1):
(1) Industries dependent on local markets – most of the industries, including a lot of food and beverage and petroleum production.
(2) Livestock processing – export oriented.
(3) Processing of oil and gas into chemical products for export from the province.

In the last decade and a half, many of the city's consumer goods industries have become more oriented to the potential of northern markets, not only in Alberta, but also in the Territories. Edmonton hopes to benefit substantially from servicing northern development, which could stimulate much manufacturing, e.g. food and drink, construction materials, metal products, pumps and other machinery for the oil industry, mobile and modular homes, and work clothing (Edmonton Planning Department, 1973, xi–xiv). Some firms have also widened their markets to the West in general, and even become competitive elsewhere in Canada or abroad (Crowston, 1971, 41–6). Other developments in Edmonton have included the broadening of the petrochemical complex. Moreover, the building projects in this sector described above will benefit the city substantially and exploitation of the Athabaska tar sands will also feed into the Fort Saskatchewan plants. Despite growth and expansion in Edmonton's manufacturing sector, it is nevertheless the tertiary activities that have been expanding most rapidly (Seifried, 1977).

Edmonton has a number of industrial districts (figure 6.4). In all of them, substantial warehousing and distribution functions are mixed with manufacturing. The central areas (*4* and *5*) now have little manufacturing other than printing. Other older districts (*2, 3, 6*) are also fully utilized. The north-east (*3*), along the rail tracks, is the meat packing area. South of the river, there is a concentration of metals and activities related to the oil and gas industry.

Calgary's manufacturing sector is somewhat smaller than Edmonton's (18,000 workers in 1974), but it has been growing faster (Calgary Department of Business Development, 1974, 10–11). The food and beverage sector plays a comparable role, occupying nearly a quarter of Calgary's manufacturing workers and processing Albertan farm produce. Metal-fabricating is almost exactly the same size in the two cities, which means that it is perceptibly more important to Calgary, with about 15 per cent employment and value added. Calgary's other large sector is printing and publishing (about 10% on both measures). For the rest, the city has a variety of activities, none of which is itself particularly large in scale. The similarities to Edmonton are suggested by the early stimulus of rail in the 1880s (Smith, 1962, 315–18) and by Barr's (1975, 20) categorization of Calgary's present manufacturing into:

(1) Processing of regional farm products for both local and national markets.

(2) Oilfield equipment for Alberta and the north.

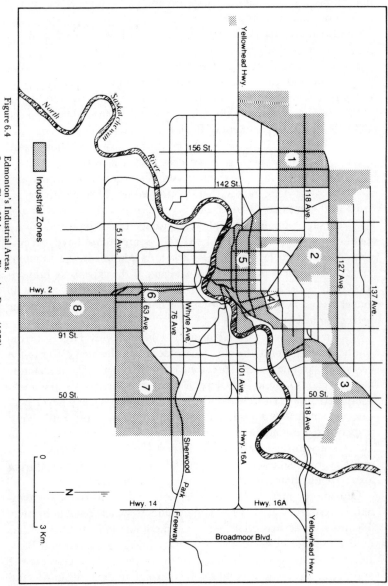

Figure 6.4   Edmonton's Industrial Areas.
Source: City of Edmonton Planning Dept. (1973)

(3) A wide range of light industrial products for a regional population, these products having a high friction of distance which affords protection from distant producers.

Barr also notes that Calgary ships over half of its manufactured products outside Alberta (p.36).

An interesting feature in Calgary is the lack of industries that process oil and gas. Calgary built up its importance in the oil industry as a result of the early discoveries, which were in the south of the province, especially developments in the Turner Valley in the 1930s (Alberta, Department of Business Development and Tourism, 1975, 9; Zieber, 1975, 77–80). The city's established position before the 1947 Leduc discovery allowed it to maintain its central position afterwards, but it has done so in administration, consultants and specialized services, rather than in processing. Manufacturing related to the industry is large, but is concerned with equipment and services, supplying for example rigs, storage tanks, pipe and equipment for wells (Zieber, 1975, 81–3). Some items have become competitive in the international market. As administrative functions have concentrated increasingly in Calgary at the expense of Edmonton (Zieber, 1975, 115), so processing has moved north. Calgary no longer has an active oil refinery and is not expected to expand in the petrochemicals sector.

Within Calgary, manufacturing is confined very largely to the southeastern sector of the city, with older plants located closer to the city centre and new areas spreading outwards in mixed manufacturing, warehousing and distribution areas. To the east, a new area, composed almost entirely of industrial multiples, is being developed, catering for the city's numerous small operations. In the south–west, a specialized mobile home complex has grown up on the site of an old military airfield. ATCO, the largest Canadian company in this industry, has its base there. In general, however, the manufacturing areas are not characterized by spatial specialization.

Outside the metropolitan centres, Alberta's industry is predominantly resource-based, with some products which service farmers. The only major exception is the mobile home industry, which has used a number of de-activated military bases (McEwen and Barr, 1977). Food-processing is found in many places, wood-processing and pulp mills are located in small centres, mainly in the north, and there are also some farm machinery and fertilizer plants in rural areas. This limited base does not necessarily imply a slow growth rate. In fact, Leigh and Carter (1972) showed that in the early 1960s manufacturing grew most rapidly in the rural south and north-east. Some of Alberta's smaller cities have quite important manufacturing activities. Lethbridge's food and beverage activities, for example, especially meat processing, are on a very large scale. The latter industry has been moving south in the last decade much to Lethbridge's advantage (Bullen, 1972, 72–81). Irrigation in southern Alberta has been an important element in Lethbridge's food and beverage expansion. Medicine Hat, another food processing centre, has recently acquired several large chemical plants, while Red Deer also stands to gain from the nearby ethylene plant now under construction.

INDUSTRIAL DEVELOPMENT POLICY IN THE PRAIRIES

Each of the three Prairie provinces has its own independent policy on economic development. Pro-business, Conservative Alberta strongly encourages the private sector. Mildly Socialist, NDP Saskatchewan sees a more positive role for the public sector. Until the 1977 election, Manitoba had a similar philosophy to Saskatchewan but the new Tory government has brought some changes. When all is said and done, however, the policies being pursued look remarkably similar. Common Prairie problems for the manufacturing sector have brought forth like responses.

The key element of policy in every province is unquestionably the desire for diversification, a recognition of the need to break away from the cyclical influences of primary activities. This involves the determination to process the region's resources to a greater degree, as well as the establishment, and expansion, of a much wider range of manufacturing activities. Manitoba has articulated this desire in its 'Guidelines for the Seventies' (1973, 127–9), noting that some items imported into Manitoba could probably be produced there. Preference is shown for high-wage industries and those which could develop linkages within the province. Saskatchewan (Saskatchewan, Department of Industry and Commerce, no date, 11) considers that manufacturing 'has a crucial role to play in stabilizing and diversifying the province's economic base and thus lessening our dependence on the unpredictable resource industries'. In Alberta, the message is no less clear. Premier Lougheed (1974, 3) has consistently stressed the vulnerability of the economy, arguing that the province's basic goal in its industrial strategy must be 'to diversify and become less dependent upon the sale of unprocessed resources, particularly non-renewable resources' (p.4).

In each province, the department responsible for industry has studied the potential of various manufacturing sectors. In Manitoba, the most diversified already, the Ministry of Industry and Commerce would like more high-technology manufacturing. Scope is seen for firms whose product is fairly insensitive to freight costs, such as aircraft parts, drugs, electronics and computers. Products of this type would be shipped to national and international markets. The province considers its steady growth, industrial tradition, pleasant way of life and reasonable wage rates as providing an attractive environment. Manitoba could also make more of the products used locally, such as tractors, farm implements and cables. A third type of activity, considered to have potential right across the Prairies despite being constrained by the domestic market, is in food processing. Manitoba, in common with Saskatchewan and Alberta, would like to see changes in freight rates to encourage Prairie manufacturing. The province also feels that federal policy on aerospace could be more sympathetic to its needs and less supportive, at its expense, of Montréal.

Saskatchewan's Department of Industry and Commerce is placing most emphasis on the iron and steel sector. This industry is the subject of a subsidiary agreement with the federal Department of Regional Economic Expansion (1977, 176–8) signed in 1974. The agreement covers iron ore exploration, research, the possibilities of a direct ore reduction plant and the expansion of steel making, opportunities for foundries and metal fabricating, and the cost of infrastructure for steel developments. A detailed study by DREE has not been released, but Parsons (1978) has assessed the prospects for western steel developments. In all probability, expansion of this sector will take place in the near future and IPSCO has announced proposals along these lines. The other opportunity, a more long-term project, is in industrial fermentation. It involves processing of farm produce for food, fuel and pharmaceuticals (Saskatchewan, Department of Industry and Commerce, and Canada, DREE, no date). Like Manitoba, Saskatchewan sees scope in import substitution – making such products as chemicals, mobile homes and clothing – but little detailed work has yet been done on these activities. Uranium processing, based on northern Saskatchewan mines, does look likely, however.

In Alberta, the focus has clearly been on petrochemicals. Because they have already resulted in some major projects, the results of research and policy decisions have largely been discussed above. There seems to be a recognition that further developments at the present time may be restricted by market conditions and problems of international competitiveness. In comparison with the Gulf Coast of the United States, for example, Alberta is a high cost producer because of both capital and wage elements. Meanwhile, within Canada, further expansions at Sarnia have increased the competition (*Edmonton Journal*, 1977). Albertans were upset that the federal government opted, through Petrosar, which is partly owned by the Canadian Development Corporation, to engage in a major development there at Alberta's expense. Alberta hopes for considerable further processing of agricultural products and, to this end, has a subsidiary agreement with DREE for nutritive processing. This agreement, however, is only for the support of new or expanding plants outside Calgary and Edmonton (Canada, DREE, 1977, 194–6). The Department of Business Development and Tourism would like to encourage more 'brain power' industries, based on research and specialized skills. The Alberta Heritage Savings Trust Fund (using revenue from oil and gas sales) is investing along these lines – in health research and oil sands technology, for example (Alberta Heritage Savings Trust Fund, 1977). In sectors related to oil and gas, a few specialized firms have already sprung up fairly naturally, and the province hopes to encourage spin-offs from medical research.

All three provinces provide a range of technical, management and marketing services to businessmen and are particularly interested in fostering home-grown entrepreneurs. This preference is a reaction to the feeling of dependence which is so resented in the region, and it is explicitly stated as a policy goal (Manitoba, 1973, 135; Saskatchewan, Department of Industry and Commerce, no date, 14; Lougheed, 1974, 2). This does not imply a closed door for outside investors, but indicates a desire for a higher proportion of manufactures to be locally controlled. Small businessmen receive a lot of attention from all provinces as a result. Development corporations in Alberta and Saskatchewan are designed to make capital more readily available, acting generally as a lender of last resort. All three provinces are interested in encouraging their own entrepreneurs to appear, to widen their knowledge and experience and to be able to obtain the wherewithal to run a successful business.

Sponsorship of the small businessman and of local ownership is closely bound up with the major element of spatial strategy found in every province, that of decentralization from the metropolitan sector. The decline of rural areas and high rate of rural-urban migration evident for a number of decades is seen as a trend to be fought. Manitoba developed its 'Stay Option' to allow its residents to remain where they prefer to live (Manitoba, 1973, 13), Saskatchewan wishes to 'develop the full socio-economic potential of all sizes of communities' in the province (Saskatchewan, Department of Industry and Commerce, 13) and Alberta seeks to balance growth across the province (Lougheed, 1974, 8). Unlike Ontario and Québec, where the spatial pattern of development tends to be separated from policy on industrial growth and the two are the responsibilities of separate departments, decentralization in the Prairies is a major element of economic strategy.

In contrast to the other two provinces, Manitoba has established regional development corporations. Seven of them in the southern part of the province receive 50 per cent funding from the provincial government. They operate under a local board of directors, reflecting local needs in rural economic development. Since 1974, the regional development branch of the Department of Industry and Commerce has also maintained regional offices so that departmental services are easily accessible to the public. In Saskatchewan, regionalization of the effort to develop manufacturing has not yet proceeded very far. For one reason, manufacturing is limited and neither Regina nor Saskatoon is very strong itself. For another, DREE's industrial development grants extend to the whole province. Although the province would like to spread manufacturing, it cannot really afford to do so when even its metropolitan areas have limited opportunities. Thus most of the rural development effort is being given to the improvement of infrastructure and to the tertiary sector. Business services are provided, however, through eight regional offices.

Alberta's approach to the question of decentralization has evolved since 1972 and places the emphasis on encouraging local communities and businessmen to help themselves. It is mainly the responsibility of the Regional Development Branch within the Department of Business Development and Tourism (Blake, 1977). The branch has ten economic development representatives, each resident in one of the ten regions into which the province (outside Calgary and

Edmonton) is divided for the purpose. The representatives encourage local initiatives, linking businessmen to advice and aid available within the government, and encouraging communities to set up development committees and prepare their own economic plans. Of course, a lot of the work does not involve manufacturing, which is only one element of the scheme. Communities can also make use of an industrial land programme, under which the province will buy and service land for a municipality. The latter buys lots only as required and so is spared both initial capital costs and risk. (Alberta Housing Corporation *et al.*, 1977).

Northern problems are generally somewhat more difficult to cope with than those of the rural south. Generally, manufacturing is a minor element in a broad socio-economic programme. DREE is very much involved in these areas and has agreements with each province (Canada, DREE, 1977, 116–93). The focus of these agreements is on human as well as economic development. Help for native peoples in the north is an important element of policy. Encouragement of careful resource use is also stressed.

Clearly the three Prairie provinces are taking active roles in the economy. In all of them, this has led to equity positions in the economic sector. The province of Manitoba owns several firms that its former government bought in preference to allowing them to go out of business (e.g. Churchill Forest Industries and Flyer Industries, a bus manufacturer). The new government, however, is trying to divest itself of such companies. Saskatchewan is in the process of buying out potash companies, because it feels the foreign owners have not been giving adequate returns to the province and because they play an important role in diversifying the rural economy. While such actions by NDP governments can be expected, Conservative Alberta has been at least as energetic, taking over a regional airline (Pacific Western), investing in steel, and assuming a major role in petrochemicals. Such actions are justified on the grounds of an inadequate response from the private sector; Premier Lougheed still maintains that his government wishes to keep out of such investments (1974, 17). Alberta's commitment to private enterprise, however, is mainly seen in its generous tax policy and its encouragement of private initiative rather than in a passive interpretation of its own role. The province is determined to make good use of the high returns currently being obtained from oil and gas revenues. In the short time before these decline, it hopes to see its objectives fulfilled and if the private sector does not move towards them, the government is not hesitating to take over.

CONCLUSION

From an economic point of view, the three Prairie provinces exhibit many similarities and face several common problems. On the policy front, therefore, industrial development follows much the same line with appropriate provincial differences. For future industrial growth, much depends on the extent to which the western provinces (often including British Columbia) can work together to achieve a better deal within federal Canada. The Western Opportunities Conference in 1973 did much to increase co-operation and to air grievances. The decentralization of DREE and the establishment of the Western Region office in Saskatoon has brought economic planning closer to home. After decades of complaints about transport and freight rates, the Hall Commission Report may lead to action that removes discrimination against the Prairies. But Ontario and Québec are not likely to sit back quietly if manufacturing activity moves west, especially if any companies actually relocate. Because many of the key factors (energy, transport, land, tariffs, grants to industry, immigration) are controlled at the political level, the extent to which manufacturing increases in the West will be determined more by political than economic decisions. The outcome is perhaps the most interesting question concerning the next 20 years of Canadian industrial development. In Friedmann's terms, can the Western counter-élite successfully challenge the establishment?

Increased Prairie power seems likely. Strength in resources and riches from oil and gas can only increase western influence. But the Prairie Provinces will not become another Ontario. Their manufacturing sector will probably remain relatively small and tied quite closely to the resource base. Within the areas of its competence, Prairie manufacturing could become more independent and innovative but attempts to expand on all fronts could well be disastrous. Specialization and trade should assure continued prosperity.

REFERENCES

Alberta (1975), *News Release*. Edmonton: 22 September.
Alberta, Department of Business Development and Tourism (1975), *Industry and Resources 1975*. Edmonton.

Alberta Heritage Savings Trust Fund (1977), *Annual Report 1976–77*. Edmonton: Alberta Treasury.

Alberta Housing Corporation *et al.*, (1977), *Alberta Industrial Land Program*. Edmonton.

Appana, M. (1975), 'An analysis of factors influencing the location of manufacturing industries in the Prairies', Unpublished M.A. Thesis, University of Manitoba.

Artibise, A. E. J. (1975), *Winnipeg: A Social History of Urban Growth, 1874–1914*. Montréal: McGill-Queens University Press.

Barr, B. M. (1972), 'Reorganization of the economy since 1945', in P. J. Smith (ed.), *Studies in Canadian Geography: The Prairie Provinces*, (Toronto: University of Toronto Press), 65–82.

Barr, B. M. (1975), 'The importance of regional inter-industry linkages to Calgary's manufacturing firms', in B. M. Barr (ed.) *Calgary: Metropolitan Structure and Influence*, (Victoria: University of Victoria), 1–50.

Barr, B. M. and Fairbairn, K. J. (1976), 'Inter-industry manufacturing linkages within Alberta', *B. C. Geographical Series*, 22, (Vancouver: Tantalus), 37–65.

Barr, B. M. and Fairbairn, K. J. (1977), 'Calgary and Edmonton manufacturers' perception of economic opportunity in Alberta', *B. C. Geographical Series*, 24, (Vancouver: Tantalus), 9–24.

Bellan, R. C. (1958), 'The development of Winnipeg as a metropolitan centre', Unpublished Ph.D. Thesis, Columbia University.

Blake, R. H. (1977), 'Comments on balanced population and economic growth policy for Alberta', Paper given at the Canadian Association of Geographers' Annual Meeting, Regina, 7 June, mimeo.

Buckley, Helen (1965), *Manufacturing Industry in Saskatchewan: A Study in Growth and Future Prospects*. Saskatoon: Centre for Community Studies, University of Regina.

Bullen, A. M. (1972), 'An examination of economic factors affecting the location and operation of the beef packing industry in Canada with particular reference to Alberta', Unpublished M.Sc. Thesis, University of Alberta.

Burghardt, A. F., (1971), 'A hypothesis about gateway cities', *Annals, Association of American Geographers*, 61, (June), 269–85.

Business Life (1977), 'Edmonton: Canada's emerging young giant is just reaching its prime', May.

Calgary, City of, Department of Business Development (1974), *Manufacturing in Calgary*.

Canada, DREE, (Department of Regional Economic Expansion), (1973a), *Western Region: Economic Circumstances and Opportunities*. Ottawa.

Canada, DREE (1973b), *Saskatchewan: Economic Circumstances and Opportunities*. Ottawa.

Canada, DREE, (1976), *Climate for Development: Western Region*. Ottawa.

Canada, DREE, (1977), *Summaries of Federal-Provincial General Development Agreements and Currently Active Subsidiary Agreements*. Ottawa.

Canada, Grain Handling and Transportation Commission (1977), *Report: Grain and Rail in Western Canada vol. 1*. Ottawa: Queen's Printer.

Crowston, M. A. (1971), 'The growth of the metal industries in Edmonton',

Unpublished M.A. Thesis, University of Alberta.

Economic Council of Canada (1977), *Living Together*. Ottawa

Edmonton, City of, Planning Department (1973), *Industrial Land in Edmonton*. Edmonton.

Edmonton Journal, (1977), 'Lougheed's 6-point plan for economy', 12 March.

Financial Times of Canada (1973) 'Preparing for the Calgary Conference: the biggest thing since World War II?', 23 July, 9.

Hastie, R. (1974), 'Development of the apparel industry of Winnipeg', in T. J. Kuz (1974), 129–45.

Ironside, R. G. (1970), 'Plant location and consequences: the case of the Hinton pulp mill, Alberta', *Tijdschrift voor economische en sociale geographie*, *61*, (July/August), 215–22.

Kuz, T. J. (1974), *Winnipeg 1874-1974: Progress and Prospects*. Winnipeg: Manitoba Department of Industry and Commerce.

Lee, T. R. (1963), 'A manufacturing geography of Edmonton, Alberta', Unpublished M.A. Thesis, University of Alberta.

Leigh, R. and Carter, D. (1972), 'Spatial patterns of economic growth in Alberta, 1961-1966', *The Albertan Geographer, 8, 49–55*.

Lougheed, P. (1974), 'Alberta's industrial strategy', Speech to the Calgary Chamber of Commerce, 6 September, mimeo.

Manitoba (1973), *Guidelines for the Seventies, vol. 1, Introduction and Economic Analysis*. Winnipeg.

Manitoba, Department of Industry and Commerce (1977), *The Economy of the Province of Manitoba*. Winnipeg.

McEwen, A. M. (1976), 'The industrial reuse of Alberta's deactivated military bases', Unpublished M. A. Thesis, University of Calgary.

McEwen, A. M. and Barr, B. M. (1977), 'The replacement process in economic development: transformation of deactivated military bases into industrial estates', *B. C. Geographical Series*, 24, (Vancouver: Tantalus), 49–65.

MPS Associates Ltd. (1975), *Transport and Regional Development in the Prairies*, A Report prepared for Canada, Ministry of Transport. vol. 1. Winnipeg.

Nelson, J. G. (1972), 'Some reflections on man's impact on the landscape of the Canadian Prairies and nearby areas', in P. J. Smith (ed.), *Studies in Canadian Geography: The Prairie Provinces*, (Toronto: University of Toronto Press), 33–50.

Parliament, R. (1974), 'Winnipeg livestock and meat processing industry: a century of development', (1974), 75–82.

Parsons, G. F. (1978), 'Steel in Western Canada: A case for industrial planning', paper presented to the Canadian Association of Geographers, London, 24 May.

Proudfoot, B. (1972), 'Agriculture', in P. J. Smith (ed.), *Studies in Canadian Geography: The Prairie Provinces*, (Toronto: University of Toronto Press), 51–64.

Saskatchewan, Department of Industry and Commerce (no date), *An Industrial Development Strategy for Saskatchewan*. Regina.

Saskatchewan, Department of Industry and Commerce, and Canada, Department of Regional Economic Expansion (no date), *Industrial Fermentation: A Saskatchewan Opportunity*. Regina.

Seifried, N. R. M. (1977), 'The changing economic structure of Edmonton 1961–1971', mimeo.

Smith, P. J. (1962), 'Calgary: A study in urban pattern', *Economic Geography*, 38, (October), 315–29.

Thompson, R. R. (1977), 'Commodity flows and urban structure: a case study in the Prairie Provinces', Unpublished Ph.D. Thesis, University of Calgary.

Underwood McLellan and Associates Ltd. and Jellicoe Resource Associates Ltd. (1975), *Industrial Opportunities in Saskatoon*. Saskatoon.

Zieber, G. H. (1975), 'Calgary as an oil administrative and oil operations centre', in B. M. Barr (ed.), *Calgary: Metropolitan Structure and Influence*, (Victoria: University of Victoria), 77–122.

7

^

British Columbia

To many people, especially Canadians east of Manitoba, British Columbia is a kind of extension to the Prairies: western Canada is lumped together as a unit. Indeed, the Department of Regional Economic Expansion operates according to this view by combining the four provinces into a Western Region with headquarters at Saskatoon. That there are economic similarities between the Prairies and British Columbia cannot be gainsaid but the contrasts are far greater. The west-coast province is almost entirely mountainous, with major north-south landforms that complicate east-west movement; it is heavily forested and tremendously dependent on its forest resource; the northern interior is still almost a frontier zone. Above all, British Columbia has a long coastline, has been settled primarily from the west and south, and is very much influenced by its 'Pacific Rim' location. To regard British Columbia as the furthest extension of the westward spread of settlement in Canada fails to do justice to the independence brought about by influences which moved into the Canadian Cordillera from the province's south-west corner.

In the early eighteenth century, British Columbia was settled by several Indian tribes but was scarcely known to the white man. In the 1770s, Spaniards arrived by sea, and so did Captain Cook. Meanwhile, Mackenzie reached the coast by an overland route in 1793. Permanent settlement, however, began only in 1843 at Fort Victoria. In the early nineteenth century, the Hudson's Bay Company discouraged settlement but did establish a system of forts and routes in the area. The first big boost to the population occurred with the 1858 gold rush to the Fraser River, which mainly attracted Americans. In the 1860s miners moved north into the Cariboo country, also exploring some other interior areas. On the coast, the influx of settlers encouraged urban settlement for supply at New Westminster, Victoria and Yale, while food requirements stimulated farming and rural development in the valleys (Siemens, 1972, 13–15).

It was only in 1886 that the Canadian Pacific Railway linked British Columbia to the rest of Canada, according to the agreement

202

under which the colony joined the new confederation. By this time, the broad outline of urban settlement in southern British Columbia had already been established. Nevertheless the rail link did much to encourage the rise of Vancouver. As the CPR terminus, it soon overtook New Westminster in importance. Victoria, the earliest settlement and provincial capital, remained the centre of commerce until the First World War, when the advantages of Vancouver's mainland position finally won out (Hardwick, 1972, 121–2). In the period of population growth that followed the railway, Vancouver Island and the Lower Fraser Valley strengthened their position within British Columbia (Siemens, 1972, 19). The southern valleys (Fraser, Okanagan, Shuswap, Kootenay area) were all fully settled by the time of the First World War. They were fairly accessible and had potential for farming, forestry or mining. Development of northern British Columbia has gradually followed, accompanied by transport improvements. The Grand Trunk Pacific pushed its route through to Prince Rupert in 1914 and its successor, the Canadian National, was actively involved in colonization in the inter-war years. Meanwhile, southwestern B.C.'s influence has been encouraged by the Pacific Great Eastern (now British Columbia Railway), which is still building lines. In fact, the extreme north-west of the province has not yet been fully opened up (Siemens, 1972, 27–31).

THE ECONOMY

The economic history of British Columbia is a classic example of the staple theory of economic growth based on furs, gold, lumber, fish and base metals (Denike and Leigh, 1972, 70). The dependence, however, is not just historic. Today it is claimed that the forest industry generates fifty cents out of every dollar spent in the province (Farley, 1972, 87). Mining is also substantial. In both of these cases, a very high proportion (over 75%) of the output is exported in unprocessed or semi-processed form (Canada, DREE, 1976, 67). Although the United States is still British Columbia's main trading partner (nearly 50% of exports in 1975 and 57% of imports through B.C. ports), the role of Japan has become extremely important. The Japanese have invested heavily in the province and take large amounts of raw material such as coal and copper. Japan took over 22 per cent of British Columbia's exports in 1975 and provided about 19 per cent of imports entering Canada via B.C.

ports (British Columbia, Ministry of Economic Development, 1977b, 27–9 and 50–1). British Columbia is, therefore, extremely dependent on the international economic climate. In the post-war years, world demand allowed rapid expansion and rising prosperity in the province, but the recession beginning in 1974–5 has hit the resource industries hard (British Columbia, Ministry of Economic Development, 1977a, 5–6). As in the Prairie Provinces, limited diversification renders British Columbia's economy vulnerable. Unlike Alberta's, however, its main strength is a renewable rather than a non-renewable resource.

In the Canadian context, British Columbians are rich. Narrow though it may be, their economy has served them very well in the post-war era. In the 1960s, the increases in population (34%) and employment (61%) in British Columbia were almost double the rates for Canada as a whole (Canada, DREE, 1973, 6–7) although they had slowed down by the mid-1970s. Personal incomes have long been higher than the Canadian average. Indeed, the major problem has been that too many immigrants have been attracted so that even a high growth of employment was insufficient to provide the necessary jobs to keep unemployment levels down (Canada, DREE, 1973, 6; British Columbia, Ministry of Economic Development, 1977a, 24–30). Historically, however, the province has seen many 'boom and bust' periods and the key question hanging over British Columbia now is whether or not cyclical problems have now become structural as a result of declining competitiveness. The British Columbia government is concerned about increasing production in third world countries, rising labour costs and relative declines in productivity. It also feels that Canadian federal policy has contributed to the problem by building up a large national debt and encouraging high interest rates which make investment expensive (British Columbia, Ministry of Economic Development, 1977a, 6–8).

MANUFACTURING

While the proportion of provincial employment in manufacturing is a little below the national average at about 19 per cent, it is higher than in Atlantic Canada or the Prairies. The province accounts for nearly nine per cent of the value added by manufacturing in Canada. This contribution, however, is dominated by primary processing, the output of which is largely exported. Not surprisingly, forest-related industries play a major role, the wood industry and paper and allied groups being roughly comparable in terms of value added. They account in combination for about 46 per cent of the provincial total (see Table 7.1). Because of relatively low employment in pulp and paper, the two groups in combination are less important as employers, taking about 43 per cent of manufacturing workers in the province. Third in importance is the food and beverage sector. Together, however, primary metal, metal fabricating, machinery, and transport equipment are substantial (20% of value added, 23% employment). Other industries are relatively small.

Forest-Based Manufacturing

The forests of British Columbia form the basis of wood, pulp and paper manufacturing and provide a huge resource of raw material. The province has well over 50 per cent of Canada's merchantable coniferous timber, totalling around 261,000 million cubic feet (Canada West Foundation, 1975, 8). Broadleaved timber resources are small. The main species in order of importance are spruces, hemlock, balsam, lodgepole pine, western red cedar and Douglas fir. Most desirable for lumber and plywood, the Douglas fir is no longer as readily available as it once was. Spatially, the forests are noticeably influenced by topography and climate. The higher mountainous areas, especially large stretches of the Coast Mountains and the Rockies, lack forest cover. The western flanks of the mountains receive more rainfall and have richer forests than the eastern ones, while some of the interior valleys are arid. On a broad scale, rainfall declines from west to east while temperatures become lower from south to north, so that the most favoured forest areas are in the south-west. The coastal forest has most of the Sitka spruce, western hemlock, cedar and Douglas fir. Growth, too, is faster on the coast and trees attain a higher stature (Farley, 1972, 88–92).

From her rich forest resource British Columbia supplies some 45 per cent of the Canadian timber harvest (Hayter, 1976, 216). As figure 7.1 shows, even this cut is not fully utilizing the resource. The south-west has little scope for expansion but elsewhere there are possibilities, these being considerable in the north. British Columbia has strengthened its role in Canada since 1950, its proportion of the

TABLE 7.1
BRITISH COLUMBIA:
PRINCIPAL STATISTICS BY INDUSTRY GROUP, 1975

	No. of Establishments	Employees No.	%	Value of Shipments $000	Value Added $000	%
Food and beverage industries	494	18,228	13.3	1,407,440	451,275	13.3
Tobacco products industries	—	—	—	—	—	—
Rubber and plastics product industries	79	1,224	0.9	41,065	20,662	0.6
Leather industries	14	*	*	*	*	*
Textile industries	58	1,239	0.9	44,504	19,662	0.6
Knitting Mills	6	*	*	*	*	*
Clothing industries	42	2,261	1.7	47,761	26,248	0.8
Wood industries	592	38,655	28.2	1,873,877	764,297	22.6
Furniture and fixture industries	196	1,990	1.5	65,410	34,205	1.0
Paper and allied industries	64	20,225	14.8	1,558,843	797,123	23.6
Printing, Publishing and allied industries	366	6,883	5.0	215,243	142,008	4.2
Primary Metal industries	37	8,333	6.1	389,855	197,170	5.8
Metal fabricating industries	373	9,097	6.6	444,897	209,077	6.2
Machinery industries	125	5,611	4.1	207,371	103,557	3.1
Transportation equipment industries	170	8,072	5.9	358,834	158,500	4.7
Electrical products industries	66	3,647	2.7	136,405	62,406	1.8
Non-metallic mineral products industries	142	4,189	3.1	216,952	112,912	3.3
Petroleum and coal products	8	1,035	0.8	565,286	110,772	3.3
Chemical and chemical products industries	87	3,153	2.3	260,340	130,166	3.9
Miscellaneous manufacturing industries	212	2,526	1.8	55,913	34,593	1.0
Total all industries	3,131	137,138	99.7	7,905,664	3,383,285	99.8

* Not available due to confidentiality restrictions.

timber cut rising from only 30 per cent at that date. Similar developments can be seen in processing (sawmills and planing mills from 58.6% in 1950 to 65.5% in 1970; veneer and plywood mills

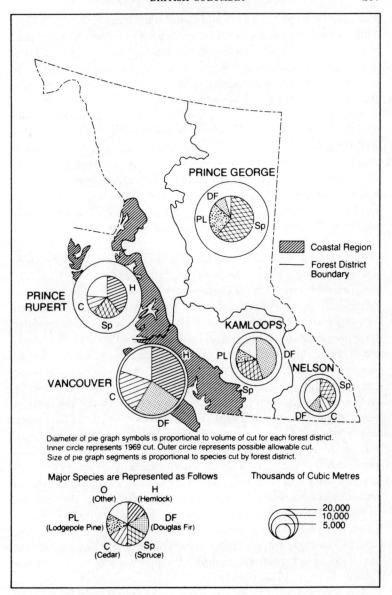

Diameter of pie graph symbols is proportional to volume of cut for each forest district.
Inner circle represents 1969 cut. Outer circle represents possible allowable cut.
Size of pie graph segments is proportional to species cut by forest district.

Figure 7.1   Present and Potential Forest Harvest in British Columbia.
             Source: A. L. Farley (1972)

from 55.2% to 67.0%; pulp and paper mills from 9.1% to 22.8%). Such growth was encouraged by an expansion of home and export markets, technological developments, stricter wood utilization laws, and exhaustion of competing regions (Hayter, 1976, 215–16). A government policy of sustained-yield harvesting has helped guarantee the resource for the long-term. The crown forests have been managed in two alternative ways following recommendations of the 1945 Sloan Report. The Forest Service maintains Public Sustained Yield Units and makes timber available to loggers. On the other hand, the use of very large areas is granted in perpetuity to companies under Tree Farm Licenses. This guarantees a material source, but the forests must be managed according to provincial guidelines (British Columbia, Task Force on Crown Timber Disposal, 1974, 62–6). As noted above, the industry growth rate slowed down in the mid-1970s.

Although sawmills are ubiquitous in the province, there are clear spatial concentrations. The industry, which grew along with logging, started near Victoria in the mid-1800s but the coastal areas of southern Vancouver Island and the Lower Mainland had more than an early start to commend them. Rich timber resources, cheap water transport (both for supplies and for exports) and good road and rail connections have all helped this area retain a major role in sawmilling. As Farley (1972, 102) notes, the 'locations that have persisted through time are those that have been strategically well-located with respect to timber supplies and to the assembly of those supplies at the mill site'. In the interior, rail lines have been important, but the cost of reaching markets was a major disadvantage in the early years. Although settlement of the Prairies provided the first real opportunities for the interior mills in the early twentieth century, they remained relatively marginal and so subject to cyclical variations of considerable magnitude. One response to the vagaries of the market was the cheap, portable mill. Now, as interior British Columbia becomes less marginal to world markets, these are giving way increasingly to permanent sites. During the 1960s and 1970s, there has been concentration into a few major nodes such as Prince George (Farley, 1972, 100–7).

It is only recently that British Columbia has improved from a very low level of wood processing. In 1950, only nine per cent of Canadian pulp and paper was produced in the province as compared to nearly sixty per cent of sawn lumber. In 1960, the pulp and

paper industry was still confined to coastal locations, where it relied
on excellent resources of wood and water. Since 1947, however,
fifteen kraft pulp mills have been built and, in the 1960s, much of the
growth has been in the interior (Hayter, 1976, 215). Changes in the
energy situation have helped this increased locational freedom.
Mills now produce more of their own thermal electricity than
formerly, while the B.C. electricity grid has also become more
widespread (Wolforth, 1965). As already noted, this expansion has
carried the province's share of Canada's pulp and paper output to
nearly 23 per cent. The changes represent a higher use of British
Columbia's resource and a movement to areas that were perhaps
marginal at former levels of demand.

An important feature of the last few decades has been the
integration of all wood processing activities. Sawmills now use their
residues for wood chips, which along with sawdust have become the
major form of material for the pulp mills. This trend has given a new
lease of life to the larger old sawmills (Farley, 1972, 113). Government policy has been quite influential in this respect because of the
desire to achieve a fuller utilization of the resource. Moreover,
permission for pulp mill expansions in the interior has been
conditional on the availability of wood chips and sawdust (Barr and
Fairbairn, 1974, 25). Much of the integration and re-organization
has taken place through the operations of a few very large corporations. It has led also to geographical concentration into a few major
wood-using complexes such as Prince George, the new town of
Mackenzie and Port Alberni. What has happened is illustrated by
the largest firm, MacMillan Bloedel, which has been studied by
Hayter (1976).

The company is an amalgamation of three local companies all
founded in the early twentieth century. MacMillan Export was a
lumber trading concern, Bloedel, Stewart and Welch a logging
company, and the Powell River Company produced newsprint. In
the 1940s, each company had extended its range of activities
vertically; in the 1950s they became one organization. As a result of
the mergers, management was reorganized and became more
efficient by building on the strengths of each constituent unit. The
company also combined many of British Columbia's prime sites on
the Georgia Strait and concentrated expansion at such centres as
Port Alberni, Harmac and Powell River. A reorganization of
product movement greatly reduced transport costs, and some

operations were closed down. All of these changes helped MacMillan Bloedel to expand and to improve efficiency based on prime resources and sites. By the late 1960s, the company was moving into more highly processed items (paperboard, boxes, fine paper, etc.) and into other areas within and outside Canada.

Somewhat untypical is the fact that MacMillan Bloedel has not moved into the British Columbian interior. Most of the new kraft mills there were established on a joint venture basis by foreign-owned corporations or companies with considerable foreign capital. Generally, they moved in to secure supplies of pulp for further processing in the large markets of the United States, Europe and Japan (Barr and Fairbairn, 1974, 20–1). The companies, however, did work on an integrated basis, almost always owning some sawmills for chip supply. Usually, they had markets guaranteed by parent companies (Barr and Fairbairn, 1974, 23–4).

The trend towards integration of wood-using industries in British Columbia has included more advanced forms of processing but the industry continues to concentrate on the raw and semi-processed end of the market. One reason for this is the reliance on export markets and the fact that most importing countries place high tariffs on processed items. This is true, for example, of paper. Thus British Columbia exports much pulp but little paper (Barr and Fairbairn, 1974, 24). Higher rail rates on finished products have a similar effect. The growth of the Canadian market is encouraging further processing, particularly in plywood, particle board and containers (Farley, 1972, 116). Although British Columbia produces a quality product, however, it is a long way from the large central Canadian market, where it must compete with well-established local producers who also have resources close at hand.

Other Manufacturing

Quite a large proportion of British Columbia's remaining industries are closely related to the resource sector in one way or another. The substantial food and beverage sector, including a large fish canning industry, mainly processes local items. There is also some metal refining, although substantial mineral output, including coal, still goes out of the province in unprocessed form. Ingram (1958) noted that many firms in the machinery and transport equipment industries were established to supply the resource sectors, especially forestry, while Shearer (1971) argued that growth in both secondary and tertiary sectors has been dependent on resources. These features, then, reinforce the importance of the forest to the province.

Most of British Columbia's other manufacturing sectors can be related to the growing size of the local market and its isolation from established production points (McGovern, 1961, 196–7). As in Alberta, British Columbia's population and expendable income have grown rapidly in the post-war years so that demands for consumer goods and construction materials have been high. In cases where freight costs from Ontario or elsewhere are too high to offset advantages of cheaper production, local suppliers have an opportunity to build up a good business. Munro (1971, 101) claims that, as of 1963, only three important plants were neither closely tied to the resource sector nor to the local market. All three were Californian-owned branches and served the whole Canadian market.[1] In general, the isolation of the province makes it very difficult to develop non-resource-related products that compete in wider markets either within Canada or abroad.

Nesbitt (1973, 105–16) has distinguished three types of manufacturing other than primary processing. His categories are based largely on destination of shipments, using 1967 data, and are related by him to stages of development. After a first stage of primary processing, a region develops localized industries related to its own market, both households and business. Industries linked to the primary sector, which in British Columbia are virtually all backwardly linked, characterize stage three. As a region develops further, it acquires the ability to compete with imported products from a wider range of industries. Competition is strong because these import-substituting industries are characteristic of developed areas and usually benefit from scale and external economics. British Columbia in 1967 was not very fully developed in Nesbitt's terms. As measured by value of shipments, nearly 54 per cent of manufacturing was primary processing, about 27 per cent localized, only 7 per cent backwardly linked and about 12 per cent import substituting.[2]

[1]Two produced locks, one electrical products.
[2]For a full explanation of Nesbitt's definitions and a list of 3–digit industries in each category, see Appendix.

THE SPATIAL PATTERN OF MANUFACTURING

In a sense, British Columbia's structure can be outlined in very simple terms. There is a small highly populated core region around the Georgia Strait and a large periphery consisting of the rest of the province. In the core area live some 75 per cent of the population: Vancouver dominates the provincial economy and Victoria is the seat of political power. Elsewhere, population is widely scattered and only a few cities reach a population of 20,000. This simple core-periphery contrast, however, does mask some differences among the various peripheral regions.

Using census regions but separating out Metropolitan Victoria and Vancouver, Denike and Leigh (1972) have examined a number of economic features using data from the 1960s. First, they considered regional economic structure in terms of major employment categories (1961 Census data), which were factor analysed to give the results shown in table 7.2 (pp. 75–7). Because forestry is present everywhere, it does not show as a separate factor. Most important is the 'urban service' component dependent upon employment in services and trade. The other two factors relate to mining and

TABLE 7.2
ECONOMIC SPECIALIZATIONS AND SIMILARITIES OF REGIONS, BASED ON COMPONENT SCORES (1961 DATA)

		Urban-service component	Resource component	
			Agriculture	Mining
Urban-service regions				
Metropolitan Vancouver		1.39	−0.14	−1.14
Metropolitan Victoria		2.13	−1.08	−0.23
Forest-mining regions				
East Kootenays	(1)	+0.06	−0.01	2.54
West Kootenays	(2)	+0.11	−0.35	+0.55
Forest-agriculture regions				
Okanagan	(3)	−0.05	1.45	−1.22
Fraser Valley	(4)	−0.46	1.08	−0.24
North-Central Interior	(8)	−0.39	+0.05	−0.26
Kamloops-Thompson	(6)	−0.15	+0.33	+0.21
Forest-based regions				
Vancouver Island	(5)	−0.42	−0.70	−0.37
Lower Coast	(7)	−1.90	−0.92	−0.76
Northwest Coast	(9)	−0.54	−1.41	+0.24
Agriculture and mining region				
Peace	(10)	+0.21	1.73	+0.67

Sources: Leigh and Denike (1972), 77.

agriculture. Denike and Leigh show four types of peripheral region, distinguished by differences in their resource base (Table 7.2).

Regional economic growth was then examined, using data for 1961 to 1969 on population, personal income, total employment and manufacturing employment (pp. 77–80). Principal components analysis was employed. It indicated two dimensions of growth – one general and one associated with manufacturing. The latter was most pronounced on Vancouver Island and in the Lower Fraser, where general growth was slow. Manufacturing also grew fairly rapidly in the fast-growing north-central interior. In the 1960s, general growth was most rapid in the north, while the south-west grew at moderate rates and the south-east slowly. In general, 'selective decentralization of population and economic activity to interior regions' took place (p.79).

In the final section of their analysis, Denike and Leigh considered the stage of development attained by the various regions within the province (pp. 80–2). This was done by relating the level of capital investment to certain other indices for the 1960s. A strong relationship between investment and income indicates an elementary stage (1) of development; at a more mature stage (2) the region offers shops and services so that investment correlates with retail sales; a well-developed economy (stage 3) has greater industrial self-sufficiency so that investment is related to manufacturing employment; finally, at the highest stage (4), interrelationships are so great that investment correlates with population growth. Admittedly, this approach is rather crude but it does distinguish between British Columbia's regions in a reasonable way. Metropolitan Vancouver, for example, comes out in the highest category while the Lower Coast and the Northwest Coast are at the most elementary stage. The Okanagan region, however, agricultural and long settled, also comes out as being in an early stage (2), which seems less appropriate. The North-Central Interior, with spectacular growth, has shown a close relationship between investment and manufacturing stage (3) but in the Kootenays this correlation was negative, suggesting that the region was returning to a more resource-based economy. Apart from Vancouver, the most developed areas are Victoria and Vancouver Island, neither of which, however, is at the Vancouver level.

On the basis of all these forms of analysis, Denike and Leigh drew up the map shown as figure 7.2. The small core (heartland) includes

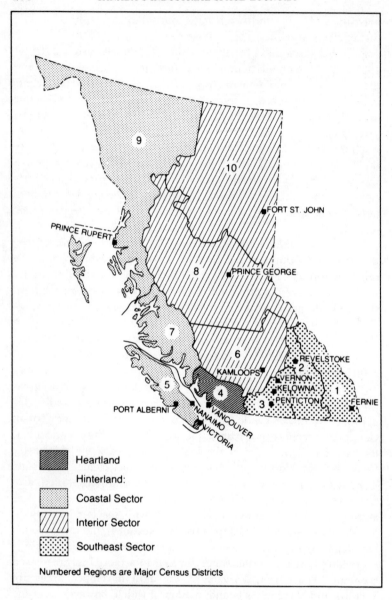

Figure 7.2   An Economic-Geographic Map of British Columbia.
Source: K. G. Denike and R. Leigh (1972)

Vancouver, Victoria and the Lower Mainland. The interior is divided into three sectors. The coastal area has a very narrow economic base including little other than forestry. Growth has been slow except for manufacturing on Vancouver Island. The southeastern sector has agriculture and mining but neither is growing: there is no major urban settlement, and the regional economy is fairly stagnant. The remaining, interior, sector has been quite dynamic in the last decade. It has importance in forestry, mining and agriculture, has received substantial public investment, and is moving towards a greater degree of linked development with strong urban growth. Prince George has been growing rapidly, with considerable new manufacturing employment largely in wood, pulp and paper industries.

Using the same census-based regions, Nesbitt (1973) has focused more specifically on manufacturing. With an emphasis on stages of development, he categorized British Columbia's industries into four groups as outlined above. Table 7.3 shows how the groups are distributed within each region. It particularly illustrates the dominance of primary processing everywhere except in the two metropolitan areas and Peace River (Division 10). Like Denike and Leigh, Nesbitt showed variations in the British Columbian hinterland but the two studies were not entirely in conformity. The slow-growing southeastern sector not only has the Kootenays (Division 1 and 2) with overwhelming dependence on primary processing but also the Okanagan (Division 3) with a more diversified structure, including especially a reasonable proportion of localized industries.

In the Kootenays, isolation and difficult transport conditions restrict the prospects for diversification from the wood and metal refining base (British Columbia, Department of Economic Development, 1976, 20). Cominco, however, has its research base as well as smelters at Trail and is planning an expansion despite the fact that ores are being brought over increasingly great distances. The Okanagan scarcely has less limitations. These southeastern areas are far from markets and must compete even in the West with much more strategically located centres. The beauty of the area may attract certain highly specialized activities dependent upon the brain power of a few people who choose to live there, but the scope in this direction would seem to be limited.

Apart from Division 6, the rest of the peripheral area is all highly dependent on primary processing, largely wood-based industries. Nesbitt (1973, 277–8) was surprised to find a very restricted base for the Prince George area but expected to see greater expansion of the

TABLE 7.3
INDUSTRIAL STRUCTURE OF B.C. CENSUS DIVISIONS, 1967,
BY PERCENTAGE OF VALUE OF SHIPMENTS

	Primary Processing	Localized	Backwardly Linked	Import Substituting	Total %
Census Division 1	92.32	7.29	0.27	0.12	100
Census Division 2	93.50	6.38	—	0.12	100
Census Division 3	64.03	23.25	3.93	8.79	100
Metropolitan Vancouver	26.32	41.08	10.02	22.58	100
Rest of Division 4	66.42	25.43	4.06	4.09	100
Metropolitan Victoria	35.20	34.79	27.36	2.65	100
Rest of Division 5	92.95	4.51	2.35	0.19	100
Census Division 6	82.26	16.04	1.30	0.39	100
Census Division 7 & 9	97.83	1.80	0.30	0.07	100
Census Division 8	91.21	6.73	0.81	1.24	100
Census Division 10	36.90	62.30	0.44	0.37	100
Total Province	53.87	26.82	6.97	12.34	100

Source: Nesbitt (1973). Tables XV, XVIII, XX and XXI

NESBITT'S CATEGORIES OF MANUFACTURING AS APPLIED TO BRITISH COLUMBIA

Nesbitt's categories of manufacturing as applied to British Columbia.

Primary Processing. Industries which are present mainly because of the resources themselves. The minimization of assembly costs is critical. The Alcan smelter at Kitimat, using imported materials, is also included because hydro-electric power is crucial to its location.

Localized Industries. Products are not important in inter-regional trade. For some reason, these products are difficult to transport and therefore locate near the market. Localized industries exceeded the B.C. average in both the following ratios:

(1) B.C. shipments as a proportion of total B.C. production.

(2) B.C. shipments as a proportion of the B.C. production met by all Canadian manufacturers in the industry.

Such industries also must not process primary products nor fulfil the requirements for the backwardly linked group.

Backwardly Linked Industries

These supply the primary processing and resource sectors.

Import Substituting Industries

This group is characterized by:

(1) The importance of economics of scale

(2) External economies

(3) Importance of labour as an input.

Such industries concentrate mainly in developed areas and their products feature prominently in interregional trade.

The difference between localized and import substituting industries is primarily one of degree. The import substituting group faces strong external competition and its proportion of total B.C. sales for its products is below the provincial average.

TABLE 7.4
CLASSIFICATION OF
BRITISH COLUMBIA MANUFACTURING INDUSTRIES
INTO FOUR GROUPS BASED ON THE THEORETICAL FRAMEWORK

Industry Group	S.I.C. Code	Industry Group	S.I.C. Code	Industry Group	S.I.C Code	S.I.C. Code
Primary			(B) 304	Import		(B) 318
Processing			(B) 308	Substituting		(B) 321
Industries			(H) 328	Industries		(B) 324
	111		(B) 341		(H) 101	(B) 325
	112		(B) 345		(B) 124	(H) 329
	147		(B) 347		(H) 125	(B) 331
	2511		(B) 348		(H) 128	(H) 334
	2513		(B) 3511		(H) 131	(B) 335
	252		(H) 353		(H) 1391	(B) 337
	259		(B) 359		(H) 1392	(B) 338
	271		(B) 3651		(H) 143	(B) 339
	295		(B) 369		(B) 169	(B) 3512
	378		(B) 372		(B) 172	(B) 352
			(B) 375		(H) 179	(B) 354
Localized			(B) 3791		(B) 197	(B) 355
Industries			(H) 3814		(B) 211	(B) 3561
	(H) 103		(H) 3815		(B) 215	(B) 3562
	(H) 105		(H) 384		(B) 216	(B) 3652
	(B) 123		(B) 397		(B) 218	(H) 374
	(H) 129		(H) 3983		(H) 2292	(H) 376
	(B) 133		(B) 3995		(H) 2299	(H) 377
	(H) 141		(H) 3997		(H) 239	(B) 3799
	(H) 145		(B) 3998		(H) 243	(B) 3811
	(H) 221				(H) 244	(H) 3813
	(B) 223	Backwardly			(H) 245	(H) 382
	(B) 2541	Linked			(H) 246	(H) 383
	(H) 258	Industries			(H) 247	(B) 385
	(H) 261		174		(B) 264	(H) 3931
	(H) 266		175		(H) 268	(H) 3932
	(B) 272		213		(H) 274	(B) 395
	(B) 2731		256		(H) 288	(H) 3982
	(B) 2732		305		(B) 291	(B) 3985
	(B) 2733		311		(B) 292	(H) 3986
	(B) 286		315		(B) 296	(B) 3988
	(B) 287		323		(B) 297	(H) 3989
	(H) 289		327		(B) 301	(H) 3996
	(B) 294		336		(B) 306	(H) 3999
	(B) 298		371		(B) 307	
	(B) 302		373		(B) 309	
	(B) 303				(B) 316	

(B), (H) = localized or import substituting industries producing goods mainly for business (B) or household (H) use

backwardly linked group. This has been gradually taking place. Meanwhile the extreme north-west (Division 10) has severe limitations because of the distance to market and the difficulties of attracting labour (British Columbia, Dept. of Economic Development, 1975, 3–4).

Manufacturing in the Core Area

A more diversified manufacturing structure in British Columbia is confined to the small Lower Mainland area with an extension to Victoria. Very largely, it is Greater Vancouver which houses the industry yet even here Steed (1973, 237) argues that the structure is narrow. In comparison with other large metropolitan areas, Vancouver has a high proportion of resource processing. Amongst its major industries are sawmills, veneers and plywood mills, sash and door plants, fish processing, meat packing and butter and cheese factories. In forest industries, Vancouver is gaining prominence as a centre for corporate head offices, which provide an important source of expanding employment opportunities and income growth; they generate considerable multiplier effects, especially through the attraction of ancillary research and development, financial, consulting, legal and marketing services (Hayter, 1977, 4). There has also been diversification into more fully processed items such as corrugated boxes, paper bags, tissues, folding cartons and fine papers.

As Table 7.3 shows, there is in addition an important sector which is backwardly linked to the resource sector. The manufacture of cans, for example, supports fish processing and fruit and vegetable canning businesses, machinery is supplied to the forestry sector, and much of the shipbuilding is also linked to the movement of wood. In Greater Vancouver is concentrated a high proportion of the manufacturing which provides items for B.C. producers. The metropolis also has a large market-oriented (localized) sector, taking advantage of the concentrated urban market in the Georgia Straits area but shipping to the rest of the province as well. Important industries include dairies, bakeries, breweries, printers and publishers, petroleum refineries, cement plants and machine shops. Metropolitan Vancouver's 72,000 workers make it Canada's third most important manufacturing centre (fourth in value added behind Hamilton).

The pros and cons of a Vancouver location have not changed much since McGovern (1961) discussed them. The coastal location gives significant transport cost advantages. Not only are imports by water facilitated but competition by water keeps the cost of overland transport down. Thus, for example, steel from eastern Canada has been supplied more cheaply than at Calgary or Edmonton. The West Coast location has become increasingly important as trade with the Pacific Rim countries has grown. On the other hand, the vast distances to large manufacturing areas provides a degree of protection for consumer goods and for some items required by the resource sector. Local producers of bulky, low-value products or perishable items receive a natural bonus in this respect. Rapid growth of the metropolitan, British Columbian and Albertan markets have all encouraged such industries since the war.

A major problem in Vancouver is a shortage of serviced industrial land, and consequent high land costs. Despite a certain amount of industrial park development in the last twenty years, this remains a difficulty (Steed, 1973, 251–5; Greater Vancouver Regional District, 1976, 19–52), although the British Columbia Development Corporation is attempting to improve the situation. In their detailed 1976 discussion of the industrial community's views on the topic, the Regional District concluded that 'it was a widely accepted viewpoint that the main problem with industrial development in the region is a lack of alternative industrial locations' (p.51). Constructive competition, it was felt, could improve the quality of sites and of the region's industry. Manufacturing has not received high priority in regional planning and is still frowned upon by many of the inhabitants, who wish to enhance Vancouver's environmental and aesthetic attractions. Strong initiatives by the Greater Vancouver Regional District (1977), however, indicate a much more positive development, including the appointment of an industrial commissioner. A remaining problem, common to the whole province, is high labour costs and a relatively bad record of industrial strife.

The main industrial areas dating from the early years of Vancouver were dominant until the 1960s (Hardwick, 1972, 126). They included False Creek to the south of the late nineteenth century city, and the area along the harbour to the east. New Westminster was another important node of sawmills and fish canning. Since the Second World War, however, population has sprawled and several formerly independent settlements have been absorbed into the metropolitan area. New manufacturing plants, especially larger ones, required other sites, and sawmills, refineries and paper plants have spread eastwards along the Fraser. Some suburban industrial areas were also established. Meanwhile, the older districts have

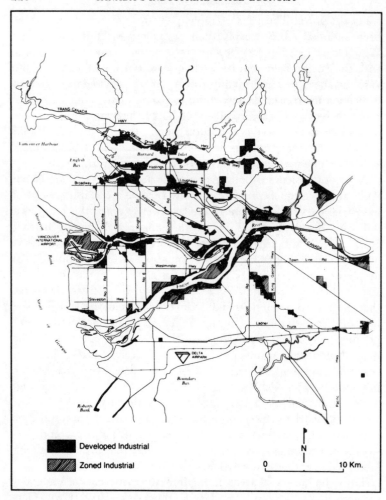

Figure 7.3   Vancouver's Industrial Areas.
Source: Greater Vancouver Regional District, Planning Department; Industrial Areas in Greater Vancouver. Map published in 1977

declined and industry has frequently been replaced by other activities (figure 7.3).

Steed (1973, 239–40) has noted that Vancouver has a high proportion of suburban manufacturing associated with the rather specialized locational requirements of a few large plants. Wood processing and paper mills gain substantially from waterfront properties for material inputs, exports and water. There are fish processors in Richmond, shipyards in North Vancouver, chemical plants and petroleum refineries at the eastern end of Burrard Inlet. Most have required large tracts of land, waterfront sites and a degree of isolation because of pollution problems. Nevertheless, plants of all sizes tend to be widely distributed rather than the more common tendency for smaller plants to be central and larger ones further out.

Within Greater Vancouver, Steed (1973) has analysed the locational change in terms of time zones for travel from downtown. In 1955, the central zone (10 minutes from the centre) showed a concentration of clothing, knitting, electrical products, printing, publishing and textiles. Clothing industries relied on cheap upper-storey space in old warehouses, and on accessible female workforce. The other major group, printing, supplied the downtown office market. In the following decade, only the clothing and knitting groups continued to concentrate in the centre, while others dispersed. Thus the Vancouver situation is quite comparable to Toronto (see chapter 5). In Vancouver, however, this central zone still gained plants from 1955 to 1965 by an excess of new plants over closures (p. 244). Nevertheless, the major gains were further out in a 16–25 minute zone while losses occurred in the 11–15 minute one.

The changing locational pattern of plants from the mid – 1950s to the mid – 1960s was a result largely of trends in a few sectors. Many food processing plants in the inner core went out of business while new ones located further out, mainly in the 16–35 minutes zone.[1] Wood processing added plants in the same intermediate zone while furniture, metals and machinery migrated out and added new suburban plants (p. 243). The main features of the changing pattern included an eastward shift of manufacturing in the core while the False Creek area declined. Meanwhile, rapid growth from a small manufacturing base took place in North Vancouver and along the north shore. Although the largest suburban growth was along the north arm of the Fraser, Surrey and Delta in the south also expanded rapidly. Most suburban growth was in the form of new plants rather than migration from the inner areas (pp. 246–51).

A more recent survey shows that decentralization is continuing, as other urban uses push manufacturing from the central parts of

[1]Steed's definitions of births, deaths and migrations are somewhat wider than usual. See his pages 241–3.

Vancouver (Greater Vancouver Regional District, 1976, 12–13). It is expected that high land costs, high rents, congestion and labour problems will affect other Vancouver locations soon. In addition, population (and hence markets and labour) has spread to the south and east, where larger industrial sites are available. Industrial employment targets for 1986 envisage a rise in the percentage of regional industrial employment in the southern sub-area (Delta, Surrey, White Rock) from 6.9 per cent in 1971 to 17.0 per cent in 1986. In the north-east (Coquitlam, Port Coquitlam, Port Moody) a similar trend (3.7 to 7.3%) is expected while Vancouver is to fall from 54.7 to 41.1 per cent (Greater Vancouver Regional District, 1977, 28). (Wholesaleing, transport and utilities are included in these figures.)

INDUSTRIAL DEVELOPMENT POLICY

As in the Prairie region, so also in British Columbia, dependence on primary activities has led to a strong policy emphasis on diversification. Here, too, manufacturing is important for promoting both fuller processing of the province's resources and also more varied industries of all types. The Ministry of Economic Development has identified manufacturing sectors in which it feels there are real opportunities for private investment. Most promising are considered to be smoked salmon, hydraulic excavators, front end loaders, diesel engines, electrical switchgear and protective equipment, A-C generators, transformers and intermodal freight containers (British Columbia, Ministry of Economic Development, no date). The Ministry has examined these industries in detail as part of its effort to widen the province's manufacturing base. It is now attempting to find firms that will go into business.

Relative to other provinces, British Columbia's advisory and consulting services to manufacturers place more emphasis on marketing and exports than on other elements of management. This is a logical reaction to the long distances which make penetration of Canadian markets very difficult. Assistance is provided for manufacturers to take part in trade missions, and a market development assistance programme also helps firms to investigate or work in new markets. Various other aids to manufacturers provide information and counselling similar to that offered elsewhere in Canada, with a focus on small businesses (British Columbia, Dept. of Economic Development, no date).

The Ministry of Economic Development (formerly a department) was established only in 1975 and has gradually widened its approach to include a broad co-ordinating role concerned with all aspects of economic development. Spatial elements of policy have been relatively unimportant until recently, although there has always been a group concerned with industrial locations. This unit is now being expanded to help municipalities with industrial development, but, so far, it is difficult to predict the results of these changes. The tradition of municipality involvement in industrial development in British Columbia is weak. There are few industrial commissioners and, in the past, the province has not taken positive steps to encourage their establishment. Neither has the province, in contrast to many others, had regional development offices. Nevertheless, an overall policy of decentralization from the Georgia Straits urban area has recently become evident and spatial policy has become more explicit with a new subsidiary agreement between British Columbia and DREE.

This agreement on industrial development signed in July 1977 outlines the most comprehensive subsidiary agreement on regional industrial development yet signed by DREE (Canada and British Columbia, 1977). Its objectives 'are to encourage greater sectorial and spatial diversification' in the province and to 'achieve a more balanced level of development among the different areas of the province'. The major focus is on steps to remedy the dominant role of the Lower Mainland Region in the provincial economy (Canada and British Columbia, 1977, Schedule A, 3). British Columbia's objectives in economic development strategy are listed as:

(1) increasing the opportunities for productive employment and more generally, ensuring greater balance between actual employment and the numbers of people actively seeking work;
(2) maintaining and enhancing the real incomes of British Columbians;
(3) providing stability of employment and real incomes in the province;
(4) achieving a greater degree of regional balance in provincial economic development.

In view of the current situation in the province, these objectives translate into a strategy of increasing 'secondary manufacturing and support activities in the less densely populated areas of the Province.' Thus the agreement essentially applies to a 'target area' outside the Lower Mainland and southern Vancouver Island.

The actual programmes provided under the agreement are quite comprehensive and are expected to cost $70 million dollars over a five-year period. This is in addition to a further $20 million of financial assistance by the British Columbia Development Corporation and $20 million of DREE incentive grants. The programmes cover:

(1) *Research* studies by consultants to identify development opportunities, including those in the service sector; studies on the viability of such opportunities; and special reports on the ability of communities and regions to cope with development.

(2) *Community Industrial Development* will consume the bulk of the financing. A regional approach to industrial development is desired with well trained people and good facilities in each region. Growth centres are identified and adequate industrial land is to be provided in them. Orderly and efficient growth is to be promoted through the use of industrial parks and industrial malls. Attempts will also be made to encourage higher value added manufacturing throughout the province. The components of this programme include:

(a) Assistance to regional industrial commissions for staff and administration. At first 90 per cent of costs will be provided but this will diminish to 50 per cent. This represents a new thrust in the province and it should be noted that a broad regional approach is to be taken. The regional commission will be responsible for an economic development plan and for co-ordinating the activities of the communities and sub-districts in the region.

(b) Low interest loans will be made to key communities for the servicing of industrial parks. The communities will be the larger regional service centres that have a demonstrated growth potential, adequate labour force and the infrastructure for further development.

(c) For smaller communities there will be low interest loans for industrial sites. This will provide land for identified opportunities.

(d) Loan financing will also be available for industrial malls but this support is regarded as exceptional.

(e) Similarly, communities may be aided in the building of advance factories.

(3) *Industrial Assistance* is for small enterprises. Interest-free forgivable loans will encourage modernization, expansion or establish-

BRITISH COLUMBIA 225

ment of small businesses which are too small for qualification under the usual incentive programmes.

(4) *Public Information* about the agreement is to be paid for out of its budget.

An interesting feature of this very comprehensive subsidiary agreement is that it is to be administered by an Industrial Development Committee consisting of provincial and federal representatives. The provincial minister appoints two regular members from the Ministry of Economic Development and one *ex-officio* member from the British Columbia Development Corporation. From the federal side are one regular member from DREE and another from Industry, Trade and Commerce plus an *ex-officio* member from the Federal Business Development Bank. If the regular members cannot reach a decision unanimously, the subject is turned over to the ministers for personal consideration.

Reference has been made to the British Columbia Development Corporation. Although funded by the provincial government, the corporation has a majority of directors from private enterprise. It was set up in 1973 with the objective of encouraging economic development throughout the province. The British Columbia Development Corporation is unique in Canada in having the ability to combine finance and land in a package for industrialists. Not only is the corporation assembling its own land for industrial parks in such communities as Prince Rupert and Kamloops but it is also the administering agency for other provincially-owned land such as the parks of B.C. Hydro and B.C. Rail. This land function could be particularly important in view of the shortage and high cost of industrial land in the province (British Columbia Development Corporation, no date).

CONCLUSION

In a sense, economic development for British Columbia has come easily. Her rich resources and natural attractions have brought people and capital without a great deal of effort on the part of the existing inhabitants. Until the defeat of W.A.C. Bennett's Social Credit party by the NDP in the early 1970s, governmental economic policy had mainly consisted of keeping British Columbia as attractive to private business as possible. On the other hand, the resource-based economy is vulnerable and has suffered some serious setbacks due to changing market conditions over the years. Attitudes and circumstances in the 1960s led to a more positive role in the economy by Mr Barrett's NDP government and this has not been revoked by the current business-oriented Social Credit regime under Mr Bennett Jr. British Columbia has recognized a need to diversify, to protect its agricultural land and environment, and to plan the regional dimension of development. These objectives have not been met in the past by unbridled free enterprise, with the result that positive government policies are now in operation. Further, the economy has turned sour recently: continued expansion has not been automatic. This again forces the government to take action or to accept the consequences of even higher unemployment rates, plant closures and reduced exports. All the signs are that British Columbia has now fully joined the mainstream of the Canadian planned economy. The results of its experiment in regional industrial development will also be awaited with interest as it represents the most comprehensive provincial attempt at the regional planning of industry in Canada.

REFERENCES

Barr, B.M. and Fairbairn, K.J. (1974), 'Some observations on the environment of the firm: locational behavior of Kraft pulp mills in the interior of British Columbia', *Professional Geographer*, 26, (February), 19–26.

British Columbia, Department of Economic Development (1975), *The North East Report 75*. Victoria.

British Columbia, Department of Economic Development (1976),*The Kootenay Report 76*. Victoria.

British Columbia Development Corporation (no date), *The British Columbia Development Corporation*. Vancouver.

British Columbia, Ministry of Economic Development (1977a), *British Columbia Economic Activity: 1976 Review and Outlook*. Victoria.

British Columbia, Ministry of Economic Development, (1977b), *The Manual of Resources*. Victoria.

British Columbia, Ministry of Economic Development (no date), *Manufacturing Opportunities in B.C.*, Vancouver.

British Columbia, Task Force on Crown Timber Disposal, (1974), *First Report. Royalties and Other Levies for Harvesting Rights on Timber Leases, Licenses and Berths in British Columbia*. Victoria.

Canada and British Columbia (1977), *Canada – British Columbia Subsidiary Agreement. Industrial Development*.

Canada, DREE [Department of Regional Economic Expansion] (1973), *British Columbia: Economic Circumstances and Opportunities*. Ottawa.

Canada, DREE (1976), *Climate for Development: Western Region*. Ottawa.

Canada West Foundation (1975), *Western Canada: Location of Primary Wood Using Industries, 1973*. Calgary.

Denike, K.G. and Leigh, R. (1972), 'Economic geography 1960–70', in J.L. Robinson (ed.), *British Columbia*, (Toronto: University of Toronto), 69–86.

Farley, A.L. (1972), 'The forest resource', in J.L. Robinson (ed.), *British Columbia*, (Toronto: University of Toronto), 87–118.

Greater Vancouver Regional District (1976), *Industrial Development: Views and Issues of the Industrial Community*. Vancouver.

Greater Vancouver Regional District (1977), *Industry and the Livable Region: Guidelines for Industrial Development*. Vancouver

Hardwick, W.G. (1972), 'The Georgia Strait Urban Region', in J.L. Robinson (ed.), *British Columbia*, (Toronto: University of Toronto), 119–33.

Hayter, R. (1976), 'Corporate strategies and industrial change in the Canadian forest product industries', *Geographical Review*, 66, (April), 209–28.

Hayter, R. (1977), 'Forestry in British Columbia: the resource basis of Vancouver's dominance', Mimeo.

Ingram, J. (1958), 'Industrial development in British Columbia: Past, Present and Future', *Canadian Mining and Metallurgical Bulletin*, (Sept.), 1–5.

McGovern, P.D. (1961), 'Industrial development in the Vancouver area', *Economic Geography*, 37, (July), 189–206.

Munro, G.R. (1971), 'The Import-competing sector', in R.A. Shearer *et al.* (eds.), *Trade Liberalization and a Regional Economy*, (Toronto: University of Toronto), 88–174.

Nesbitt, J.G. (1973), 'Regional differences in the structure and growth of manufacturing in British Columbia', Unpublished M.A. Thesis, University of British Columbia.

Shearer, R. (1971), 'The Economy of British Columbia', in R.A. Shearer *et al.* (eds), *Trade Liberalization and a Regional Economy*, (Toronto: University of Toronto), 3–42.

Siemens, A.H. (1972), 'Settlement', in J.L. Robinson (ed.), *British Columbia*, (Toronto: University of Toronto), 9–31.

Steed, G.P.F. (1973), 'Intrametropolitan manufacturing: spatial distribution and locational dynamics in Greater Vancouver', *Canadian Geographer* 17, (Fall), 235–58.

Wolforth, J. (1965), 'Comments on the current energy uses of the pulp and paper industry of British Columbia', *Canadian Geographer*, 9, (Spring), 104–7.

8

Municipal Industrial Development

Municipal officials everywhere are concerned about income. Their policies depend on a solid tax base and so they are understandably interested in the nature of that base. The rationale for an industrial (economic or business) development programme is largely founded upon the recognition that a community which relies entirely on residential taxes will find it difficult to provide adequate services for its population. The industrial commissioner is responsible for keeping the business sector healthy and preferably growing. In so doing, he ensures large commercial and industrial tax returns. A secondary, but important, rationale for this function is the desire to provide sufficient jobs for the municipality's young people. Without some attention to this problem, a community may find itself in the position where its young people are forced to move elsewhere to find work. Nor surprisingly, most Canadian cities with a population above about 30,000 have a commissioner, and many smaller ones are active as well. Although numerous variations are found, the scope of the role and the approaches to the job have many similarities across the country.

Traditionally, the major focus of the work has been on manufacturing – hence, the common title of 'industrial commissioner'. More recently, especially in the 1970s, an increasing number of communities have found it necessary to expand the role to include the economic sector as a whole. Currently, commissioners are more and more being considered as business development officers. Their job includes the stimulation of all kinds of business – tourism, restaurants, retailing, wholesaling and transport, as well as manufacturing. Some are concerned with land acquisition (e.g. Regina, Saskatchewan), downtown renewal (e.g. Cambridge, Ontario), or municipal airports (Tillsonburg and Kingston, Ontario). Currently, the profession is grappling with the need to broaden its perspectives and educate its members for the wider involvement with total community development (O'Connell, 1976).

The Industrial Developers Association of Canada (IDAC) is the professional group which represents the industrial commissioners. It is not, however, solely concerned with municipal officials and the proportion of its membership from provincial and federal governments is growing. Also included are development officers with organizations such as rail and utility companies, and from the private sector (banks, developers and consultants). IDAC is relatively new, being formed in 1969. The association provides a means of communication across the country and has also developed an educational programme at the University of Waterloo. In-career education is seen as a major means of coping with the continuous changes in the work of a commissioner (Cooksley and Walker, 1974; Macpherson, 1976, 18, 78; Walker, 1977). Many members of IDAC also belong to the larger United States based American Industrial Development Council (AIDC), which is much older and provides a fuller range of services. In many ways, IDAC represents a spin-off from AIDC and relationships are cordial. Professional contact is further fostered by provincial associations in several provinces.

ORGANIZATION

Municipal industrial development in Canada, in contrast to the United States, is most commonly undertaken by local governments. The commissioner is in charge of, or occasionally a part of, a department responsible ultimately to council. There are a few cases where the job is handled by the Chamber of Commerce (e.g. Niagara Falls, Ontario), or by a development corporation with its own board (e.g. Moncton, New Brunswick). Under a city department, the work of the economic commissioner must conform to overall city goals and actions, which should encourage a fully integrated approach to community development. In addition, there is always the opportunity for the commissioner to make his point of view known and to see that business requirements are reflected in municipal policy. A commissioner who is not at city hall is able to represent the business community more fully, to be an advocate for the private sector. On the other hand, he is an outsider rather than a part of the process of the city's economic planning. It is hard to see how a commissioner outside of city hall can claim to be working for the good of the community as a whole as opposed to the special interests of the business community. The view that an industrial commissioner is essentially an economic development planner, concerned with seeing that development fits in with overall community objectives, is growing in Canada and is noticeably stronger than it was at the beginning of the decade. The main problem with a city hall post seems to be the danger of direct political intervention or breach of confidentiality by elected officials. Especially in discussion with companies considering a location in the community, such interference could be damaging. On the other hand, the majority of councillors in most places recognize the danger. And certainly no commissioner can do much in direct opposition to strong elected officials, even though he may be violently opposed to their viewpoint. All in all, success demands a good working relationship between councillors, city civil servants and the commissioner.

Local economic development efforts have historically been associated with larger urban centres, but rural areas and small towns have also become involved. This often necessitates an organization which cannot correspond to a particular local authority. Some municipalities have combined to fund an organization that represents them all, for example, the Windsor – Essex County Development Commission in Ontario. More commonly, provincial governments have been active in encouraging such commissions. The earliest were those in southern Manitoba, with 50 per cent provincial funding, but mainly locally-elected boards. More recently, Québec and New Brunswick have been active in promoting regional commissions and others are being established in British Columbia. Of necessity, these commissions face the problem of balancing their efforts amongst the constituent municipalities. Political considerations inhibit the spatial concentration of development efforts within their boundaries even when this might suggest itself as the most appropriate strategy.

Such internal conflict can be resolved, if at all, only if and when regional economic commissions match regional governments. With the advent of regional municipalities in some parts of Canada, this has, in fact, happened in some cases. Ontario has set up a number of two-tier regional governments in some of which the economic development function is at a regional level. One example is the Regional Municipality of Durham to the east of Toronto. Under this arrangement, there is political power to operate a regional development strategy even though certain constituent municipalities may not be in favour of it. The Ontario government has not made up its mind as to the wisdom of this arrangement: in most of the regional governments, economic development was not made a regional function. Experience, so far, has been too short to come to any empirical conclusions. Québec's urban communities (Montréal and Québec City) are also regional governments of a similar type with corresponding functions.

ASPECTS OF THE JOB

No two development commissions operate in exactly the same way so that a discussion of roles must of necessity be somewhat idealized. What follows, then, covers some of the essential elements even though, in any given municipality, the combination and emphasis will vary.

Planning

The kind of planning traditionally carried out by industrial commissioners has been quite narrow, relative to the range of topics that requires consideration. This is partly because long-term forecasts and the community plans that are based on them are usually prepared by the planning department. It is difficult, however, to see how population and economic forecasts can be made without some consideration of the policies the development commissioner might be expecting to follow. If, for example, the commissioner is planning a sustained campaign for expansion of certain sectors and has reasonable expectations of success, this will have implications for population growth and for other sectors on which demands will be made. Long-term projections based on past trends just assume that no initiatives will come from the development office! For adequate community planning, surely the commissioner must become intimately involved with such matters, and there are indications of some moves in this direction.

In two areas of long-term planning many industrial commissioners are currently involved. The first of these is the selection of appropriate sectors of growth in the community. Such a selection requires, ideally, a thorough evaluation of the locational advantages and disadvantages of the community in order to concentrate on sectors for which this balance is most encouraging. On the basis of a recent evaluation, for example, Edmonton's development department suggests a concentration on head offices for resource-based companies, financial institutions, high technology industries, consulting and research companies related to resources, industries using petro-chemical materials, increased transport services, and some attention to activities related to a growing local market. It must be admitted, however, that many communities in central and south-western Ontario have never conducted such an exercise in a serious way because growth has occurred quite naturally in the past.

Closely related to expected growth trends is the second aspect of forecasting commonly carried out by industrial commissioners, the estimation of future requirements of industrial land. This is impor-tant because of the widely-held view that a store of serviced land is essential to any community's success in development (Gillies, 1974, 207–9; O'Connell, 1976). Usually, it has become policy for the community to own some of its own industrial land. Thus a forecast of requirements must be made. These forecasts normally are closely related to, if not entirely governed by, past demands for land but clearly they should tie in with estimates of the future which consider both changes in the community's attraction and in its development policy. A recent study for St Catharines (St Catharines Business Development Dept., 1975) evaluated trends in population, assessment, existing land use by manufacturing firms, estimates of expansion requirements by existing firms and likely demands by new firms as a basis for a 15-year projection. Thus, past trends were modified by reasonable speculation about the future.

In spatial planning, the industrial commissioner has often con-fined his interests to the location and planning of industrial parks, an area in which the Canadian practitioner is now fairly expert. But, is this enough? Almost all elements of urban land use bear some relationship to economic viability. Even if a commissioner is solely concerned with manufacturing, he must take an interest in the location of residences (workforce) and transport routes (for both workers and trucks). With a trend towards a broader involvement in most aspects of business, it is hard to see how a vital involvement with the overall spatial configuration of the community can be avoided.

All of these arguments lead to a view that economic development and planning must be more closely related if not joined together. Either the development office must take on a larger role in economic planning or at least be closely related to the economic planners on a regular basis. Unfortunately, there is a high degree of mutual mistrust between the two professions in Canada at present. On the one hand, developers argue, with some truth, that the planners know little about economics and are only concerned with controlling the private sector. On the other side, and also with some truth, planners consider most commissioners to be completely business-oriented and to be uninterested in the quality of life of the average citizen. Somehow, these conflicts must be resolved and mutual understanding and respect built up.

Industrial Park Development

It has become the norm in Canada that any municipality seriously interested in industrial development should have an industrial park (Gillies, 1974, 20). Most development commissioners are therefore concerned with planning and running such parks and some provinces have produced manuals which help them in the task (Québec, Ministère de l'industrie et du commerce, 1974). Most of the parks in Canada, however, still do not conform to the narrow definition of a strictly controlled area in a park-like environment. Rather they are industrial districts operating under less tight controls (Vann, 1974, 167–70 and 192–4). Nevertheless, standards required by municipalities are becoming increasingly stiff as demands for an improved environment grow.

There are many private industrial parks in Canada, but the proportion of municipally owned ones is increasing in response to the widespread feeling that they help to keep the price of serviced land down. Municipalities recoup the cost of raw land plus the expense of providing such services as roads, water, gas, sewerage, and electricity, but no profit is made. Choice of site seems to be based primarily on two features, fairly level available land and accessibility. Accessibility mainly means access to major highways for trucks, although the secondary element of accessibility for workers is considered. This second element could well become more important as energy costs push up the expense of commuting.

An industrial commissioner usually has considerable influence on the design of the park even though he operates in close co-operation with the planning and engineering department. This is important because he should be the official in the municipality who is most familiar with the demand for industrial space, being fully aware of popular lot sizes and the most probable nature of future requirements. The decisions taken about lay-out are quite important because they will determine the pattern of service provisions, so that any miscalculation of demand could be expensive.

The quality of development is controlled in various ways. In a study of several industrial parks in midwestern Ontario, Vann (1974) looked at some of these. *Land use controls*, *via* zoning, are used everywhere and normally keep heavier, noxious industries out of the park. Commercial activities are also usually restricted to a limited type of activity, which serves the needs of the industries or their employees. The typical park has substantial warehousing, distribution and industrial service functions, as well as manufacturing. It is also possible to limit activities by *performance* controls, such as upper limits on noise, effluents, air pollution or vibration. Vann (pp. 175–6) found such limits to be mainly ill-defined, but they could be made quite specific.

Restrictions on the buildings themselves are now commonly imposed. Certain building materials are often requested, while others are disallowed. In particular, building fronts may usually not be of concrete block. The degree of control in this area varies considerably, however, with Kitchener insisting on certain types of finish for exterior walls (Vann, 1974, 181; Gillies, 1974, 226). *Site* restrictions are more numerous, including landscape requirements, limits to outdoor storage, a minimum level of parking (usually based on number of workers), setbacks, and proportion of the site to be covered by buildings. The features are usually established by means of legal devices, especially purchase agreements, deed restrictions, covenants and conditions established in the lease.

Controls over parks have been increasing and many industrialists prefer to operate in this type of environment because they are protected from bad neighbours. The better industrial parks are now as attractive as many residential areas. In fact, the sharp separation of land uses which grew up in the early twentieth century as a response to the unpleasantness of earlier industrial environments should be questioned. It has sometimes led to large tracts of industrial land far removed from the residences of many workers. With the current careful controls on industrial parks, it would seem that residence and industry could be located closer together again and that smaller industrial parks (100 acres or so) located within different sectors of the municipality could be established. If performance controls were used to filter out inappropriate plants, the only possible problem would come from trucks. These, however, can usually be routed along certain corridors and could avoid residential areas. Such an arrangement would reduce employee travel and help to lower the inordinate amount of energy wasted on commuting. It might also bring industry into the consciousness of the average citizen again (City of Toronto Planning Board, 1974, 41).

In the past, most firms have bought rather than leased sites in industrial parks, but in the last few years leased space in multiple occupancy buildings (industrial malls) has become important. Most industrial parks now have some such space and malls are also springing up in other parts of many communities. Owned normally be private developers, these buildings cater for small operations. Recent studies (Smith and Werb, 1977) show the average lessee employs fewer than ten people and occupies under 10,000 sq. ft. of floor space. For small firms, this kind of space proves to be cheap, saves capital for operating costs, and provides flexibility for expansion. There is some evidence that malls are now playing an important role in the 'incubation' of new firms in suburban areas, replacing the old multi-storied factories of the inner city. Malls are most used by wholesalers but many industrial services also find the space ideal. Types of manufacturing that favour this kind of space are restricted: metal fabricating, machinery, printing and publishing being the most common. It should be noted that these manufacturing operations frequently provide services to other firms. In less developed parts of the country, malls are now being considered as a development tool. This approach is being used successfully in Prince Edward Island, for example. Generally lower rents are allowed with a most favourable first year grading up to a commercial rent at the end of five years. This arrangement helps new firms to establish themselves with reduced capital costs.

Prospecting

Ten years ago, many industrial commissioners would have argued that their primary function consisted in attracting manufacturers to move into their community from outside. This view is less prevalent today, but the prospecting role remains important. New factories are tangible evidence of success and particularly useful in convincing local politicians of a job well done!

The practical elements of prospecting are covered in Bessire (1970, 201–92), which is still used widely in Canada. While part of the work may consist in responding to unsolicited enquiries about the community, an organized campaign consists of identifying companies that may be interested in locating a plant there and trying to persuade them to do so. The identification process should ideally be related to the activities considered appropriate on the basis of the economic plan. Frequently, the initial contact is made by writing to North American companies involved in the relevant business and informing them of the advantages of the community. Increasingly, approaches are now also made to European companies. Any replies are followed up by visits to the company, by sending more specific information on the community, and/or by an invitation to company executives to visit the community.

An important document prepared by commissioners is the community profile. It contains all important information on the community that is likely to be required by businessmen. Included usually are details on location and climate, history, population, labour, administration and governmental services, public services, transport, financial institutions, trade, manufacturing, industrial services, education and recreation. Guidelines for this and other publicity documents have recently been drawn up by Mignault (1977).

Often, special studies for a particular client will also be needed. These will cover topics peculiar to the firm and requiring individual research.

Servicing the Business Sector

In practice, most industrial commissioners spend a much higher proportion of their time with businesses already located in the community than with potential new ones. This is as it should be because a high proportion of job creation does, in fact, come from existing firms and from new entrepreneurs who already live locally. But even where expansions are rare, the commissioner may have a vital role to play in keeping existing enterprises viable and preventing businesses from moving away or going out of business.

The extent to which the office of the commissioner becomes involved in general advice and counselling will depend largely on the activities of the local Chamber of Commerce, which, as a businessman's organization, usually has programmes of this type.

The commissioner should certainly be aware of available programmes and courses. There are two areas which require particular attention. The first is diagnostic and involves knowing the local firms well enough to spot problems in order to tactfully offer advice before minor difficulties become major ones. The second concerns counselling related to investment decisions. Current practice indicates that many commissioners act as a kind of financial consultant to the small businessman. They should be aware of source of funds and be able to help prepare a case either for financial agencies or incentive-granting agencies such as the Department of Regional Economic Expansion. A recent publication by Bergeron (1977) greatly helps in the task.

The industrial commissioner should also be closely involved in the continuing process of spatial adaptation in his community. As plants age and the industrial areas of yesteryear lose their attraction, many of the firms in these areas need help. If a municipality does not concern itself with updating the old areas or providing new sites, it is likely that it will lose plants. The main response to date has been the provision of new industrial parks in the suburbs. In the meantime, the older areas have declined and often been taken over by commercial or residential land uses. Now there is some concern as to whether or not this process should be halted because of the needs of some industries for central locations, and for the preservation of working class districts near the older industrial areas (City of Toronto Planning Board, 1974). This problem faces many eastern Canadian cities, though it is less troublesome in the more recently developed West. A close involvement with land use planning and zoning policy will be essential in allowing flexibility for adaptations to take place.

Perhaps one of the greatest dangers today as the economic development practitioner becomes more sophisticated and more involved with broad elements of economic planning is that the commissioner loses touch with the local business community. This would be disastrous, inasmuch as he should be the main person responsible for seeing that essential business needs are met by the community, whether it be by sensible zoning, the design of an industrial park or urban transit policy. In contrast the commissioner should be a catalyst for creativity in the local business sector, not only helping to provide the right environment but introducing new ideas for product development, introducing businessmen to others in the community who could supply or require their services or products, and generally encouraging entrepreneurial activity.

An Educational Role

Most development commissioners take some part in educating the community about economic development even if it consists only in answering questions or supplying information to school children. As the person most responsible for achieving a good climate for business, it could be argued that more attention should be placed on this role. As businessmen become more sensitive to community attitudes towards economic development, these attitudes themselves are becoming a location factor of some importance, especially in a choice between communities within the same region. But what is a good business climate and how can it be achieved?

It is a common fallacy amongst professionals to believe that their job is so vital that everyone automatically accepts its importance. Today, however, there are proponents of no growth and slow growth, and few who accept economic growth as an unmitigated blessing. In order to make the case that jobs are needed, the developer must recognize some of the disadvantages that could accompany them. Growth may push up land prices, cause congestion, damage the environment and disrupt neighbourhoods. On the other hand, most of these dangers can be partly or completely overcome. A community will welcome business when its members can see that the advantages of new developments outweigh the disadvantages.

The development commissioner should undertake to see that this is the case. He will need to keep in touch with several groups, starting with elected officials and the municipality's own staff. As representatives of the community, these people must be well briefed. The community at large deserves attention through meetings and the media but this is not easy except in providing general information. Many special interest groups develop which are opposed to development and the commissioner must be prepared to engage in debate with them. They may not be convinced but others in the community will see that all the right is not on their side. Finally, the businessmen themselves may need to be educated to think about responsible practice *vis-à-vis* the community, so that harsh criticisms of them do not prove to be true.

Perhaps the profession should take special steps to improve its contact with young people. They require discussion not only on development but also on business and jobs. Attitudes in many schools tend to be anti-business and especially to encourage the view that blue collar work is completely undesirable. Partly because of this, skilled labour is in short supply in many parts of Canada and forecasts suggest that the situation will worsen (Economic Council of Canada, 1975). Given the shortage of jobs for many university graduates and the good pay of many skilled jobs, this situation is surprising. It could well be the result of pressures at school, which encourage potential skilled workers to go to university, where they are often out of place and obtain poor degrees. Industrial commissioners could certainly concentrate some attention on the schools to the profit both of the future business climate and of the manpower situation.

AN EMERGING WIDER ROLE

Despite the importance of manufacturing in the traditional job specification of an industrial commissioner, all the evidence points to a move in the direction of development departments which concern themselves with all types of business. This makes sense because of both the close inter-relationships of all aspects of the urban economy and the fact that non-manufacturing sectors are providing an increasing proportion of new jobs (see chapter 1). On the first point, it has already been stressed that good planning for one sector can be made only if due consideration is given to all others. As for the second, if industrial commissioners ignore traders, hotel owners and industrial service firms, they could put themselves out of a job, especially in smaller centres outside southern Ontario and Québec.

It has already been stressed that the business development department should be a planning department, but its role is wider than that of traditional municipal planning. It must be activist in the sense that it is responsible for encouraging its plans to material-ize rather than just designating what and where things should happen and setting up criteria which control the character of the happening. The development group is responsible for stimulating the business sector to do what the community as a whole (through its plans) would like.

This view of municipal development is hard to reconcile with the possibility of having the work carried out by a private commission and particularly by a business group such as a Chamber of Commerce. The thesis here is that economic development as it is now practised in Canada, and as it should be practised, is not for the benefit of the businessman but for the community at large. The commissioner should not be a spokesman for the private sector but a public servant trying to ensure that the private sector benefits the community to the full. The roles may at times be similar because a healthy business sector is vital to a prosperous community. But what is good for business is not always good for everyone else. Nevertheless, the scope for the private sector in research, consulting, planning and development is considerable. The key point is that it will be carried out according to criteria laid down by the public authorities.

In becoming established in this somewhat new position, the economic development profession is becoming more sensitive to the various interest groups in a city. While the complaints by environmental and citizen groups about economic growth were once considered to be the railings of a few eccentrics, now their arguments are heard even if not always consented to. What is happening is that quality of development is becoming more important than its size (O'Connell, 1976). Sensitivity is essential if the developer is to maintain credibility in the face of changing public attitudes. Moreover, it should be part of his educational role to convince the private sector where necessary that attractive factories, clean air and good working conditions are important. On the other hand, the commissioner must also represent the legitimate complaints of the private sector to the community. All in all, a difficult but vital task! The situation could be improved by advisory boards which included a diverse membership as opposed to purely politicians and businessmen. If citizens' groups and unions were also involved, the meetings could play a major education role in themselves.

CONCLUSIONS

Municipal industrial development is becoming more complex for those who once had a mandate to increase jobs by helping manufacturers to expand or set up a new plant. Societal attitudes have changed as the value of growth for growth's sake has been questioned. As a result, the development commissioner faces opposition groups and must work within a policy framework that is less favourable to private enterprise. In the meantime, the problems of the Canadian economy have slowed growth down. Add to this the fact that the development department is now responsible for a wider range of activities than before, and it can be appreciated that the profession is facing a major transition.

Wisely in these changing times, the Industrial Developers Association of Canada has chosen to place a good deal of emphasis on continuing education. Not only does it sponsor the programme at Waterloo but it also runs an annual conference which has a strong educational focus. Its small publication programme is moving in the same direction. While these efforts are producing better commissioners more appropriate to the times, a new professional focus has not yet fully emerged. The association has not established its professional territory or set up meaningful accreditation for its membership. Only in Québec have major steps been achieved in this direction. There, the provincial association has a voice in the appointment of new commissioners.

In the context of professional identity and good economic development for Canada, the question of the inter-relationships of the three levels of government requires attention. A tendency remains for IDAC to act as though it were essentially an association for municipal commissioners, when in fact an increasing proportion of its members work at a much larger scale. Partly as a consequence, provincial and federal officials closely bound up with development see little in the Association for them. In the long run, such a separation of personnel could be very counterproductive. For one thing, personal acquaintances across the governmental barriers are likely to help in cases where two or more levels of government deal with each other. Perhaps more importantly, it is hard to imagine good federal programmes drawn up by officials who are unaware of the reality of operations at provincial or municipal levels. At the same time, a municipal development commissioner cannot really appreciate his own situation until he has looked at it from a much broader perspective than the one from his own office. Intergovernmental relationships are of course a feature of all aspects of urban policy in Canada (Gertler and Crowley, 1977, 211–14, 452–6). One must hope for a future profession in which movement among the three levels of government takes place to a much greater degree than it does now.

REFERENCES

Bater, J. H. and Walker, D. F. (1977), 'Industrial services: literature and research prospects', in D. F. Walker (ed.), *Industrial Services*, (Waterloo: University of Waterloo, Department of Geography), 1–25.

Bergeron, P. G. (1977), *Capital Expenditure Planning for Growth and Profit*. Ottawa: The Canadian Institute of Chartered Accountants.

Bessire, H. D. (1970), *The Practice of Industrial Development*. El Paso, Texas: Hill Printing Co.

Buck, W. P. (1977), 'Cost and time to develop industrial land', *Bulletin, Industrial Developers Association of Canada*, 9, (April).

Cooksley, R. J. and Walker, D. F. (1974), 'The advanced educational programme of the Industrial Developers Association of Canada', *Journal, American Industrial Development Council*, 9, (July), 39–49.

Economic Council of Canada (1975), *Looking Outward: A New Trade Strategy for Canada*. Ottawa.

Gertler, L. and Crowley, R. (1977), *Changing Canadian Cities: The Next 25 Years*. Toronto: McClelland and Stewart.

Gillies, A. J. (1974), 'Municipal industrial development with special reference to Kitchener', in D. F. Walker and J. H. Bater (eds.), *Industrial Development in Southern Ontario*, (Waterloo: University of Waterloo, Department of Geography), 199–230.

Macpherson, R. (1976), 'Rethinking industrial development', *Executive*, (September).

Mignault, D. (1977), 'Documents publicitaires de la promotion industrielle', Unpublished Economic Development Diploma Essay, University of Waterloo.

O'Connell, D. S. (1976), 'Strategies for achieving and managing economic growth in cities', *Bulletin, Industrial Developers Association of Canada*, 9, (November).

Québec, Ministère de l'industrie et du commerce (1974), *Guide de développement des parcs industrials*. Québec.

Smith, J. and Werb, W. M. (1977), 'Industrial malls: a modern home for the service sector', in D. F. Walker (ed.), *Industrial Services*, (Waterloo: University of Waterloo, Department of Geography) 78–102.

St Catharines, Business Development Dept. (1975), *A Working Paper on Future Industrial Land Requirements: St Catharines*. St Catharines, Ontario.

Toronto, City of, Planning Board (1974), *A Place for Industry*. Toronto: City Planning Board, Industry Work Group.

Vann, R. (1974), 'Industrial parks in Mid-Western Ontario' in D. F. Walker and J. H. Bater (eds.), *Industrial Development in Southern Ontario*, (Waterloo: University of Waterloo, Department of Geography), 167–97.

Walker, D. F. (1977), 'Continuous education or impending decline? The choice for the industrial development profession', *Bulletin, Industrial Developer's Association of Canada*, 10, (December).

9

Conclusion

Manufacturing has never held as important a place in Canada as in most developed Western countries and its role is declining. Nevertheless it is still vital to the country and its current weak position is a cause for concern. In chapter 1, manufacturing in Canada was shown to be relatively inefficient, suffering from a lack of indigenous innovation and a multiplicity of product lines, which make scale economies difficult to obtain. In consequence, Canada has a trade balance characterized by very large exports of primary products and resource-based manufactures such as pulp and paper, and massive imports of finished products. Although the problem has been recognized for decades, the situation has not changed significantly. Indeed, dependence on the resource sectors could increase.

Looking into the future, Kettle (1977) sees problems for Canada's trading position on all fronts. Cartels, of which the Organization of Petroleum Exporting Countries is the best known, have been formed to control a number of raw materials and foods in the 1970s. They have succeeded in raising the price of a number of products which Canada imports and Kettle argues that primary producers may combine on the basis of several, rather than just one, commodity in the future. Higher prices on exports are vital to many Third World countries, and so they can be expected to take a tough line. On the manufacturing front as well, many new nations are competing on the world market in industries that depend on semi-skilled and skilled low-cost labour. The plight of Canada's textile, clothing and shoe industries can only get worse. Moreover, the range of products subject to cheap imports will increase – many electronic components and items are already in the same class.

As imports increasingly threaten home producers in Canada, export markets are becoming tougher with the increasing number of common markets in the world. While Canada is trying to reduce dependence on the United States, countries in the rest of the world are combining for the benefits provided by free trade. At the same time, each group is protecting itself against outside competition. As Kettle notes, the six existing common markets (including Comecon) have 30 per cent of world population and 40 per cent of the world's gross product. Canada, with its population of under 23 million is trying to go it alone in a competition of giants. It is possible that, in the long run, trade barriers in the world will be reduced under the General Agreement on Tariffs and Trade (GATT) negotiations. As the Economic Council (1977, v) notes, however, in the difficult economic circumstances of the late 1970s the mood is one of protectionism.

Canada's manufacturing is fairly highly protected already and most economists have argued that its competitive weakness and foreign dependency is the result. Moves in the direction of free trade will cause major problems of restructuring, affecting particularly Québec's textile and clothing towns but also many Ontario centres (Economic Council of Canada, 1975, 62–83). Nevertheless the holding operation against much cheaper products can surely not go on forever. It would make much more sense to concentrate on industries with greater potential, and especially to encourage more research and innovation, which could lay the foundations for truly competitive companies.

Canada spends very little on research and development, only 1 per cent of GNP as compared to 2.4 per cent by West Germany and 2.5 per cent by the United States (*The Financial Post*, 1978a). These figures reflect long-standing dependency attitudes concerning Canadian manufacturing, attitudes which have encouraged import of foreign ideas and the companies which can market them. The Science Council of Canada is currently campaigning for an industrial strategy 'which begins with the premise that we cannot be good in everything, that we need to take advantage of our strengths, and that we need to pay particular attention to areas that reflect uniquely Canadian conditions' (Science Council Committee on Industrial Policies, 1977). Gilmour (1978, 32) goes so far as to argue that 'Canadian secondary manufacturing finds itself faced with the threat of extinction, except in the manufacture of products which must be produced locally'.

Research and specialization should bring a long term solution to Canada's difficulties, providing world competitiveness is achieved. There is much evidence to suggest, however, that Canada's standard of living is too high at present to achieve competitiveness in many areas. Manufacturers complain about wage rates that are higher than those in the United States and among the highest in the world (Economic Council of Canada, 1977, v), yet the country

imports more money than any other country to finance a persistent
balance of payments gap. The situation is so bad that in 1978 it is
expected that Canadians will spend $1.2 billion dollars more on
interest payments to foreigners than the latter lend to the country
(*Financial Times of Canada*, 1978). These facts all point to a conclusion that the Canadian standard of living is artificially high and a
decline is to be expected. The forecasters expect some gloomy years
ahead. On the other hand, only more realistic life-style expectations
will allow international competitiveness to be re-established.

It is within this context of national weakness that one must view
the regional variations of manufacturing in Canada for, if the sector
as a whole has problems, the prospects for less advantageous regions
must be quite harsh. An expanding economy provides scope for
regional policy by creating income and increasing market size: thus
manufacturers can build new plants, some of which may be in
different areas. But in a stagnant market, the opportunities for new
investment and change in the spatial pattern of manufacturing are
limited. Even in the West, with its expanding population, there have
been closures in secondary manufacturing because of a slow-
growing national market and a lack of international competitiveness.

A strong shift of population and disposable income towards the
West is currently under way in Canada, however, and it is beginning
to affect manufacturing to a perceptible degree. The Atlantic Region
felt the effect of distance to the main Canadian market in the early
part of the twentieth century and never established many of this
century's growth industries. Now Québec is finding its position
increasingly difficult to hold. Its importance in manufacturing is
declining, it has many older plants, and Montréal, once the
unquestionable business centre in Canada, has lost its position to
Toronto. So far, however, the West has not managed to make strong
inroads into Ontario's manufacturing dominance. The Prairies in
particular have a low proportion of manufacturing and their economic strength is based very much on resources, while their secondary
sector is very heavily oriented to resource processing.

Can the western position change? A growing regional market is
attracting an increasing number of branch plants in consumer
industries, but the fact that central Canadian markets remain so
much larger is an inhibiting factor to major changes in this area.
The greatest possibilities would appear to be in an extension of the

traditional field of supplying the resource sector. The scale of projected developments in Alberta and the western northlands is incredible. The Alaska Highway pipeline, designed to bring Alaskan gas along the Highway route through Canada to the United States, is a $10 billion dollar project controlled from Calgary. The demand for pipe for this project will be enormous. On the Athabaska tar sands two plants are projected at around $4 billion a piece. In addition, there is considerable traditional oil and gas exploration and development taking place. These mammoth construction projects will have major impacts on the manufacturing sector by demanding metal products, machinery, construction materials, food products, modular housing and other items. They could attract new plants to the area and encourage existing and new companies in the West (*The Financial Post*, 1978b).

In the future distribution of activities, much depends on the extent to which corporate and political power relations in Canada can be changed. As noted in chapter 2, the corporate élite in the country has established its position mainly via finance and commerce. It is based in Toronto and Montréal and has managed to retain control by investing in other sectors and participating at a directoral level in most major developments across the country, including those by foreign-based multinationals. An independent western group with strength in resources has, however, been growing with a base mainly in Calgary and to a less extent in Vancouver. The Alaska Highway Pipeline is its first major success against eastern opposition but it could be one of many. Certainly, it now has the ability to influence manufacturing more fully. In petrochemicals, under considerable government influence, Alberta has made inroads although it has had to fight hard against Ontario. More and more gains are being made and it is hard to imagine that the trend will not continue at least to the point where all discrimination, especially over freight rates, is removed. The latter would help the food processing industry develop further in the Prairies at the expense of Ontario. It is likely that Alberta and British Columbia, at least, will receive enough of a boost to expand significantly into highly competitive production of a wider range of resource-based and resource-supply activities. There are elements of this already in such items as logging machinery and prefabricated homes.

Future regional trends in manufacturing depend in large degree on the resolution of Canada's constitutional problems. Québec currently has a separatist government committed to a referendum which will allow its population the chance to vote for or against independence. The province has always pressed for more powers than other provinces because it feels inhibited in its ability to preserve and enhance the Québecois language and culture. Thus, regardless of the results of the referendum or the party in power, it can be expected that pressures to decentralization will strengthen. In fact the new leader of the Liberal opposition, Claude Ryan, has bemoaned Québec's lack of control in key areas of public policy as well as in indigenous private enterprise (Ryan, 1976, 588).

The Québec case may be the most serious, but other voices are also being raised against the existing character of the Canadian confederation. The tensions are strongest in the West, where discrimination in favour of central Canada has often been claimed and occasional suggestions for independence are made (Blackman, 1977). While Graham (1977, 473) argues that 'provincialism outside of Québec is largely economically oriented, particularly with respect to development policy', there certainly are pressures for greater decentralization (Emerson, 1978). It would appear that Usher's (1978, 67) claim that most English Canadians would prefer Québec's separation to a weakening of the federal government's power is a minority one, certainly outside Ontario.

The degree of decentralization of power will be important in affecting manufacturing location because it is likely that provinces would initiate policies to increase their manufacturing sector if they were able to do so. If some degree of regional protection were developed, the manufacture of consumer oriented products could well become more decentralized, especially to the West. Moreover, resource-serving sectors could also increase more rapidly in the West. Meanwhile Ontario, and probably Québec, would lose, although Québec might make some gains at Ontario's expense. Greater regional self-sufficiency has been proposed as a strong policy option by the Canadian Federation of Independent Business-men. In the view of a growing number of Canadians, then, even a decentralized policy under DREE is not enough. A broader discussion of economic policy is desired (Fréchette, 1977, 439–40).

Within provinces, signs of rebellion against the rich cores are also evident in such regions as northern Ontario and Cape Breton Island. The likelihood of major restructuring within any province in the foreseeable future, however, is slight. Certainly some decentralization of activity is probable under the influence of both federal and provincial policies, which are trying at least to maintain backward and rural areas. The long-term tendency for manufacturing to concentrate in major metropolitan areas could in fact slow down or even be halted as a result of policy decisions and high costs of land and labour. There is little sign of change from the concentration of head offices and power structures, however, so that even with a spread of fabricating, the existing dependency relationships will remain. Given the current mood, a greater degree of local initiative may be fostered in the small business sector and this may help to counter the alienation of modern corporations. Certainly 'indigenous industry' has attracted the attention of policy makers across the country.

In the larger metropolitan areas, the place of industry in the central city could stabilize as the authorities question the need for a continuous decline. The greater attraction of the suburbs can be expected to remain, however, unless the expansion of residential building stops or policies to halt the spread are introduced. It is easier and cheaper to build factories on new land than to convert that which is already developed, and to date the case for conserving land has been given little weight. Attitudes may change in the next twenty years. On the other hand the quality and attractiveness of industrial areas is improving and with industrial parks becoming ubiquitous, that trend is not likely to be reversed.

As development practice becomes more sophisticated and professional, the key problem would appear to be that of co-ordination between the various governmental levels and amongst different groups at the same level. The agreements being signed between provinces and the federal government help to encourage an articulation of objectives and co-operation in their attainment. At the provincial-municipal interface, most provinces now have considerable influence via financial inputs and planning controls, although Ontario's municipal development officers are more independent than others. Suspicions remain, however, and a true spirit of co-operation is rarely found. Apart from a certain amount of inevitable jealousy, lack of understanding could be a major problem. Rare is the man or woman who has worked in development at more than one tier of government in Canada. The gulf between the Municipal officer, with relatively local objectives, and the person trying to help a province or the whole country is particularly wide.

Moreover, the type of person employed is often different: ex-businessman or politician in the former case, university graduate, often with a master's degree, in the latter. The current programme of the Industrial Developers Association of Canada does help to bring the two groups together but many provincial and federal officials intimately connected with economic development do not participate. One possible solution would be to introduce far more job interchange, insisting on experience at all three levels of government as part of a training for a career in the field. This would all link in with the establishment of a true development profession, something currently under discussion.

At any given level of government, two relationships require particular attention. First is that between planning and economic development and, second, that between sectoral and spatial aspects of development. They are intertwined because planners are particularly involved in the spatial elements of development. Most development officers in Canada work for governments and are concerned with encouraging development for the people in their area. This task is essentially a part of what is known as planning except that it involves a more active role of encouraging business to help fulfill public objectives. Clearly, then, relationships between planners and development officers must be good. In practice, it is not. Background and education are important elements in this unfortunate situation. Most planners in Canada have tended to be weak in economics and unsympathetic to business. On the other hand, development officers are often ex-businessmen or graduates in engineering, economics, commerce or business. Somehow, ways must be found to establish more common ground in the educational process and to encourage regular interaction in the career situation (e.g. joint seminars, conferences etc.)

In sectoral and spatial aspects of development, a similar problem has arisen at provincial and federal levels. The difficulty is that these two elements are frequently under two different ministries, which of course fosters institutional inflexibility and ministerial rivalry. The case of DREE and Industry, Trade and Commerce at the federal level is one example of conflict. Québec and Ontario also both have separate ministries associated with spatial planning and economic development. Although co-ordination is attempted, the people concerned again have different backgrounds and viewpoints. Fortunately, many of the other provinces are avoiding this extreme separation and the smaller size of their civil service does in any case help interaction. Despite this, much needs to be done to help sectoral officers to understand the spatial perspective.

Whatever happens in the future, Canada's industrial development will certainly be an interesting field for study and a fascinating one in which to work. For the practitioner, there will be the challenge of rising above some of the difficulties expected to arise in these changing times. While researchers need to monitor future expectations continuously, there is still much work to be done in interpreting the past. It is amazing how little is known about Québec in the later nineteenth and early twentieth centuries, about the history and development of most Canadian firms, and about the industrial history of many cities. We also need more up-to-date evaluations of post-second World War industrial growth in most centres with the exception of Toronto. This book has attempted a review of what has been done but at the same time it is a testimony to what still needs to be examined. If it stimulates essential research and innovative development practice, it will have fulfilled its purpose.

REFERENCES

Blackman, W. J. (1977), 'A Western Canadian perspective on the economics of Confederation', *Canadian Public Policy*, 3, (Autumn), 44–53.
Economic Council of Canada (1975), *Looking Outward*. Ottawa: 1975.
Economic Council of Canada (1977), *Bulletin*, 2, (December), i–vi.
Emerson, D. L. (1978) 'Comments', *Canadian Public Policy*, 4, (Winter), 71–6.
The Financial Post (1978a), 'Build our R and D – or see unemployment rise', 4 February, 4.
The Financial Post (1978b), 'Special Report. Pipeline progress: tapping oil and gas supply', 25 February.
Financial Times of Canada (1978), 'Big foreign loans bleed economy', 9 February, 20–26.
Fréchette, Pierre (1977), 'L'économie de la Confédération: un point de vue québecois', *Canadian Public Policy*, 3, (Autumn), 431–40.
Gilmour, James (1978), 'Industrialization and technological backwardness: The Canadian dilemma', *Canadian Public Policy*, 4 (Winter), 20–33.
Graham, J. F. (1977), 'Comments', *Canadian Public Policy*, 3, (Autumn), 470–547.
Kettle, John (1977) 'Direction Canada – International Trade: We're in bad shape', *Executive*, (February), 30–9.
Ryan, Claude (1976), 'Un cas pertinent: le Québec', *Canadian Public Policy*, 2 (Autumn), 587–95.

Science Council Committee on Industrial Policies (1977), *The Condition of Canadian Manufacturing Industry: A Statement of Concern*. Ottawa.

Usher, D. (1978), 'The English response to the prospect of the separation of Québec', *Canadian Public Policy*, 4, (Winter), 57–70.

Index

ADA (Area Development Agency), 59–64, 66, 70, 93–5
ADB (Atlantic Development Board), 59, 95
AIDC (American Industrial Development Council), 229
APEC (Atlantic Provinces Economic Council), 66
ARDA (Agricultural Rehabilitation Development Programme), 59, 63
ATCO, 192
Abitibi, 127
Acadian Coast, 89
Accelerated Capital Cost Allowances, 60
Agriculture (farming): in Atlantic Provinces, 81–2; area of land for, 13–14; in central Canada, 51; exports, 6; implements for, 185, 186, 192; numbers engaged in, 4; in Ontario, 107, 131, 156; in Prairie Provinces, 170–1, 175; in Québec, 112–13
Agricultural Rehabilitation Development Programme (ARDA), 59, 63
Air Canada, 9
Alaska Highway Pipeline, 246
Alberta (Province): coal in, 15, 54, 171; compared with British Columbia, 204, 211; Conservative Government in, 193, 197; Gas Ethylene Ltd, 187; gas in, 15, 54, 170, 187; Gas Trunk Co, 187; Heritage Savings Trust Fund, 54n, 195; incomes in, 41; Industrial Development Policy in, 193–4, 195, 246; and labour situation, 179; manufacturing basis of, 186–8; and migration, 39; oil in, 54, 170, 175, 187; and petrochemical industry, 175, 179; population of, 39, 171; productivity in, 43; pulp and paper in, 176;

spatial pattern in, 188–93; steel plants in, 184, 187; wealth of, 54
Alcan, 113, 216
Alma, 113
Aluminium refining, 108, 113, 116
American Industrial Development Council (AIDC), 229
Amherst, 80, 88, 100
Annapolis–Cornwallis Valley, 81, 89
Antimony, 82
Appalachians, 107, 112
Area Development Agency (ADA), 59–64, 66, 70, 93–5
Argus Corporation, 110
Arvida, 113
Asbestos, 15, 110, 116, 127
Athabaska tar sands, 15, 190, 246
Atlantic Development Board (ADB), 59, 95
Atlantic Development Council, 95
Atlantic Provinces Economic Council (APEC), 66
Atlantic Provinces/Region, 78–103; and area/regional development policy, 61–2, 63, 64, 65–7; as major problem area, 44, 74, 78, 245; and directorships, 56; employment in, 41–2; entrepreneurship in, 53–4, 84; federal policies for, 73, 92–7; future of, 101; incomes in, 58, 93; industrial history of, 78–81; labour quality in, 43; location effect on, 51, 83; physical facts of, 81–3; population of, 39, 50, 83, 85–6; productivity in, 43; proportion of manufactured goods in, 36; size of firms in, 84; spatial patterns in, 86–92; value added in, 36, 83; *see also* New Brunswick, Newfoundland, Nova Scotia and Prince Edward Island Provinces
Aurora, 142

253

Automobile industry, 4, 13, 81, 87, 106, 137, 153, 156, 157

Balance of trade, 1, 3, 7, 245
Barrie, 142
Bathurst, 89
Bècancours Industrial Park, 116
Bell Island, 80, 82, 91
Belledune, 89
Bennett, W. A. C., 225
Bismuth, 82
Blackbourn, A., 144–5
Bleury, 119
Brandon, 184
Brantford, 136, 145, 154, 155
Bridgewater, 89
British Columbia (Province), 202–27; and Alberta, 204, 221; coal in, 15; Development Corporation, 219, 224, 225; economic history of, 203–4; employment in, 41–2, 204; farming in, 14; and federal grants, 73; forestry in, 36, 202; governments of, 225–6; incomes in, 41, 204; industrial development policy of, 222–5; joins Dominion, 7; manufacturing in, 204–22; and migration, 39; population of, 39, 203; and Prairie Provinces, 202, 204; productivity in, 43; Railway, 203; regional commissions in, 230; settlement of, 202–3; spatial patterns in, 212–22; value added in, 36, 204; wealth of, 45, 54
British Empire Steel Corporation, 54, 80
Burlington, 142, 151, 152
Burrard Inlet, 221
Business Development and Tourism, Department of (Alberta), 195, 196

CIL, 189
CPR (Canadian Pacific Railway), 9, 202–3
CPR–Cominco, 110
Cadmium, 82
Caisses, 111
Calgary, 17, 172, 180, 188–9, 190, 192, 246
Cambridge, 141, 144, 145, 154, 155–6, 228
Canadian Chemical Industries, 189

Canadian Development Corporation, 26, 27, 158, 195
Canadian Federation of Independent Businessmen, 247
Canadian General Electric, 27
Canadian Industries Ltd, 136
Canadian National, 9, 56, 203
Canadian Oil, 158
Canadian Pacific, 56
Canadian Pacific Railway (CPR), 9, 202–3
Canadian Shield, 15, 51, 112, 175
Canso, Strait of, 90
Cape Breton Development Corporation (DEVCO), 90, 100
Cape Breton Island, 15, 80, 82, 89–90, 247
Cars, see Automobile industry
Cartels, 243
Chambers of Commerce, 229, 236, 240
Chatham, 144
Chemicals: in Alberta, 187, 189, 193; in Atlantic Provinces, 81; in Manitoba, 182; in Ontario, 136, 137, 153, 154, 157, 159; in Québec, 106, 108, 116, 117, 120; value added in, 11, 13
Chicoutini, 114, 125
China, 21
Churchill Falls, 83, 91
Churchill Forest Industries, 197
Clothing industry: in Alberta, 189; as employer, 11; in Manitoba 177, 181, 182; in Ontario, 51, 133, 137, 141, 148, 149, 154; plight of, 243; in Québec, 105–6, 108, 116, 117, 119, 120; in Saskatchewan, 185
Coal, 15, 54, 80, 82, 90, 107, 171, 203, 210
Cochrane, 187
Cominco, 215
Common Markets, 243–4
Confederation (1867), 4, 50, 107
Conservative governments, 193, 197
Consumer goods, 87, 177, 189–90
Contrecoeur, 120, 122, 124
Copper, 15, 82, 160, 184, 203
Coquitlam, 222
Cordillera, Western, 15, 202
Core-periphery concept, 46, 48, 50, 86
Corner Brook, 91, 92
Corporate Élite, 55, 246
Cotton, 53, 79

Credit Unions, 111

DEVCO (Cape Breton Development
Corporation), 90, 100
DOFASCO (Dominion Foundry and
Steel Co), 151
DREE, *see* Regional Economic
Expansion, Department of
Dartmouth, 98; *see also*
Halifax–Dartmouth
Delta, 221, 222
Denike, K.G., 212–14
Development grants, 60, 196
Development officers, 229, 249
Dockyards, 86, 88
Dome Petroleum, 187
Dominant corporations, 55–6
Dominion Foundry & Steel Co
(DOFASCO), 151
Dominion Steel and Coal Corporation,
90
Dorval Airport, 119
Dow Chemical Co, 187
Durham, 230

EDP (Enterprise Development
Program), 31
Economic Council of Canada, 15–18,
29–30, 43, 178, 244
Economic Development, Ministry of
(British Columbia), 222–3, 225
Economic shadow concept, 52
Edmonton, 170, 172, 180, 182, 187,
188–91, 231
Edmunston, 89
Education, 21–2
Efficiency of manufacturing, 15–19
Electrical products: in Atlantic
Provinces, 81; in Manitoba, 182; in
Ontario, 137, 151, 154, 155, 157,
159; in Québec, 106, 116, 117; in
Saskatchewan, 185; value added in,
11, 13
Electronics, 86–7
Employment, 1, 2, 10–13, 41–2, 104,
133, 204
Empress, 187
Energy, 4, 7, 14–15, 82–3; *see also*
Hydro-electricity
Engineering, 117
Enterprise Development Program
(EDP), 31

Entrepreneurship, 22–3, 53–4, 81, 84,
179–80
Erie, Lake, 152
Ethylene plants, 158, 187, 193
European Economic Community, 29
Exports, 4–7, 36, 50, 156, 203, 210, 243

FRED (rural development programme),
59, 99
False Creek, 219, 221
Farming, see Agriculture
Federal Business Development Bank, 31,
225
Federation of Independent Business,
Canadian, 30
Fisheries, 5, 14, 50, 78, 82, 91, 112–13,
203
Flin Flon, 175, 184
Florenceville, 89
Flyer Industries, 197
Food and beverage industries: in
Alberta, 186, 189, 190, 192, 193; in
British Columbia, 205, 210; in
central Canada, 51; and freight
rates, 246; in Manitoba, 181, 182; in
New Brunswick, 88; in Ontario,
133, 153, 154, 157, 159, 160; in
Prairie Provinces, 175; in Québec,
105, 113, 114, 115, 117; in
Saskatchewan, 184, 185; value
added in, 11
Foreign Investment Review Act, 1973,
26
Forests and forestry: areas of, 6, 14; in
Atlantic Provinces, 82; and balance
of trade, 4; in British Columbia, 36,
202, 203, 205–10; in Manitoba, 184;
in New Brunswick, 78; in Ontario,
137, 159; in Québec, 112
Fort Garry, 182
Fort Saskatchewan, 189, 190
Fournier, P., 110–1
Fraser River/Valley, 202, 203, 213, 219
Fredericton, 62, 86, 88, 94
Free trade, 29–30, 243–4
Freight flows and rates, 172–5, 177–9,
194, 246
French Canadian culture, 109–11
Friedmann, John, 48–50, 56, 198
Fund for Rural Development, (FRED),
59, 99
Furniture, 13, 115, 156, 182
Furs, 5, 50, 203

GATT (General Agreement on Tariffs and Trade), 244
Gabarus Bay, 90
Galt, 136
Gander, 91
Gas, 14–15, 54, 83, 170, 171, 187, 189
Gaspé Peninsula, 112
General Agreement on Tariffs and Trade (GATT), 244
General Development Agreements, 68–9, 122, 124
General Investment Corporation, 121
Georgia Straits, 209, 212, 218, 223
Georgian Bay, 61, 62, 144
Gold, 15, 202, 203
'Golden Horseshoe', 136
'Golden Triangle', 154
Goose Bay, 91
Gordon, Walter, 27
Granby, 125
Grand Falls, 91, 92
Grand Mère, 115–16
Grande Prairie, 176
Grants, Federal, 73
Great Lakes, 131, 134
Greater Vancouver Regional District, 219, 221
Gross Domestic Product, 1, 2
Growth, components of, 46–8
Guelph, 141, 145, 154, 155
Gypsum, 15

Halifax, 53–4, 88–9, 95
Halifax–Dartmouth, 62, 64, 67, 86–7, 94, 95, 97, 100
Hall Commission, 177–8, 198
Hamilton, 107, 133, 134, 136, 142, 143, 144, 145, 150–2
Harmac, 209
Heritage Savings Trust Fund, Alberta, 54n, 195
Hinton, 176, 188
Hudson's Bay, 171; Company, 5, 202
Hydro-electricity, 14, 51, 82, 108, 112, 116, 153

IDAC, see Industrial Developers Association of Canada
IPSCO, see Interprovincial Steel and Pipe Corporation
Imperial Oil, 158
Imports, 7, 17, 152, 203, 243

Incomes, 39, 41, 58, 83, 92, 93–4, 204, 244
Industrial Commissioners, 228–41
Industrial Developers Association of Canada (IDAC), 228–9, 241, 249
Industrial Enterprises Incorporated, 99
Industrial Estates Ltd, 98, 99
Industrial Funds Act (1961), 121, 123
Industrial Park Development, 233–5, 248
Industry and Commerce, Department/Ministry of (Manitoba), 194, 196
Industry and Commerce, Department of (Saskatchewan), 194
Industry and Tourism, Ministry of (Ontario), 161, 162
Industry, Trade and Commerce, Department of, 16, 30, 225, 249
Innovation, 23–4, 26, 48–9, 108, 250
Interprovincial Steel and Pipe Corporation (IPSCO), 184, 187, 194
Iron and steel industries: in Atlantic Provinces, 79, 80, 82, 84, 90; in Ontario, 7, 133, 150–1, 153; in Québec, 105–6, 107, 121; in Saskatchewan, 69, 194; see also Steel industry
Iron ore 15, 80, 82, 91, 107, 113, 160; works, 115, 153
Irving family firms, 88

Japan, 29, 203, 210
Jewellery industry, 149
Joffre, 187
Joliette, 125

Kamloops, 225
Kildonan, 182
Kingston, 164, 228
Kitchener, 136, 141, 142, 144, 145, 154–5, 234
Kitimat, 216
Kootenay area, 203, 213, 215
Korea, North, 21

La Mauricie, 115–6
La Tuque, 115
Labour quality, 43, 46, 143–4
Labrador, 63, 82–3, 91, 113
Lac St Jean, 113, 114, 127
Lachine Canal, 9, 118

Land use, 232, 234
Lauzon, 114
Laval University, 114
Lead, 15, 82, 160, 184
Leather industries, 105, 108, 114, 120,
    137, 154
Leduc Oilfield, 170, 186, 192
Leigh, R., 212–14
Lethbridge, 193
Liberal governments, 63, 66
Liverpool, 89
London, 136, 142, 143, 156, 157, 164
Lord Selkirk, 182
Lougheed, P., 193, 197
Lower Mainland Region, 208, 215, 218,
    223
Lumber, 14, 50, 53, 203
Lynn Lake, 175

MAGI (Metropolitan Area Growth
    Investment Ltd.), 64, 97
McBain Co., 89
Machinery industries: in Alberta, 186–7;
    in British Columbia, 205; in
    Manitoba, 181; in Ontario, 142,
    151, 152, 154, 159; in Prairie
    Provinces, 177; in Québec, 106, 114;
    value added in, 13
Mackenzie, 209
MacMillan Bloedel, 209–10
Mainland Investments Ltd, 64
Malls, industrial, 235
Manitoba (Province): governments of,
    193, 197; incomes in, 39, 41;
    industrial development policy of,
    193, 194, 196–7, 230; labour quality
    in, 43; manufacturing base of, 170,
    180–2; metal processing in, 175,
    181; population of, 39; productivity
    in, 43; pulp and paper industries in,
    176; spatial pattern in, 182–4; value
    added in, 36
Manufacturing belt, 57
Maritime Provinces, see Atlantic
    Provinces/Region
Medicine Hat, 193
Metal products: in Alberta, 186–7, 189,
    190; in British Columbia, 205, 210;
    in Manitoba, 181, 182; in New
    Brunswick, 88; in Ontario,.137, 141,
    151, 152, 153, 154; in Prairie
    Provinces, 175, 177; in Québec, 106,

107, 113, 114, 116, 117; value added
    in, 11, 13
Metals and metal ores: in Alberta, 189;
    and balance of trade 4; in British
    Columbia 203, 205; export of, 7;
    location of, 15, 51; in Manitoba 181,
    182; in Ontario, 159; in Prairie
    Provinces, 171; value added in, 11,
    13
Metropolitan Area Growth Investment
    Ltd (MAGI), 64, 97
Michelin plants, 84, 88, 89
Mineral products (non-metallic), 153,
    182, 188, 189
Mirabel International Airport, 125
Mobile homes, 177, 192
Molybdenum, 15
Moncton, 67, 68, 86, 88, 95, 229
Montréal: corporate élite in, 246; and
    DREE 68, 124–5; growth of, 50,
    53–4; intra-urban patterns of,
    118–20; regional dominance of, 111,
    117, 121, 159; as regional
    government, 231; relative decline of,
    118, 122, 124; and Toronto, 56, 104,
    117
Motor vehicles, see Automobile industry
Multinationals, 21, 22, 24
Multiplex Corporation Ltd, New
    Brunswick, 64, 97, 99, 101
Municipal industrial development, 166,
    228–42

NDP, see New Democratic Party
Nackawic, 89
Nanticoke, 151
National Policy (1879), 9, 19, 51–3, 79,
    80
Nationalisation, see Public ownership
Nesbitt, J. G., 211, 215–6
New Brunswick (Province): and area
    development policy, 61, 94;
    Development Corporation, 98–9,
    101; exports from, 36; forestry in,
    78; incomes in, 41; industrial
    development in, 100, 101;
    manufacturing in, 88–9, 98;
    Multiplex Corporation Ltd, 64, 97;
    and nuclear power station, 83;
    regional commissions in, 230;
    settlement of, 4; value added in, 36
New Democratic Party (NDP), 193, 197,
    225–6

New England, 51
New Glasgow, 80, 88
New Westminster, 202, 203, 219
Newfoundland (Province): and
    development corporations, 99–100;
    farming in, 14; fisheries in, 5, 91;
    and hydro-electricity, 82; incomes
    in, 39, 41, 83, 92; joins Dominion,
    79; manufacturing in, 91–2; Ocean
    Research and Development
    Corporation, 100; population of, 83;
    settlement of, 4; and social welfare
    programme, 73
Niagara Falls, 52, 153, 229
Niagara Peninsula, 134, 143, 144, 152–4
Nickel, 15, 153, 160, 184
Norcliffe, Glen B., 57–8
North, The (Yukon and North-West
    Territories), 39, 45, 190
North Vancouver, 221
Nova Scotia (Province): and
    Area/Regional development policy,
    61, 64, 93, 97; entrepreneurship in,
    84; exports from, 36; fisheries of, 78;
    incomes in, 39, 41, 93–4; industrial
    development in, 100;
    manufacturing in, 86–7, 89–90, 98;
    settlement of, 4; steel industry in,
    54; value added in, 36

OECD countries, 43–4
OPDQ (L'Office de Planification et de
    Développement du Québec), 121
Oakville, 142, 157
Ocean Research and Development
    Corporation, Newfoundland, 100
Oil, 14–15, 54, 83, 158, 170, 171, 187,
    189, 192; refineries, 86, 88, 114, 118,
    158, 175, 187, 189
Okanagan valley, 203, 213, 215
Ontario, Lake, 134, 152, 159, 164
Ontario (Province), 131–69; and
    Area/Regional development policy,
    61, 65, 161–6, 247, 249; compared
    with Québec, 104, 106–9, 159; as
    core region, 52–3; economic power
    of, 51, 55; employment in, 41–2,
    133; exports from, 36; farming in,
    14; and federal grants, 73; foreign
    ownership in, 138–9, 144–5;
    incomes in, 41; industrial history of,
    131–7; industrial structure of,
    137–9; iron and steel in, 7; and

manufacturing dominance of, 35,
    36, 44, 245; and migration, 39;
    municipal industrial development
    in, 166, 230, 232, 234, 248; planning
    regions of, 146–61; population of,
    36, 50, 131, 137; Prairie markets for,
    54, 172, 198, 246; productivity in,
    43; settlement of, 4; spatial pattern
    in, 139–46; effect of tariffs on, 29,
    32, 73, 244; value added in, 36, 131
Oshawa, 144
Ottawa, 66, 68, 142, 158–9, 164
Ottawa Valley, 6
Outaouais, 113
Output, manufacturing, 7, 8, 15
Ownership of industry, 19–21, 26–7,
    138–9, 144–5

Pacific Western airline, 197
Paper industry: in Alberta, 188; in
    Atlantic Provinces, 81, 82, 84, 88,
    89; in British Columbia, 205,
    208–9, 210; export of, 7; importance
    of, 14; in Manitoba, 182; in
    Ontario, 137, 143, 148, 153, 160,
    161; in Prairie Provinces, 176; in
    Québec, 106, 108, 113, 114, 115,
    116
Parti Québecois, 110, 126, 127
Patent Act 1872, 10
Peace River, 215
Peterborough, 144
Petrochemical plants, 119, 143, 157–8,
    175, 179, 187, 188, 190, 195, 197,
    246
Petroleum and petroleum refineries, see
    Oil and oil refineries
Petrosar, 158, 195
Pine Falls, 176
Platinum, 15
Polarization theory, 48–59
Polymer Corporation, 158
Population: of Alberta, 171; of Atlantic
    Provinces, 50, 83, 85–6; of British
    Columbia, 202–3; of Canada, 4; of
    Ontario, 50, 131, 137; of Prairie
    Provinces, 170; provincial statistics
    of, 36, 38–40; of Québec, 50, 104; of
    Saskatchewan, 184
Port Alberni, 209
Port Cartier, 113, 125
Port Colborne, 153
Port Coquitlam, 222

Port Moody, 222
Potash, 15, 171, 185, 197
Powell River, 209
Power Corporation, 110
Power stations, 83
Prairie Provinces/Region, 170–201;
    agriculture in, 6; and British
    Columbia, 202, 204; and capital
    requirements, 179–80;
    characteristics of, 44, 170–1, 245;
    employment in, 41–2; and freight
    rates 172–5, 177–9, 246; industrial
    development policy in, 193–8; and
    labour situation, 179;
    manufacturing in, 175–93;
    population of, 170; proportion of
    manufacturing goods in, 36;
    settlement of, 54, 170; value added
    in, 36; vulnerability of, 171–2; see
    also Alberta, Manitoba and
    Saskatchewan Provinces
Prince Albert, 176
Prince Edward Island (Province),
    Comprehensive Plan for, 68; and
    development corporation, 99;
    farming in, 81; incomes in, 39, 41;
    and industrial malls, 235;
    settlement of, 4; and social welfare
    programme, 73; value added in, 36
Prince George, 208, 209, 215, 216
Prince Rupert, 203, 225
Printing and publishing, 114, 120, 148,
    149, 159, 182, 185, 187, 190
Productivity, 16–17, 42–4, 104
Public ownership, 27, 110, 127, 193, 197
Pulp industry: in Alberta, 188, 192; in
    Atlantic Provinces, 81, 82, 84, 88,
    89; in British Columbia, 205,
    208–9, 210; export of, 7, importance
    of, 14; in Manitoba, 182; in
    Ontario, 137, 143, 160, 161; in
    Prairie Provinces, 176; in Québec,
    106, 108, 113, 115, 116

Qu'Appelle Valley, 69
Québec (City), 114–15, 125–6, 231
Québec City–Windsor axis, 47, 52, 104
Québec (Province), 104–30; and
    area/regional development policy,
    65, 66, 74, 120–7, 230, 231, 241,
    247, 249; asbestos in, 15; compared
    with Ontario, 104, 106–9, 159; as
    core region, 51, 53; distribution of

manufacturing in, 111–20;
    employment in, 41, 104; and federal
    grants, 73; Group of Enterprises
    Inc., 123; incomes in, 39, 41;
    Industrial Development
    Corporation, 122–3; industrial
    strength and structure of, 104–11;
    industrial weakness of, 54, 127, 245;
    manufacturing dominance of, 35,
    36, 44, 55; and migration, 39;
    Ministry of Industry and
    Commerce, 116, 120–3; peripheral
    regions of, 112–14; population of,
    36, 50, 104; prairie markets for, 54,
    172, 198; productivity in, 43, 104;
    separatism in, 56, 110–11, 127,
    246–7; settlement of, 4; effects of
    tariffs on, 29, 32, 73, 244; trading
    patterns in, 36; value added in, 36,
    104, 113

RDIA, see Regional Development
    Incentives Act 1969
Railways, 7, 9, 50, 54, 74, 203
Ratcliffe, A. T., 70
Ray, D. M., 45–8, 52, 56, 142–3, 144
Red Deer, 193
Regina, 184, 185, 196, 228
Regional Development Incentives Act
    (RDIA) 1969, 63, 64, 66–8, 70, 95
Regional diversity, 35–77, 245
Regional Economic Expansion,
    Department of (DREE): and
    Atlantic Provinces, 66, 95, 97, 99;
    and British Columbia, 223–5;
    decentralisation, 68, 198, 202, 247;
    early years of, 65–7; expenditure
    by, 70–3; and industrial
    commissioners, 237; and ministerial
    rivalry, 249; and Ontario, 164, 165;
    and Prairie Provinces, 178, 197;
    purpose of, 63; and Québec, 122,
    124–5, 126; reorganisation of, 66,
    68–70; and Saskatchewan, 194, 196
Research and development, 23–4, 25,
    244
Richmond, 221
Rivière du Loup, 7
Royal Bank of Canada, 56
Royal Commission on Canada's
    Economic Prospects, 15
Rubber industry, 13, 106, 154
Ryan, Claude, 247

SIDBEC, 121, 122
STELCO (Steel Company of Canada
    Ltd.), 150, 151
SYSCO, 90
Sackville, 98
Saguenay, 113, 127; river, 108
St Andrews, 98
St Augustin, 115
St Boniface, 182
St Catharine's, 144, 153, 154, 232
St Félicien, 113
Ste Hyacinthe, 125
Saint-Jean, 125
Saint-Jérome, 125
Saint John (New Brunswick), 62, 64, 67,
    80, 81, 86, 88, 94, 95, 97, 99; river,
    89
St John's (Newfoundland), 67, 95
St Lawrence Boulevard, 119, canal
    system, 9; Lowlands, 112; river,
    115, 116, 120, 131, 159; Seaway, 9,
    74; valley, 6
St Maurice river, 108, 115
Saltfleet, 151, 152
Sarnia, 143, 157–8, 195
Saskatchewan (Province): agriculture in,
    184; coal in, 15; and General
    Development Agreement, 69;
    government of, 193, 197; incomes
    in, 39, 41, industrial development
    policy in, 193, 194, 195, 196–7;
    labour quality in, 43;
    manufacturing history of, 184—5;
    metal processing in, 175; population
    of, 38, 170, 184; potash in, 15;
    productivity in, 43; pulp and paper
    in, 176; spatial pattern in, 185–6;
    value added in, 36
Saskatoon, 68, 184, 185–6, 196, 198, 202
Sault Ste Marie, 133, 160
Scale of manufacturing, 16, 25
Science Council of Canada, 23–4, 25, 30,
    244
Sept Iles, 113, 114, 125
Service sectors, 86
Shawinigan, 115–16, 125–6
Sherbrooke, 116–17, 125–6
Shield, Canadian, 15, 51, 112, 175
Shipbuilding, 50, 79, 86–7, 88, 114, 120
Shuswap valley, 203
Silver, 15, 82
Sloan Report (1945), 208
Small business sector, 30–1

Smallwood, Joey, 91, 99
Social Credit Party, 225–6
Social welfare programme, 73
Sorel, 120, 125
Special Areas, 64, 95, 96
Specialization, 16, 25
Springhill, 80, 88
State action, 7
Steel Company of Canada Ltd.
    (STELCO), 150, 151
Steel industry, 54, 117, 120, 184, 185,
    187, 197; see also Iron and steel
    industries
Stellarton, 98
Strathcona, 189
Sudbury, 160
Sugar refining, 53, 79, 80, 143
Sun Life of Canada, 56
Sun Oil, 158
Superior, Lake, 107
Surrey, 221, 222
Sydney, 80, 81, 90, 100

TEIGA (Ministry of Treasury,
    Economics and Inter-governmental
    Affairs), 161, 162
Talbotville, 157
Tariff policy, 1, 9–10, 17, 19, 23, 25, 29,
    32, 51, 73, 244
Technology, 21–5
Témiscamangue, 127
Textiles: in Atlantic Provinces, 79, 80; in
    Ontario, 137, 141, 148, 154, 156,
    159; plight of, 243; in Québec,
    105–6, 108, 114, 116, 117, 120; in
    Saskatchewan, 185
The Pas, 176, 184
Thompson, 175, 184
Thorold, 153
Thunder Bay, 161, 164
Tillsonburg, 228
Timber, 5–6, 50, 131, 175, 177, 205–8
Tobacco industry, 106
Torbay, 91
Toronto: corporate élite in, 246; and
    DREE, 68, 164; dominance of, 134,
    136; and industrial parks, 235, 237;
    manufacturing in, 146–50, 250;
    metal working in, 107; and
    Montréal, 56, 104, 118; spatial
    pattern in, 141–5; and U.S. capital,
    52
Trade unions, 109–10

Trail, 215
Trans-Canada highway, 119
Transcona, 182
Transport equipment: in Alberta, 187; in Atlantic Provinces, 84; in British Columbia, 205; in Manitoba, 181, 182; in Ontario, 153, 155; in Québec, 106, 117; in Saskatchewan, 185; value added in, 11, 13
Trans-Québec Autoroute, 116
Treasury, Economics and Inter-governmental Affairs, Ministry of (TEIGA), 161, 162
Trenton plant, 88
Trois-Rivières, 115–16, 125–6
Trudeau, Pierre, 63
Truro, 7, 88
Turner Valley, 192

United States: automobile pact, 4; capital, 51–3, 55; dominance of, 7, 9, 23, 48, 243; exports to, 156, 203, 210; imports from, 152, 203; investment, 108, 139, 144–5; and manufacturing efficiency, 15–19; and patents, 10; pipelines from, 118; and subsidiary firms, 21, 152; and tariffs, 10, 73; trading relationship, 29
Uranium, 160, 185, 194
Urban polarization, 56–9

Valleyfield, 125
Value added in manufacturing, 10–13, 17, 36, 83, 104, 113, 131, 204

Vancouver, 203, 212, 213, 215, 218–22, 246
Vancouver Island, 203, 208, 213, 215, 223
Varennes, 119–20
Victoria, 202, 203, 208, 212, 213, 215
Vietnam, 21
Villeneuve, Paul Y., 46–8, 56

Waterloo, 142, 145, 154–5, 229, 241
Welland, 153
Western Opportunities Conference (1973), 198
Wheat, 5, 6, 7, 50, 107, 170
White Rock, 222
Windsor, 52, 104, 136, 141, 142, 144, 156, 157
Winnipeg, 170, 172, 177, 180–3
Wood products/processing: in Alberta, 188, 192; in British Columbia, 208–10; in Manitoba, 182; in Ontario, 141, 143, 154, 160, 161; in Québec, 106, 113, 115; in Saskatchewan, 185; value added in, 13
Woodstock, 142
Woodward, R. S., 70

Yale, 202
Yarmouth, 89
Yukon and North-west Territories, see North, The

Zinc, 15, 82, 160, 184